THE METRICS OF TEACHER EFFECTIVENESS AND TEACHER QUALITY RESEARCH

Most developed nations measure the performance of teachers in audit evaluations of school productivity. Accountability metrics such as "teacher effectiveness" and "teacher quality" dominate evaluations of student outcomes and shape education policy.

The Metrics of Teacher Effectiveness and Teacher Quality Research explores how these metrics distort analyses of student achievement, sideline broader contextual and systemic influences on learning, reinforce input-output analysis of schooling, and skew the educational debate. Focusing on recent phases of school education policy reform, this book utilizes qualitative data from classroom teacher participants to examine how and why issues of teacher effectiveness and teacher quality figure so prominently in policy reform and why pressing matters of social class, school funding, and broader contextual influences are downplayed. The authors use this information to suggest how teachers can develop their role as pedagogic experts in a highly scrutinized environment.

This book will be of great interest to education academics and postgraduate students specializing in teacher performance, accountability and governance.

Andrew Skourdoumbis is an associate professor in education. His research engages with the quantitative findings of teacher effectiveness research and subsequent implications for policy development in pedagogic practice. His work examines global reform efforts in education and also teacher effectiveness/teacher quality and their impact on teaching and learning.

Shaun Rawolle is a senior lecturer in education. His research includes the way that education from schools, vocational education and training, and higher education is constituted, measured and impacted through education policy and by economic thinking. He draws on Pierre Bourdieu, contractualism and the social contract of education in his work.

THE METRICS OF TEACHER EFFECTIVENESS AND TEACHER QUALITY RESEARCH

Sidelining the Issues That Really Count

Andrew Skourdoumbis and Shaun Rawolle

LONDON AND NEW YORK

First published 2020
by Routledge
2 Park Square, Milton Park, Abingdon, Oxon OX14 4RN

and by Routledge
52 Vanderbilt Avenue, New York, NY 10017

Routledge is an imprint of the Taylor & Francis Group, an informa business

© 2020 Andrew Skourdoumbis and Shaun Rawolle

The right of Andrew Skourdoumbis and Shaun Rawolle to be identified as authors of this work has been asserted by them in accordance with sections 77 and 78 of the Copyright, Designs and Patents Act 1988.

All rights reserved. No part of this book may be reprinted or reproduced or utilised in any form or by any electronic, mechanical, or other means, now known or hereafter invented, including photocopying and recording, or in any information storage or retrieval system, without permission in writing from the publishers.

Trademark notice: Product or corporate names may be trademarks or registered trademarks, and are used only for identification and explanation without intent to infringe.

British Library Cataloguing-in-Publication Data
A catalogue record for this book is available from the British Library

Library of Congress Cataloging-in-Publication Data
A catalog record for this book has been requested

ISBN: 978-0-367-46061-7 (hbk)
ISBN: 978-0-367-46063-1 (pbk)
ISBN: 978-1-003-02671-6 (ebk)

Typeset in Bembo
by Apex CoVantage, LLC

CONTENTS

1 Framing the scene   1

   Introduction 1
   1.1 Scoring teachers' work 1
   1.2 What's wrong with the metrics of teacher effectiveness and teacher quality? 3
   1.3 Why work with Pierre Bourdieu and Michel Foucault? 4
   1.4 School effectiveness and school improvement 6
   1.5 The structure of the book 7
   References 11

2 Simplifying the complex   12

   Introduction 12
   2.1 Teacher effectiveness and teacher quality (TE and TQ) 13
   2.1a Quality teaching 14
   2.2 Teacher effectiveness research 15
   2.3 Data 16
   2.4 Student achievement 18
   2.5 School and teacher productivity 19
   2.6 Disparaging a public education system 22
   2.7 Teachers are the problem 25
   2.8 Evaluating systems and people 27
   2.9 Conclusion 29
   References 30

3 Reform   33

   Introduction 33
   3.1 The political and economic question 33
   3.2 Schooling and education in the new world 36
   3.3 The impact of reform/s 37
   3.4 Accountability 37
   3.5 New managerialism 38
   3.6 Choice 39
   3.7 Privatization 40
   3.8 The education production function 41
   3.9 Conclusion 43
   References 44

4 Improve or else!   47

   Introduction 47
   4.1 The knowledge-based economy 47
   4.2 The skills students need 48
   4.3 The seduction of comparison/s 49
   4.4 De-centring responsibility 50
   4.5 Competitiveness and educationalization 51
   4.6 A new form of leadership 52
   4.7 Inspection 53
   4.8 Parents 55
   4.9 Student voice 57
   4.10 Individualizing the teacher subject 58
   4.11 Conclusion 59
   References 59

5 The case of teacher effectiveness research   63

   Introduction 63
   5.1 Models and algorithms 63
   5.2 A tapered view 67
   5.3 An economizing "doxic" discourse 69
   5.4 Symbolic orders of control 73
   5.5 Governing teaching work 76
   5.6 Conclusion 78
   References 78

6 "Making the difference" – sidelining the contingent   81

   Introduction 81
   6.1 Master narratives – There Is No Alternative (TINA) 81
   6.2 Four education policy case studies 86

6.3 Symbolic policy forms 95
6.4 Conclusion 96
References 97

7 Instruction, skills or pedagogy – inventing the new teacher   100

Introduction 100
7.1 Standards and outcomes 100
7.2 Instruction versus pedagogy 103
7.3 Skills and competencies 106
7.4 The pedagogical encounter 109
7.5 Hardwiring perfection – role intensification 111
7.6 Conclusion 112
References 113

8 Pedagogic adaptability   117

Introduction 117
8.1 The relational 117
8.2 Identity and agency 119
8.3 Pedagogic adaptability 120
8.4 Adaptive teaching 121
8.5 Power contingencies: socio-economic status and class 124
8.6 Caring 126
8.7 Conclusion 127
References 128

9 Implications   131

Introduction 131
9.1 The performative habitus in teaching 131
9.2 A new teacher education: "best practice/s" 133
9.3 Disruptive innovation 135
9.4 Continuous achievement 138
9.5 Conclusion 140
References 141

10 Concluding comments   144

Introduction 144
10.1 Capacity 144
10.2 Becoming 146
References 148

Index   149

1
FRAMING THE SCENE

Introduction

This book is based on our collective interest in school improvement and comes as a result of discussions and research on measures of teacher effectiveness and teacher quality and how they have come to have such a large impact on both the public discussion of what schools and teachers should be concerned with and a marked shift towards understanding education and schools as key parts of economic systems. What interests us is the way that technical measures, such as "Teacher Quality" and "Teacher Effectiveness", have slipped into public discussions with surprisingly limited critical commentary about their use or effects, or ways that they connect to the broader social contract that connects schools, principals and teachers to students, parents and the broader public. Underpinning this book is a research project that asked questions of policy makers, economists, teachers and principals about a central framing discourse in Australia, that of productivity, which is used as a way of providing a rationale for change to economic systems and reorienting social institutions like education so that they better reflect economic orthodoxy. The major economic policy body, the Productivity Commission, has undertaken major reviews of different parts of Australia's education system, a central plank of which has been an attempt to systematize the measurement and reporting of the performance of different sectors and to provide a consistent form of data for the consideration of policy makers.

1.1 Scoring teachers' work

Media coverage of schools has turned from general concerns about who teaches the next generations to discussions about the measurement of teachers. While there are other targets of discussion, teacher effectiveness (TE) and teacher quality (TQ) are regularly held to be key influences that impact student achievement scores, which then flow into the comparisons of nations' performances on large-scale tests. TE and TQ are often described in the media in general terms, suggesting that this is a discussion of ideal qualities that a teacher should possess, but they are also measures, tied to different traditions of measurement, and are often linked. In a specific way, TE and TQ are the objects of contest and competition within education, and their meaning and importance are not static. While we treat this in more detail throughout this book, "teacher quality" points to the desirable personal attributes that are possessed by a teacher, which might be innate or learned, such as the capacity to empathize, motivate or engage students, knowledge about subjects or ways of teaching, or dispositions towards fairness or social justice. In contrast, "teacher effectiveness" points to the efficiency with which a teacher enables students to learn, either in terms of how quickly students can come to learn something, or how much learning can take place over a given time period. This might be measured in relation to different desired outcomes, from test scores, knowledge, competencies or skills. Alongside these measures, media and public debate also cover terms that offer a counter to TE and TQ, such as "quality teaching", which point to what good teaching looks like in a classroom, as measured against different dimensions of desirable classroom interactions, such as connectedness, intellectual quality, supportive environment or recognition of difference. The distinction between "teacher" and "teaching" is important in relation to measurement in that it shifts the targets from what a teacher possesses (their "teacher capital") to what they can actually do in practice (how they draw on their teacher capital and convert this into student learning).

Public and media discussions about TE and TQ elaborate on the potential they each have to improve the selection of teachers, and then the learning of students, in order to be more efficient in the use of resources and to make Australia's education system competitive with other national systems. Both are tightly connected to student learning, and in policy discussions this connection is measured by TE and TQ to model how education as a system works, in conjunction with other variables, as a way to identify targets for policy intervention. Alternatively, a different policy purpose proposes that TE and TQ might be used as a form of accountability and employed in a variety of possible ways, from low stakes uses such as basic feedback to reflect on practice, through to increasingly high stakes targets for performance, attached to KPIs, performance reviews, employment, contract negotiations between governments for the renumeration of teachers, right up to the possible closures of schools or the wholesale restructuring of entire systems.

Despite the obsessions of measuring teachers condensed in TE and TQ, there is no single measure of a teacher's TE and TQ that travels with them through their career, marking them, their capabilities and their performance as they move from school to school. There is a contrast in this to the metrics that accompany the work of people in other professions, like academics in universities, that mark the research productivity of academics with single scores such as the h index or g index, but not the teaching, leadership or service components of their work. This can be explained by important debates about what inputs ought to be included in measures, but also acknowledgement of the multiple contributions that teachers make to students' lives beyond academic performance.

There is a sense that TE and TQ are used mainly as a kind of rhetorical device in media coverage, as a way to point to or frame a specific problem to be scrutinized, agonized about, intervened with and obsessed over as opposed to other targets that might be less politically palatable, such as addressing continual changes to curriculum, teacher overload, teacher attrition, relative declines in teacher salaries, the need for some teachers to teach out of field, or the move from selective to comprehensive to universal provision of education in many nation states. The same can be said about the impact of technology companies, privatization and marketization of education. Rarely, if ever, are the actual metrics of TE and TQ explored, and there is hardly any discussion of the connection between the metrics of TE and TQ and the broader sociological elements that permeate the field of education.

1.2 What's wrong with the metrics of teacher effectiveness and teacher quality?

This book is about the positioning of classroom teachers by policy makers and in the media as both the major problem and solution to student learning as measured on national and international tests. This involves reconstructing how classroom teachers came to be positioned as the central problem and the way that the problem has been framed in relation to measures like TE and TQ. The book is also a direct deconstruction of this move, and, to do this, we use both the work of Michel Foucault and Pierre Bourdieu to examine the effects of accountability metrics, such as TE and TQ, on school and teaching practice. The work of Michel Foucault gives us notions of "governmentality" and "regime of truth" with which we explore how existing techniques of power, exerted by systems of authority, control teaching practice and "governmentalize" the complexities linked to schooling. From the work of Pierre Bourdieu, we draw on the concept of "social fields", understood as spaces that are structured around specific practices, like research, or teaching and learning, and where there is also competition for key stakes and positions. We use social fields to explore school effectiveness/school improvement (SESI), in which TE and TQ are central stakes. Here we talk in particular about a SESI field, or field of SESI, as a space of competition in which agents compete to best account for the measurement and performance of teachers, schools and school systems, in order to provide advice as to how to improve their performance. We then look at the relations between this field and other related fields, like the field of schooling, the field of education research and the field of education policy. To expand on this theorizing, we explore in particular how the "logic(s) of practice" and "doxa" of the SESI sub-field complement Foucault, helping to expose (1) the inadequacies of restrictive inquiries into school education that overlooks organized controls and (2) illustrates the dangers connected to the makings of a research doxa. In drawing on aspects of these theorists, we hope to shed some light on the influence of dominant fields like economics on evaluations of school productivity that discounts the organized controls and unique aspects (distribution of capital, habitus) of fields like school education, and provide specific cross-field effects that act to shape and distort such fields. The use of two Bourdieuian notions, namely a "logic(s) of practice" and "doxa", will also highlight dominant political mobilizations that channel debate about public education towards the "what works" inputs connected to TE and TQ. This will be achieved by showing that national and international policy discourse nominates classroom teachers and their pedagogy as the topmost treatable inputs in the education equation.

While important as policy mechanisms, when misapplied, measures of TE and TQ are distorting influences on teaching work, and over-reliance on them in decision-making misdirects funding and attention from education system goals, and in particular equity and social justice goals. This book calls out the reliance on such measures and offers a modest proposal to move beyond their obsessions. The book as such and in short explores the theoretical foundations of these two research constructs and maps their policy influence over time as trademark indicators of performance within education effectiveness research.

1.3 Why work with Pierre Bourdieu and Michel Foucault?

Löic Wacquant suggests that it is 'no accident that Michel Foucault and Pierre Bourdieu are the world's two most cited and utilized authors in the social sciences today: both are critical thinkers and thinkers of power' (2004, p. 98). In merging work by Michel Foucault and Pierre Bourdieu, specifically aspects connected to their conceptions of power, we hope to add to an understanding of how power operates in the evaluation of teacher performance and school productivity. Cronin (1996) claims that contemporary society is beset by 'crises of legitimation' where 'operations of power have become detached from recognizable structures of political responsibility and accountability' (p. 55). This has resulted in what Cronin suggests is an absence of an 'appropriate conceptual framework for analysing how power functions in modern society' (Cronin 1996, p. 56). By this he means that the alienation felt by many in contemporary society is not solely a symptom of the decentred nature of democratic institutions. As Cronin makes clear:

> these very institutions and the discourses of legitimation on which they are based seem to function as instruments of impersonal forms of power that resist straightforward analysis and escape political control.
>
> *(1996, p. 56)*

In this book we take the view that teaching practice and the work of schooling is shaped by powerful contextual forces which are economic, political, historical and social in nature. These forces include struggles that are broadly political and revolve around debates such as what the role of the teacher ought to be, interpreted through conservative, progressive or radical lenses. These forces are also about which economic views (macro and micro) about the importance of education should come to shape the education field and the role of teachers and how they should best be deployed (such as through neoclassical economics, endogenous growth theory, productivity, privatization, competition, human capital, and nudging), and how the economic functions of education should be balanced against social and other functions. These are also contextual and historical forces in that they reflect questions about what role democratic decision-making ought to play in different education systems, what values ought to be considered in decision-making, overlaid with urgency about how to embed national narratives about the possible futures of students and to nudge their choices to paths that are politically desirable. An effect of these contextual forces is that decisions about the measurement of teaching practice and the work of schooling is not best represented as a final destination but as something of a temporary settlement.

Power dynamics operate within and across these contextual forces, and they do so, we suggest, through a combination of relational (Foucault) and symbolically charged (Bourdieu) structures of domination. Foucault attaches a mobile and diffuse element to the operation of power devoid of a subject-centred or fixed location and exercise of power, suggesting that the action of power exists through flows and movement and is deployed through practices and techniques that enable people to be shaped and to shape themselves. Power is productive and helps people to make something of themselves and into something else. In this approach, TQ and TE are measures that could be embedded in practices and techniques that provide ways for teachers to be made up, known and compared. In this sense, TQ and TE shape and modulate teacher practices and in turn help to make up students. Teachers are then made through the action of power, and we argue that TQ and TE might feature heavily in these flows. In contrast, Bourdieu reinserts the subject into analyses of power by arguing for the 'substantive conception of the subject as both essentially embodied and socially constituted' (Cronin 1996, p. 56). For Bourdieu power is embodied and crystallized in the habits, dispositions and on the bodies of people like teachers and is configured differently in each field. An individual teacher's habits are built up over time and in relation to other teachers in the field of schooling, with some teachers accruing more teaching capital than others and hence more power. This apparent incommensurability, we argue, is bridged if the focus of analyses of power in a field such as education centre not only on what produces particular forms of practice but what forms of practice actually produce. Hannus and Simola (2010) in bringing Foucault and Bourdieu together in their work on the power mechanisms of education and schooling state:

> we might conclude that Foucault's most useful contribution is in providing tools for analysing the prevailing mode of governing while taking

> into account the historical, multilayered character of power and governance. . . . Bourdieu, in turn, provides better tools for researching the mode of generation of practices: how the prevailing culture and social order is transmitted and challenged, and what kinds of structure and hierarchy of positions could develop in schools.
>
> *(p. 7)*

Hannus and Simola move on to say:

> Foucault introduces multiple layers of power and Bourdieu fills them with a more specific description of the interest politics of the school. He also makes a contribution on the political level. Thus, these approaches could be considered complementary rather than conflicting.
>
> *(2010, p. 7)*

1.4 School effectiveness and school improvement

TE and TQ are subsets of what Slee and Weiner (1998) name 'effective schooling research' which 'in conjunction with its operational branch – the school improvement movement – has been adopted by policy-makers' to resolve 'alleged crises in state education' (p. 1). Slee and Weiner (1998) name the various elements of the "crises" in schools, although, as they illustrate, the major crisis of public education is about the perceived failure and under-performance of public schooling in general. Berliner and Biddle (1995) have characterized the perceived failure and under-performance of public schooling as a 'manufactured crisis' which has occurred against what we suggest is a background of 'enduring myths' (Smyth 2006, p. 302). Smyth (2006) catalogues the myths variously as:

1. That we have a crisis in schools, attributable to schools, teachers, and teacher education.
2. That the way of fixing these alleged problems is by cutting schools and higher education institutions loose from a public education system and allowing them to be disciplined by 'market forces'.
3. Furthermore, that the way of improving 'quality' in education is by requiring close adherence to arbitrarily determined standards and targets, and ensuring compliance through forms of prescribed accountability.
4. That the language, rhetoric, models and modes of thought of the business sector are preferable and more appropriate to anything that can be developed by schools, students, teachers or teacher educators.
5. That the role of parents is that of judicious consumers exercising 'choice' of school that provides the best deal for them and their children, rather than active citizens interested in a system of education that is in the interests of everyone's children, not just those most adept at working the system.

(pp. 302–303)

The school effectiveness and school improvement movement (SESI) is about providing a series of counter measures to address failure. Taken up as 'lists of factors' (Slee and Weiner 1998, p. 2), SESI research provides in the main a practical and positivist education management approach to schooling applying technicist and generic solutions to educational problems. In promoting 'models of school evaluation and change' (Wrigley 2013, p. 31), which not only individualize educational problems but also their solution, SESI downplays broader social and political structures and contexts.

This then means shifting policy maker and education system attention onto the practices of classroom teachers. Increasing the effectiveness of teachers by narrowing pedagogy 'constitutes a powerful intervention which both reshapes the nature of teaching and presages fundamental restructuring within the teaching profession of lines of power, responsibility and accountability' (Hextall and Mahony 1998, p. 135). Teaching effectiveness and its improvement are then framed upon a set of procedures that prioritizes "what works" criteria of educational enhancement. Educational practice is then:

> conceived of in a particularly mechanical way. . . . In keeping with economistic definitions of effectiveness, it is the bit that comes between 'input' and 'outputs'. It is seen largely as a set of techniques, the 'core technology', for managing 'throughput' rather than a complex and always unpredictable process of ongoing construction of educational practice. Practice is imposed rather than constructed, negotiated or asserted; it is a set of techniques to be employed by teacher technicians on malleable pupils.
>
> *(Angus 1993, p. 337)*

A feature of what Laurie Angus is referring to in his quote involves the individualizing of effectiveness and improvement with teachers increasingly 'being required to adopt individualistic, quasi-competitive orientations' (Hextall and Mahony 1998, p. 138) in their classroom practice/s. Responsibility (and also blame) about student achievement are attributed to individual teachers and schools while having little control over the system-imposed requirements of effectiveness and improvement.

1.5 The structure of the book

We have written this book so that readers gain a sense of how various contributing themes about TE and TQ in each of the chapters dominate and influence the field of school education and by extension classroom teachers. While each chapter sets the scene for following chapters, it is possible for readers to move between chapters, particularly if there are specific themes and/or issues that stimulate interest. That said, there are two main themes in the book. The first and over-riding theme is to outline the symbolic dimensions of TE and TQ and to understand their "evaluative effects", in particular, their policy effects on pedagogy and the nature and role of teacher work. This theme also situates the focus on TE and TQ in a broader history of school improvement and school effectiveness, tracing shifts downwards in the burden of proof for the impact of reform efforts and funding. The second theme is one of legitimation, namely tracing the knowledge and logic of TE and TQ as evolving research constructs with an epistemological orthodoxy rooted in economic theory. The objective of this theme is two-fold: to establish a basis for pedagogic work of classroom teachers beyond the purely instrumental, thereby elevating social justice obligations, and, furthermore, to carve out a station for the classroom teacher that respects their professional responsiveness and sensibility developing their role in a highly scrutinized environment.

Contemporary debates about the poor quality of public education positions classroom teachers in particular ways. Our take on TE and TQ is rooted in a theoretical orientation which is cognizant of the deeper hold that contemporary neo-orthodox econo-political ideologies exert on classroom teachers. Given the neo-managerialist assault of "the neoliberal approach" (see Kivisto 2018) on education and its subsequent reformulation over several successive decades, the work and performance of classroom teachers are now under scrutiny as never before. Each chapter is designed in such a way as to continually remind the reader of the distortions connected to the exacting derivations of TE and TQ, skewing the educational debate to camouflage basic school system and economic inequities. Any data that we draw upon inform the major contention of the book that the documentation of classroom teaching practice by the research constructs TE and TQ acts as a subjugating accountability device which narrows the role of classrooms teachers in school productivity calculations.

Chapter 2, for example, draws on data from a small-scale qualitative case study of Australian school and teacher productivity. The chapter is framed on two questions: what makes research constructs like TE and TQ prime indicators of school productivity, and do they capture what matters in public education? In this chapter we problematize the research constructs TE and TQ and argue that the emphasis on metricated "data" such as standardized tests is dangerously reductive and omits the broader work that teachers and schools do. The specific data utilized in this chapter relate to a small sample of teacher participant responses from the Australian state of Victoria. All of the data used in this chapter are in the form of semi-structured interviews where participants 'speak their vocality' (Gale and Densmore 2003, p. 12) about classroom practice and student achievement. We deliberately focused on teacher participants with an extensive and current history in classroom teaching work. All participants chosen are practising classroom teachers with a working history of ten-plus years. This deliberate move on our part is about acknowledging the experience of these established classroom teachers, each of which has an in-depth awareness of the shifts in education policy over time connected to "effectiveness" and "quality".

Chapter 3 explicitly addresses the "new normal" of reform in school education and along with this an education reform movement that has particular objectives and weapons at its disposal. The chapter deals with political and economic parameters that influence contemporary education worldwide and will explain why education is involved in doing the work of the economic and political. A key feature of the chapter is to show how particular reformist themes (accountability, for example) paint a negative picture of public education so as to discredit its achievements by focusing public attention on issues of supposed under-achievement.

Chapter 4 takes a closer look at how the constant of reform connects to another constant, the need to improve. The chapter considers some of the contemporary markers of a "re-worked" school education system that is driven by a new "knowledge-based economy" that has at its core the continued influx of broad-based change evinced by global economic re-structuring. This brings with it particular commitments – acute economic competitiveness, large-scale data comparisons, enhanced individual responsibility and stronger demands on social services such as education, all of which exert and have an influence over classroom teachers.

As with Chapter 2, Chapter 5 is the second to draw upon teacher participant data. The chapter brings together a toolkit drawn from the writings of Michel Foucault and Pierre Bourdieu to critically reflect on the field of teacher effectiveness research (TER) and the effects of measures of teacher effectiveness and teacher quality on school and teacher practices. The chapter traverses the specific techniques of measurement/surveillance used in TER and the regularizing discourse that accompanies it. Teacher participant responses engage with some of the unquestioned assumptions of TER and what it means to be a productive classroom teacher today.

Chapter 6 makes use of a different type of data set utilizing relevant document analysis (key education policy and research reports). The chapter discusses how TER frames up school education policy and in particular teaching practice in contemporary times. Reports to be analyzed include *Teachers matter: Attracting, developing and retaining effective teachers* (Organization for Economic Co-Operation and Development 2005) and Barber and Mourshed's (2007) *How the world's best-performing school systems come out on top*. Policy documents to be analyzed include the U.S. Department of Education's "Race to the Top" (2009) and the "No Child Left Behind" (2002) legislation. Each document is explored as a specific "case" detailing the rhetoric associated with purely objectivist rationalizations of education and the work of classroom teachers.

Chapter 7 concentrates on a term synonymous with TE and TQ, namely "instruction", to outline its distinguishing features and policy relevance. The chapter will show that the term "instruction" as opposed to pedagogy is reductive in nature and is evident of the take-up of U.S. education policy language and research. In addition, the chapter will discuss how the teacher's classroom role is configured differently now with an emphasis on developing students' skills and capabilities. The discussion incorporates the contemporary importance attached to the classroom teacher as learning facilitator and collaborator with an increased responsibility for assisting students to self-regulate their own learning by setting goals for evaluation against benchmarked performance standards and outcomes.

Chapter 8 draws the discussion away from TE and TQ somewhat by focusing more on the attributes that classroom teachers will need to develop to help them understand and undertake their role in a changing educational context. Discussion will centre on how teachers need to develop critical thinking, problem-solving, collaboration, creativity and communication capacities so that they can better engage with restrictive and often prescriptive curriculum and administration practices. The emphasis in the chapter will be on understanding relationships between subject content knowledge in schools (i.e. "opportunity to learn") and student achievement, acknowledging that all students can learn and have the opportunity to succeed. Thus, the chapter will traverse how teachers as learning collaborators and facilitators need a pedagogy that fuses content knowledge and assessment beyond standardized minimums.

Implications for teacher preparation and professional development are areas for discussion in Chapter 9. In this chapter we suggest that the work of classroom teachers is increasingly shaped and categorized in specific "performative" ways. The Bourdieuian notion of habitus is used to explore the "performative" in classroom teaching, which by extension has had particular effects within the field of teacher education and more broadly the teaching profession in terms of how practising classroom teachers engage in professional learning and development. We argue that the "performative" in classroom teaching is about "conditioning" the "right" type of classroom teacher, which can only be achieved through adherence to an education policy and research literature espousing a "best practice" approach to teacher preparation. The maintenance of professional currency by practising classroom teachers is then expected through engagement in continuous professional learning and development of a particular type and kind.

Chapter 10 rounds out our critical exploration of TE and TQ. We suggest, as others have before us, that education is in fact a process of becoming and that perhaps the most important work of classroom teachers is to help facilitate the learning potential of all of their students. This means finding 'the balance of creativity and structure that will optimize student learning' (Sawyer 2011, p. 2), which quite often is about calling upon teaching techniques and practices that are not as easily captured by the metrics of TE and TQ.

What follows then, in the chapters is not an attempt to redefine TE, TQ or indeed TER. We hope though that this book entices readers to re-engage with the concepts of TE and TQ, their metrics and to question what it is that these particular research constructs supposedly document and say about classroom teacher practice, student achievement, school and teacher productivity. At the very least we have tried to problematize notions of TE and TQ and positioned their conceptualization critically and from within a broader range of qualitative documentation of the macro and micro contexts that influence education. This, we believe, serves as a better and more important guide for persons interested in complex educational matters of teacher performance and their connection/s to student achievement.

References

Angus, L. 1993. The sociology of school effectiveness. *British Journal of Sociology of Education*, 14(3), 333–345.
Barber, M. and Mourshed, M. 2007. *How the World's Best-Performing School Systems Come Out on Top*. McKinsey & Company. Retrieved from https://www.mckinsey.com/~/media/McKinsey/Industries/Social%20Sector/Our%20Insights/How%20the%20worlds%20best%20performing%20school%20systems%20come%20out%20on%20top/How_the_world_s_best-performing_school_systems_come_out_on_top.ashx
Berliner, D. and Biddle, B. 1995. *The Manufactured Crisis*. Reading, MA: Addison-Wesley.
Cronin, C. 1996. Bourdieu and Foucault on power and modernity. *Philosophy & Social Criticism*, 22(6), 55–85.
Gale, T. and Densmore, K. 2003. *Engaging Teachers: Towards a Radical Democratic Agenda for Schooling*. Maidenhead, UK: Open University Press.
Hannus, S. and Simola, H. 2010. The effects of power mechanisms in education: Bringing Foucault and Bourdieu together. *Power and Education*, 2(1), 1–17.
Hextall, I. and Mahony, P. 1998. Effective teachers for effective schools. In R. Slee and G. Weiner with S. Tomlinson (Eds.), *School Effectiveness for Whom? Challenges to the School Effectiveness and School Improvement Movements* (pp. 128–143). London, UK: Falmer Press.
Kivisto, H. 2018. Capital as power and the corporatisation of education. *Critical Studies in Education*, 59(3), 313–329. https://doi.org/10.1080/17508487.2016.1186707.
Organization for Economic Co-Operation and Development. 2005. *Teachers Matter: Attracting, Developing and Retaining Effective Teachers*. Paris: OECD Publishing.
Sawyer, R. K. 2011. *Structure and Improvisation in Creative Teaching*. New York: Cambridge University Press.
Slee, R. and Weiner, G. 1998. Introduction: School effectiveness for whom? In R. Slee and G. Weiner with S. Tomlinson (Eds.), *School Effectiveness for Whom? Challenges to the School Effectiveness and School Improvement Movements* (pp. 1–11). London, UK: Falmer Press.
Smyth, J. 2006. The politics of reform of teachers' work and the consequences for schools: Some implications for teacher education. *Asia Pacific Journal of Teacher Education*, 34(3), 301–319.
U.S. Department of Education. 2002. *No Child Left Behind*. Government of the U.S.
Wacquant, L. 2004. Critical thought as solvent of *Doxa*. *Constellations*, 11(1), 97–101.
Wrigley, T. 2013. Rethinking school effectiveness and improvement: A question of paradigms. *Discourse: Studies in the Cultural Politics of Education*, 34(1), 31–47. https://doi.org/10.1080/01596306.2012.698862

2
SIMPLIFYING THE COMPLEX

Introduction

In this chapter we problematize the research constructs teacher effectiveness (TE) and teacher quality (TQ). We begin by suggesting that there are complexities in the field of education which are susceptible to overly simple explanations. The chapter is framed on two questions: what makes research constructs like TE and TQ prime indicators of school productivity, and do they capture what matters in public education? Some of the inherent characteristics that define these research constructs is covered towards the latter stages of the chapter, as is highlighting why accountability metrics add to critiques of teachers and public education more generally. The chapter shows that policy-making discussions about school education are repeatedly framed in deficit and/or economic terms (see Gearin 2017). A good teacher/bad teacher dichotomy is the end result, with policy makers and education researchers seeking measurement methods to identify the essential ingredients of teachers' "effectiveness" and "quality". This dichotomy is a practice that aids in sidestepping the broader socio-economic and context-related issues regarding education and schooling. A contrast is also revisited from Chapter 1 to research any changes that have focused instead on the construct of "quality teaching", which has come to fill an important, though dominated, position in the field. In addition, the chapter works with an inherent contradiction at the heart of research dealing with TE and TQ (i.e. the apparent disconnect between how teachers understand and talk about classroom actualities versus the rarefied and objectified nature of research defining effective and quality teaching). Data utilized in the chapter are drawn from a case study of four secondary school teachers concerned with understanding school and teacher productivity and their enactment in current Australian education policy. The research focused on how notions of school and teacher productivity (including the concepts TE and TQ) are understood by classroom teachers. The full data set include semi-structured interviews with the four teachers: Aaron, Chad, Heather and Vicki (not their real names).

2.1 Teacher effectiveness and teacher quality (TE and TQ)

The effectiveness and quality of teachers are about the value they bring to in-classroom student learning. Teacher quality remains a somewhat 'contested term with multiple meanings' (Naylor and Sayed 2014, p. 3); however, generally it has been associated with an individual classroom teacher's efficacy and student achievement gains. Teacher quality also often refers to designated individual characteristics, including qualifications/credentials and particular skill sets or attributes/dispositions (see Clinton et al. 2016). Teacher effectiveness conversely is about the "effect" of an individual teacher on student achievement gains. Clinton et al. (2016) summarize the distinction between teacher effectiveness and teacher quality in this way:

> These two terms are often used interchangeably in the literature, and there has been considerable debate regarding their definition and appropriate use. Generally, teacher effectiveness can be conceptualised as being on a continuum covering the extent to which a teacher is able to progress student outcomes. This is often measured using student achievement results and other summative tools. Teacher quality, however, refers to teacher attributes, such as capabilities, training, knowledge, or beliefs.
>
> *(p. 6)*

Studies into teacher effectiveness and quality (Hattie 2003) exclude all other factors when they consistently position teachers and their classroom work as the major influence on student achievement. The promise inherent in studies of this kind is that causal connections between the teaching practice/s of individual in-classroom teachers and student learning can be observed and so definitively captured and measured. Distinctive elements in the form of particular behaviours and/or actions once identified need only be systematically and routinely implemented in classrooms in order for students to successfully learn and achieve. The major methodological assumption that drives this work suggests that measures of student achievement can be directly attributed to an individual teacher's effectiveness and therefore pedagogic/instructional or teaching quality. This assumption though 'assumes that student learning is measured well by a given test, is influenced by the teacher alone, and is independent from the growth of classmates and other aspects of the classroom context' (Darling-Hammond, Amrein-Beardsley, Haertel and Rothstein 2012, p. 8). These same researchers highlight a number of other influences that also have an impact on student achievement, and they are worth listing here:

- School factors such as class sizes, curriculum materials, instructional time, availability of specialists and tutors, and resources for learning (books, computers, science labs, and more);
- Home and community supports or challenges;
- Individual student needs and abilities, health, and attendance;
- Peer culture and achievement;
- Prior teachers and schooling, as well as other current teachers;
- Differential summer learning loss, which especially affects low-income children; and
- The specific tests used, which emphasize some kinds of learning and not others and which rarely measure achievement that is well above or below grade level.

(Darling-Hammond et al. 2012, p. 8)

Contemporary school education policy often reflects the behaviours expected of teachers to optimize learning. Teacher effectiveness and quality can be established via in-classroom observations and audits of student achievement (national/international standardized tests), student and/or parent surveys and/or ratings, and tests of teacher subject and/or pedagogic content knowledge (see Clinton et al. 2016). Teacher performance evaluations to gauge individual effectiveness and quality are compared against state or national teacher and curriculum standards. Standards are often centred on aspects of professional practice and its connection to student achievement. Teacher standards vary across and, in many cases, within national jurisdictions and are usually understood as system-defined exemplars or "baselines" of behaviour and/or practice. Standards of professional practice are characterized by accountability markers or 'levels of competence expected of individual teachers' (Sachs 2016, p. 417) regarding content knowledge, instruction and planning, fostering positive and safe learning environments, reflection on practice, leadership and so on (see U.S. Department of Education 2009).

The research constructs of TE and TQ are performance identifiers and they act as symbolic carriers of surveillance about the performance of individual classroom teachers. Their accountability mechanism relies on a calculable linear cause-effect rationale. In objectifying the work of individual teachers, judgements are made about their capacity to effect change on student learning. The measure of student achievement gain or "added value" is considered an indicator of "teacher impact" and therefore performance leading to a summative evaluation of individual teacher success. We delve further into the metrics of TE and TQ in Chapter 5.

2.1a Quality teaching

In positioning the constructs of TE and TQ in the field of SESI, we note that they have come to be dominant in the field, but they are not the only constructs that have been developed. Quality teaching is a research construct in education research in Australia which draws on an alternative research path in Australia and the U.S., whose principal contention is that what ought to be focused on directly to understand the outputs of education are not just background measures of individual teachers and their effectiveness, but also a direct measure of what happens in the classroom in terms of the kind of teaching and interactions between teachers, support staff and students. This research is based on direct observation of lessons, and coding instruments are used to measure the kinds of interactions that take place. In some national settings, quality teaching has come to rival TE and TQ in public discussions about teaching and teacher preparation, but in relation to a global field of SESI, it still represents a largely dominated position.

2.2 Teacher effectiveness research

The theoretical basis upon which judgements about effective teaching are made rely on a methodological approach to inquiry that is almost exclusively framed by quantification. The work of teachers and the interactions that occur in classrooms are labelled as variables so that their isolation for purposes of objectification is made easier. Nonetheless, the complex nature and process of learning is not easily captured, as Barrow (1984) attests:

> There are a number of factors that stand in the way of success in such research. Some of them are merely contingent matters such as the practical difficulty of observing large enough truly random samples, of ensuring that participants in the research do not behave uncharacteristically because of the research, and of effectively controlling some of the variables. Those sorts of problems are acknowledged by researchers, although the implications for the value of their work are not so often acknowledged. Then there are constraints that are unavoidable in the world as we know it: for example, a student or a teacher in any field study or experiment will have his particular personality and all that that entails. We cannot nullify its effects. Thirdly, there are logical constraints such as the impossibility of actually observing cause and effect.
>
> *(p. 77)*

While TER, like all statistically laden research, allows and supposedly corrects for anomalies or accounts for influences such as socio-economic status, it can never quite overcome the imbalances of life that are constants in classrooms. As Barrow (1984) notes, in the classroom 'things are never equal' and any research design that purports to capture effective teaching falls short of dealing with the 'thousands of variables that actually are in play in a classroom setting' (p. 77). Phillips (2014) captures this as a 'phenomenon that involves real people who live in real, complex social contexts from which they cannot be extracted in any meaningful way' (p. 10). Phillips (2014) recognizes that learners have a 'gender, a sexual orientation, a socio-economic status, an ethnicity, a home culture; they have interests – and things that bore them . . . they are attracted by (or clash with) the personality of their teacher and so on' (p. 10). All these things are present and are interwoven to varying degrees, which makes the notion of their being "statistically controllable" a point of contestation.

The evidence regarding aspects of effective schooling, including TE and TQ, has its own set of particular exchanges. A precept of TER is the prioritization it gives to the statistical regularities of teaching practice and its relationship to student achievement, which often ignores context. So, when studies of TE claim, 'other things being equal' or 'when adjustments or corrections are made for' (see Rowe 2003; Ballou, Sanders and Wright 2004; Pianta and Hamre 2009), they are invariably admitting to the vagaries of their analytical mechanisms. The contextual complications of classrooms either often goes unstated in many studies of TE or is ignored altogether. Instead there is an attempt to present a clinical perspective that reflects a linear and discrete compilation of the phenomenon of teaching and its effects on learning via a defined 'set of reduced-form treatment effects' (Chetty, Friedman and Rockoff 2011, p. 6), in other words, mathematical constructs.

In prioritizing the practical, TER accepts that there are specific norms inherent in levels of student achievement that can be observed and measured. TER reduces the overall complexities, including the subjective experience of teaching and learning to what is "visible" and to "what matters" (see Robinson 2004; Hattie 2009, 2012; Muijs et al. 2014). The exclusive focus on student achievement by TER to the exclusion of all else means that the pedagogic capacities of teachers and how adept they are at enhancing learning outcomes is the only variable worth capturing in evidencing learning. Findings 'generally drawn in severely controlled contexts' (Gottlieb 2015, p. xii) have a wide education policy appeal, often assigning conclusions as incontestable facts, for example, that effective teaching leads to 'improved financial and social outcomes for the students' (Gottlieb 2015, p. xii) in the long term. We return to a fuller discussion of TER again in Chapter 5.

2.3 Data

Data and drawing upon a "scientific" evidence-base are the ongoing contemporary educational mantra (see Biesta 2010). The prescribed policy advice on how to teach best and using "what works" is generally framed by the seemingly obvious (i.e. that classroom teachers):

- Should set clear but attainable goals/aims;
- Plan for, develop and deliver structured time-paced lessons;
- Teach methodically using very clear, simple language and explanations;
- Be prepared to model solutions;
- Provide constant "hits" of positive and constructive feedback, foreshadowing what comes next in the learning sequence;

- Allow for some student collaboration, although under tight teacher regulation and observation;
- Adjust the learning experience so that individual needs are catered to and met and make sure all of this is tested at the end of a prescribed teaching sequence to "measure" or "verify" what has been learnt.

While teaching inevitably includes the list provided, the steering of classroom learning towards a singular quantifiably assessable endpoint is promoted as effective practice. The enablers of an effective and quality lesson are data sets of "tested" in-classroom teacher practices found to produce the right kind of outputs and outcomes in terms of student achievement. The data-based and performance-managed lesson is about technical delivery, where the classroom teacher is focused on "adding value". We return to this discussion in Chapter 5, where we problematize in more detail key metrics of TE.

There are two important features of data utilization about what works best in classrooms: comparison and evaluation. Both are policy instruments through which teachers and school systems are managed and held to account. The "value-add" needed is a mix of curriculum provision and teacher knowledge that both work towards a common benchmarked metric of student achievement. Herein is the unavoidable, although plausible, peculiarity of data and how it is promoted and used in education, generally 'abstracting complex qualities into simple and reductive quantities' (Lewis 2016, p. 286). The term used for such a phenomenon is "commensuration", more accurately described as the 'transformation of different qualities into a common metric' (Espeland and Stevens 1998, p. 314). We could also add here the term "singularity", where the accumulated experiences of schooling (learning, teaching and so on) are assayed to provide a single number which acts as an indicator of performance. An over-arching aspect of data proliferation in education is a set of policy assumptions about schooling aims. These are that (1) the goals and objectives of different school systems and individual teachers are commensurable; (2) economic national prosperity and well-being is aligned to school system performance, which can be ascertained through international/national standardized testing; and (3) achievement markers are linearly realized through universally understood cause-effect means (see Morris 2012). We also add that the increase in data proliferation in education has also been about re-situating the field of education so that it aligns more closely with the needs of a market economy.

An important premise central to the production and use of data in education is that it has something valuable to say about productive performance and student learning. This is usually tied to the type of teaching practice needed to enhance achievement. The stockpile of comparisons and rankings that school systems and those who work in them are now exposed to and surveilled by are about providing a reservoir of performance data that affect and change perceptions. Data and how it is interpreted and used has the power to transform. Large-scale student performance data can be used for accountability purposes and has the 'capacity to change perceptions about school and teacher performance and, in turn, to change leadership and teaching practices through systems of reward and sanction' (Sellar 2015, p. 131). Several of the major education policy reforms and reports of recent decades (see U.S. Department of Education 2009) espouse this by suggesting that there is an active relationship connecting the proliferation of performance data and the seemingly abstract elements of which it is constituted. The effects often represent an oversimplification of the contextual realities of daily school life and in particular of student achievement. An important point worth noting is the distorting effects of data that often overly simplify the very complex phenomenon of learning, either discounting the lived experience/s of people (students and teachers) or at worst, totally ignoring it altogether.

Michel Foucault has argued that the observational act with its powers of recording 'normalizes' (1977). Performance data about schools, teachers and students serve normalizing 'purposes in the constitution of knowledge and the exercise of power' (Lingard, Hayes, Mills and Christie 2003, p. 127). The inherent processes of objectification and normalization at work in TER and the data recording involved in it can be thought about in terms of "technologies of power" (Foucault 1977) as they act to subjugate and shape. Standardized tests (e.g. Trends in International Mathematics and Science Study-TIMSS; Progress in International Reading and Literacy Study-PIRLS; The Programme for International Student Assessment-PISA, amongst others) as examples of "technologies of power" and mechanisms of surveillance act as an 'apparatus of observation, recording and training' (Foucault 1977, p. 173), disciplining how students and teachers engage with curriculum and how we (the public) think about education. This accountability in and about education is about how an individual teacher and/or student 'may be described, judged, measured, compared with others' as it is the 'individual who has to be trained or corrected, classified, normalized, excluded, etc.' (Foucault 1977, p. 191). It is in this way that 'surveillance, and with it, normalization becomes one of the great instruments of power' (Foucault 1977, p. 184). Data are the technological conduit that facilitates this change through constant supervision of performance.

2.4 Student achievement

The scholastic achievement of students is in reality about mastering a series of different relationships. The relationship of student to school, student to community, student to teacher/s, student to curriculum, student to assessment, student to aspiration/s, student to expectation/s, and student to goal/s, all of which signal something about the educational level a student either finally reaches or achieves or wishes to achieve. In more recent times, the plain language of the now famous Coleman et al. Report (1966) first documented the subtle yet tangible influences affecting student achievement. The report illustrated the combination of influences at work regarding student achievement, including, although not limited to, composition of school, students' sense of control of the environment and their futures, teachers' verbal skills and student family background (see Ladson-Billings 2006). We say more about the Coleman Report in Chapter 3, Section 3.8.

Proficient levels of literacy and numeracy are what major education policy expects of student achievement as of late. Standardized achievement tests gauge student attainment. The learning trajectory is plotted and monitored over time, where gains in achievement signal successful teaching. While standardized tests are the system "snapshots" of student achievement at any one time, they perform the important function of performance management. Standardized testing of student achievement reminds us all that the education system is constantly measuring and evaluating, the latter point re-visited towards the end of this chapter. The goal is to establish student achievement growth over time.

In much of the work done on student achievement one distinctive element always seems to separate itself from the rest. There is the clear understanding that achievement cannot be explored in isolation; it occurs within some bounded context, be it school, and, more broadly, social, cultural, historic, political and/or economic contexts. For some, student achievement is partly explained by social class (see Connell, Ashenden, Kessler and Dowsett 1982); for others student achievement is a function of school autonomy (see Caldwell and Spinks 1988); and yet for others student achievement is directly connected and dependent on how well individual teachers teach (see Muijs and Reynolds 2005; Hattie 2009, 2012).

An important consideration about student achievement revolves around precisely understanding all of the interactions that exert impact on learning, which then correlates with attainment. This means acknowledging that student achievement is bound up in the myriad of influences and/or relationships found in social contexts, including why it is that external school and social influences/relationships have a powerful effect on how students react in classrooms. Misguided concerns about those relationships often centre on inadequate teacher professionalism and/or pedagogy, for example, a misreading of the social structure of which schools are also a part. In retreating from dealing with those relationships, the practices that best delineate student achievement as a set of constructed interactive and hard-to-capture practices are then overlooked.

2.5 School and teacher productivity

Another link in the teacher effectiveness and quality chain is school and teacher productivity. School and teacher productivity are measures of student achievement levels (see Skourdoumbis 2017). Productivity implies actualized value and growth which takes into account system inputs. Measures of productivity are based on narrow arithmetic functions relating various inputs to a singular output of student achievement. Productivity is commonly understood as the inputs needed in a particular process in order to obtain a given output. Productivity is then a ratio of system inputs to system outputs over a defined time period. In the field of business, for example, firm productivity is relatively easy to measure if all that is needed is basic measures of numbers of workers/employees producing an output in a period of time. In the field of education things are never that simple, as a teacher in our research suggests:

> Well, I don't work in a factory, so how can I be more productive? We have – we have improved systems to make our life easier but the whole idea of productivity is what . . . I have a shorter lunch hour or I have a [new] system to – instead of writing out a letter for excursions I can have it pre-printed and put on an electronic system?
>
> *(Chad)*

There is often confusion about how productivity should be defined in education and how best to interpret changes in achievement over time. This may be the result of applying an economic model of productivity to an educational problem, something that we consider in more detail in Chapter 3. Another teacher in our research, when talking about school productivity, suggested that while "the system" may define school productivity 'these days . . . as improvement on school results' (Aaron), for him it was more about other influences, for example:

> It might be about ensuring your enrolment from one year to the next has not declined. That to me is productivity. To ensure that students feel good within that school . . . that experience and student well-being actually matters as well as student outcomes.
>
> *(Aaron)*

Interestingly, Aaron, from his comments, is also implying that student enrolment is something in the "control" of teachers and/or schools. Another teacher in our research, when asked about school and teacher productivity, raised the matter of business models. Productivity seemed to go

> hand in hand with . . . a business model. . . . The children and the parents are the clients. The children are our . . . assets and we have to show that we are producing good results. And, so I feel education, public education, has gone off the rails with this type of attitude.
>
> *(Heather)*

The productivity of schools is dependent on more than simply the labour of teachers. Inputs in education are multi-faceted and may include the type of curriculum implemented, resources available, time allocated to learning and the pedagogic approach adopted, amongst other things. School managers and state education departments may consider school and teacher productivity purely in terms of quantifiable results. Teachers though may view things differently. As Aaron has suggested, productivity from a "systems" perspective:

> is now purely in . . . as far as I see it . . . results driven. How do I see it . . . productivity? I look at this . . . I look at teachers as now being professional human beings and the profession requires them to . . . do their best for their students and that means you're there on time, you're ready to work and you do your best with the resources available. That is productivity.
>
> *(Aaron)*

A meaningful measure of school and teacher productivity begins when the particular inputs and outputs are identified. Even so, meaningful measures of productivity in education are hard to qualify. A U.S. study of productivity by Triplett and Bosworth (2004) suggests that in education 'there is very little agreement on how to develop strong quantifiable measures of either output or productivity' (p. 268). Reasons for this vary and are mainly attributed to complications regarding

> how to adjust for the influence of non-school factors on student performance, about the importance of taking account of multiple outputs (such as the various missions assigned to the public school system and the combination of education and research in higher education), and about the long lags between education and economic returns in the form of higher earnings.
>
> *(Triplett and Bosworth 2004, p. 268)*

Aaron pointed to the multiple concerns of public education as:

> we actually care about things like welfare. Kids engaging with what we're trying to do and – you know – there's no silver bullet. There's no silver bullet in education. You're dealing with things that are so random and so human, but . . . productivity . . . a teacher's [and school's] productivity cannot . . . be based on some singular form or output . . . you know . . . student results for example.
>
> *(Aaron)*

School and teacher productivity evaluations are symbolic representations of performance. In reinforcing an empirical and often de-contextualized understanding of achievement, productivity evaluations dismiss the active 'contingencies, interests, conflicts' (Bourdieu 2014, p. 28) at work in the field of education. The abstract elements of a "science of education" is preferred over the 'in-between space/places/contexts that connect classrooms with the experiences of everyday life' (Giroux 2011, p. 75). This type of evaluative exposé of the classroom teacher or school as inadequate or in need of "fixing" is invariably about dismissing the relevance and impact of student attitudes towards schooling, behaviours and experiences of schooling and obvious family background characteristics. Chad highlights the minimization of these classroom complexities by saying that:

> everyone [thinks they] can do teaching better than teachers. They all have a context . . . and everyone has a view of how they can do it better than you can.
>
> *(Chad)*

Chad reveals some of the complexities he works with every day:

> The second thing is that every societal problem I have to solve. I suppose the third thing is that every societal problem that hasn't been solved I've been neglectful of. It's this whole view of 'if we had better personnel from the universities training them [classroom teachers] we'd have all of these – we'd have a better society because the teachers would be better'. But, in reality it's a load of rubbish.
>
> *(Chad)*

This final point made by Chad is about how some research (and policy) symbolically represents the work of teachers. Teachers are generally "not good enough", are poorly educated/trained and so are "underperforming". Perceived problems in society, even various parental responsibilities, have been assigned increasingly to teachers and an already crowded curriculum. As Chad notes, it is teachers who are being asked more and more to ameliorate the issues that society and parents no longer address, and when they cannot, blame is attributed by those who have relinquished their responsibilities. He criticizes the simplistic nature of this representation and positioning of teachers and their work, be it in policy or in some forms of research that tend to view efficiency, effectiveness and quality in linear and ordered terms.

2.6 Disparaging a public education system

The consistent message from governments of all persuasions in most Anglophone capitalist nations post-1950s about the public education system is that it is in crisis through persistent failure and under-performance. The clearest illustration of this message comes from a report commissioned in the U.S. during the Reagan era (1981–1989). The report, *A nation at risk: The imperative for educational reform* (U.S. Department of Education 1983), launches an attack on public education, declaring about the U.S. that:

> Our nation is at risk. Our once unchallenged pre-eminence in commerce, industry, science, and technological innovation is being overtaken by competitors throughout the world. This report is concerned with only one of the many causes and dimensions of the problem, but it is the one

that undergirds American prosperity, security, and civility. We report to the American people that while we can take justifiable pride in what our schools and colleges have historically accomplished and contributed to the United States and the well-being of its people, the educational foundations of our society are presently being eroded by a rising tide of mediocrity that threatens our very future as a Nation and a people. What was unimaginable a generation ago has begun to occur – others are matching and surpassing our educational attainments.

(1983, p. 9)

In the U.S., the "under-performance" and "low productivity" message in education has its modern origins in the late 1950s with the growing belief that America was losing its dominant position to the Soviet Union regarding technical and educational superiority (see Zhao 2009). Fear about declining educational standards became a political strategy. In 1958 the National Defense Education Act (NDEA) was passed. The act provided for the federal involvement in the comprehensive financing of education at all levels (public and private) within the U.S. Zhao (2009) claims that the NDEA comprehensively 'transformed the American education landscape' (p. 23) by stimulating educational innovation, increasing the talent pool in areas such as science, engineering, mathematics, technology and foreign languages and lay the foundation for a new curriculum. While the NDEA covered all levels of education, 'its major influence has been much bigger in higher education' (Zhao 2009, p. 23). We re-visit the "under-performance" and "low productivity" message again in Chapter 7 when considering how terms such as "instruction" and "pedagogy" are now used in education policy.

In England in the 1960s a similar rhetoric of crisis, failure and underperformance was unfolding, although couched more in terms of inadequate school student retention rates and declining post-compulsory examination results. Change was afoot as governmental concern about declining educational standards led to legislative reform (see Machin and Vignoles 2006). The educational challenge at the time in England centred on a value-for-money argument rooting out endemic failure and insisting on customer satisfaction. Nonetheless, it was not until the Education Reform Act of 1988 that major educational change arrived in the United Kingdom as a whole. The Education Reform Act formed the education policy vision of the then Conservative Thatcher government (1979–1990). It successfully 'inaugurated a new policy settlement in England based on marketization, a standards agenda, a traditional academic curriculum, prescribed teaching and a bureaucratic system of accountability' (Jones and Thomson 2008, p. 718). These economically driven reforms which continued apace under the Blair Labour government (1997–2007) triggered other initiatives such as parental choice, parent representation on government education bodies and linking school funding with student enrolment numbers (see Machin and Vignoles 2006). Performance management and new forms of governance soon emerged.

The Australian educational scene at the time mirrored that of the U.S. and England, although it was not until the 1970s and beyond that major educational change came to Australia. The Australian experience was tied to industry change, and the need for competitive economic advantage saw a redefinition of education's purpose. The particular crisis presented in Australia was economic in origin. A newly elected national Labour government (March 1983) in accord with the nation's peak trade union body, the Australian Council of Trade Unions (ACTU), prepared a report, *Australia Reconstructed* (1987), which canvassed the notion of maintaining international economic competitiveness. Central to this was the concern with reducing Australia's fiscal trade imbalance and enhancing productivity via new work practices. The report in its executive summary stated:

> The seriousness of Australia's current economic situation is now well appreciated throughout a significant part of the community. Furthermore there is broad agreement as to the main causes of the economic problems we now face.
>
> Ours is a middle-sized economy which is largely unable to influence international economic conditions, yet is largely subject to them. For a considerable period, the prices received for our exports have not kept pace with increases in the prices paid for our imports. That is, there has been a long-term decline in Australia's terms of trade.
>
> (ACTU/TDC 1987, p. xi)

Australia's school retention rates, like those in England, were considered low, particularly for a nation concerned with maintaining its long-term economic global competitiveness. Inadequate skill formation was also identified as a major issue, and the report made it clear that education and training must be a central pillar in any long-term vision to make Australia economically competitive. Education became synonymous with training and the development of job-ready skills. Large-scale changes were experienced in the higher, technical and school education sectors, re-orienting the field of education, including the public education system towards a 'post-Keynesian framework and the dominance of market liberal ideology' (Lingard 2000, p. 29). As Lingard (2000) mentions, the 'context for this move was the globalisation of the economy' (p. 29) combining the dual aims of a 'postmodernist performativity' and the 'leaner and meaner state emphasising efficiency and effectiveness' (Lingard 2000, p. 30) as a response to the new economic world. In this world education is increasingly

> defined as an industry, and educational institutions have been forced to conduct themselves more and more like profit-seeking firms. Policy changes across the sector have been introduced by different governments, state and federal, and in different forms. But the policy changes all move

in the same direction – increasing the grip of market logic on schools, universities and technical education.

(Connell 2013, p. 102)

The result in Australia saw it moving further than any other nation in the English-speaking world to the creation of school markets (see Campbell, Proctor and Sherington 2009). The market mechanisms of choice and competition mean that all schools compete for student and parent customers. An era of enhanced funding to non-government schools (private schools) and a 'broad loss of faith in the effectiveness of many public institutions' (Campbell et al. 2009, p. 1) is the consequence. Parents in an environment such as this are 'expected to be active and wise in choosing a school' (Campbell et al. 2009, p. 1) to safeguard against a host of perceived failures, including that of poor teaching performance.

2.7 Teachers are the problem

An important feature connected to data simplification in education is "teacher blame". The phenomenon of teacher blame has a history. It is situated within a broader controversy that Seddon (1991) claims is the 'generalized crisis of schooling' focused now more specifically as a 'crisis of teachers and teaching' (p. 359). Larsen (2010) suggests that the 'discourse of blame and derision about teachers' always arises 'in key periods of socio-economic, political and cultural change' (p. 208). She makes the claim that the parallel discourse of the 'centrality of the teacher' (Larsen 2010, p. 208) (i.e. that it is only the work of teachers and their teaching practice/s that ensures successful student achievement) represents teachers as somehow inadequate or not. Chad, a teacher in our research, made reference to this phenomenon earlier in the chapter. These 'dual discourses (the discourse of blame/derision and the discourse of the centrality of the teacher)' allows teachers to be positioned as 'deficient . . . [while] simultaneously shouldered with the responsibility of fixing societal and school problems' (Larsen 2010, p. 208). Gale (2006) highlights this particular phenomenon as well, suggesting that 'positioning teachers as the "problem"' is more broadly a 'politics of schooling' manifestation' (p. 12). This teacher problem is

> distinguishable by four sometimes contradictory accounts: (1) disappointment with student outcomes, particularly those within government systems; (2) the shortsightedness, irrelevance and inappropriateness of much school curricula; (3) teaching's ageing and potentially diminishing workforce; and (4) the inadequacies of teachers' professional development programs.
>
> *(Gale 2006, p. 18)*

Some of the teachers in our study also refer to this in these terms:

> And, so I feel education, public education, has gone off the rails with this type of attitude because ever since the productivity commission[1] did a

> whole lot of research, I think, around how hard teachers work or don't work, there seems to have been this general push that every time . . . that if we gain a pay-rise or we gain any conditions, along with that comes a productivity push that we've got to do more and more. In other words we somehow are not deserving of a basic rise . . . we just have to keep working harder for it. But the pressures of all this new information coming down on us, so from – since 2014 I could count on my hand at least ten new acronyms to learn in teaching.
>
> *(Heather)*

Heather draws our attention to the need to approach research cautiously because not all research is equal. One always has to ask is this policy seeking evidence or is the research premised on asking authentic research questions where the answer is not known and where advocacy is put to the side.

> You know, it's like – it's like you've got a whole lot of people outside the education industry telling you what to do again.
>
> *(Chad)*

As Chad indicates, there is widespread ignorance about teaching and learning, and this often is visible when people outside of the classroom and schools think they can offer informed opinions without consulting the experts. A question that arises from Chad's experience is whether the ongoing commentary by those without expertise/experience in teaching/pedagogy is a result of unconscious beliefs and bias about what it means to teach and be a teacher.

> Everything is channelled towards a set of numbers that somebody else values. That's not what teachers value more broadly.
>
> *(Aaron)*

Aaron highlights another issue facing the profession with its change in emphasis as a social good to an economic good. While this change in emphasis (e.g. what is valued is what can be measured) may work well for economics for the most part, it is an over simplification about teachers and teaching when considering students' development.

When individual teachers are singled out as the problem, they are then targeted for some form of reparatory action. The action undertaken is generally framed on shaping teachers' professional practice/s, especially teaching practice/s with stronger performance and in-classroom accountability with reporting the aim. Heather states on this point:

> The actual how we're doing our teaching and how we're reporting and the systems being put in place, they're not giving us time to just think and process. . . . [Take] online reporting [it] is meant to make our lives easier. Well,

actually, what it's done is made our lives harder and taken us away from
the teaching and learning and being with students which is our core work.
(Heather)

Chad, in reference to stronger accountability, talks of the implementation of a
"medical model" in education and the imposition of more control.

> Well, we've got control of the curriculum now, back to the 1950s . . . 'this
> is the essay you will write', 'this is the time that you will take to write it',
> 'this is the book you will read', 'this is the chapter you will be examined
> on and on these dates, around these dates', and if you don't, you're deemed
> deficient.
> *(Chad)*

Teachers are encouraged (forced?) into accepting the rudiments of 'performance cultures' (Sachs 2016, p. 414) where accountability, reporting and improved performance is demanded. The performance culture relies on the 'use of performance indicators . . . whereby student learning outcomes and teacher performance can be measured' (Sachs 2016, p. 414). In other words, using statistical data as a "cover" for the complex and contingent. Aaron states on this point:

> It's not one teacher, one student. It's one teacher, many students and in that
> you've got 25 random things happening every single minute. Not every
> single day, every single minute. So, I don't know how you control for so
> much random human behaviours. I don't know. I don't know.
> *(Aaron)*

A performance culture reporting on teacher deficiencies requires information. The objectification and subjectivation of teachers are actualized via metrification – a point previously alluded to by Aaron. The metrics used are a series of student achievement audits generally based on standardized tests and value-added scores, which we cover in Chapter 5. A performance culture co-opts the teacher into national economic agendas. Enhanced student achievement as the preferred learning outcome is the demonstrated requirement and is realized 'by improving the standard and quality of teaching' (Sachs 2016, p. 415). Aaron, in reference to standards and quality, suggests that education systems are now 'looking for numbers. They're looking for order. They're looking for quiet classrooms' (Aaron).

2.8 Evaluating systems and people

Teaching practice operates within an economic and political context that shapes and/or subjectifies. Teaching is also constituted by an array of governance arrangements. The numerical value that a classroom teacher adds to the individual learning outcomes of particular students stems from a desire for certainty about the efficacy and quality of designated teaching sessions. The work of Michel Foucault, chiefly his studies of discipline, bio-politics and government, deals with techniques of control and power that work to regulate relations between people. We have alluded briefly to some of this work earlier in the chapter. The work of Foucault can be used to think about how teachers are controlled and managed and in particular how their teaching practice/s can be closely scrutinized. The core Foucauldian notion of governmentality can be used to explain constraining modes of regulation, specifically methods (administrative and/or research) that circumscribe and evaluate practice. Importantly for Foucault, discursive statements – often dominant and assenting discourses defining and evaluating practice – deliver certitude by virtue of their acclaimed acceptance and universal adoption. The declarative and arithmetical symbolism often used in education policy making and TER pronouncing sureties of "best practice" (a notion we cover in Chapter 9) or of "what works" is a form of 'governmentalization' (Foucault 1997, p. 28) which is manifest in the expert and specialist evaluations of teaching effectiveness and quality. Governmentalization are the processes and mechanisms in place that regulate and control behaviour which can be thought about as the system of relations, techniques, frameworks – in brief, the apparatuses that "discipline" exerting control (see Foucault 1977) over people. While enacted by government in terms of installation, governmentalization becomes a process where individuals self-regulate. The self-regulation that comes with standardized testing, for instance, is an example of governmentalization.

The symbolic surety of TER as a regime of evaluation provides a foundation for "truth" about teaching effectiveness and quality. It opens a space that permits policy makers and school administrators to discern between what counts as effective as opposed to ineffective teaching. This allows for the falsification and verification of teaching practice/s according to some established "truth". In other words, evaluation and the mechanisms used therein are governmentalizing tools that permit TER and the classroom in which teaching occurs to function as a 'site of veridiction' (Foucault 2008, p. 32) and to tell the "truth" regarding the productive capacity of an individual teacher to enhance student achievement.

Pierre Bourdieu has suggested that 'objectivism destroys the specificity of all practices, which, like gift exchange, tend or pretend to put the law of self-interest into abeyance' (Bourdieu 1977, p. 171). The evaluation of a "pure" objectivism has a symbolic power connected to it suggestive of a relative autonomy or pure independence free of bias and contextual influences. Objectivism in the form of algorithmic models and quantification (categories, numeral indices, vector scales) reduces complexity and the specificity located in classrooms. The evaluative models used in TER adhere to 'systems of classification (taxonomies) which organize perception and structure practice' (Bourdieu 1977, p. 97). Bourdieu, a critic of reductive theoretical constructions to explain sociological practice/s, maintains a scepticism towards models and their 'capacity to *objectify*' (Bourdieu 1977, p. 170, emphasis in original). His reasons for doing so hinge on their incapacity to outline in detail the full picture of experience. As he states, models of objectification:

> owe their practical coherence . . . to the fact that they are the product of practices that can fulfil their practical functions only in so far as they implement, in the practical state, principles that are not only coherent – that is, capable of generating practices that are both intrinsically coherent and compatible with the objective conditions – but also practical, in the sense of convenient, that is, easy to master and use, because they obey a 'poor' and economical 'logic'.
>
> *(Bourdieu 1990, p. 86)*

If we apply this thinking to TER, we find that the complexities encompassed in schooling are usually lumped into a framework of pre-conceived constructs and experimental controls (input/output indicators, impact factors and so on). The integrated whole which forms the myriad of experiences and relationships inherent in schooling is then detached and replaced by a partial and narrowed down representation of what is actually the case. This, we say, creates another and more pressing problem: that of false representation.

2.9 Conclusion

We have argued in this chapter that the research constructs TE and TQ typically define classroom teachers and their teaching practice/s in particular ways, usually in deficit terms. While TE and TQ purportedly capture "what matters" in teaching and learning, they too are also indicative of hierarchical linear "cause-effect" research processes. Theoretically informed by algorithmic mathematical iterative research functions, notions of TE and TQ numerically define teaching practice, dispensing with the properties which combine to form social phenomena. This can only be the case if 'reference to concrete things is abandoned' (Totaro and Ninno 2016, p. 140), privileging instead a techno-rational conceptualization of classroom teaching and learning.

This instrumentalist course in research into TE and TQ aligns with broader "neoliberal tendencies" (an issue we engage in in the next chapter) around the contemporary nature of teachers' work, 'encompassing the decisions they make on both a short and long term basis about approaches to such things as curriculum design, pedagogy and assessment (to name a few)' (Mockler 2011, p. 517). Selective use of data centred around student performance levels based typically on external indicators of effectiveness and quality are linked to accountability. This type of "thin" data is 'presented in numbers and graphics and requires interpretation and meaning making, relating numbers to other types of knowledge sources' (Mausethagen, Prøitz and Skedsmo 2018, p. 38). An absent under-communicated element in how "thin" data represents teachers is the role it has in narrowing perspectives on schooling and teaching and learning. The emphasis is then towards standardized performance in learning and behaviour and adopting a "one best way" to teach and educate.

Note

1 The Australian Productivity Commission is the major Australian government review and advisory body on matters related to microeconomic policy, regulation and a range of other economic, social, educational and environmental issues. The Commission provides independent advice and information to Australian governments (federal and state) and has four main functions: to participate in public inquiries and research studies, to perform performance monitoring and benchmarking, to engage in self-initiated research and annual reporting and to advise on competitive neutrality complaints.

References

ACTU/TDC. 1987. *Australia Reconstructed: ACTU/TDC Mission to Western Europe*. Canberra: AGPS.
Ballou, D., Sanders, W. and Wright, P. 2004. Controlling for student background in value-added assessment of teachers. *Journal of Educational and Behavioural Statistics*, 29(1), 37–65.
Barrow, R. 1984. Teacher judgement and teacher effectiveness. *The Journal of Educational Thought*, 18(2), 76–83.
Biesta, G. 2010. *Good Education in an Age of Measurement: Ethics, Politics, Democracy*. Boulder, CO: Paradigm Publishers.
Bourdieu, P. 1977. *Outline of a Theory of Practice*. Cambridge, UK: Cambridge University Press.
Bourdieu, P. 1990. *The Logic of Practice*. Oxford, UK: Blackwell Publishers.
Bourdieu, P. 2014. *On the State: Lectures at the College de France 1989–1992* (Translated by D. Fernback). Cambridge, UK: Polity Press.
Caldwell, B. J. and Spinks, J. M. 1988. *The Self-managing School*. London, UK: The Falmer Press.
Campbell, C., Proctor, H. and Sherington, G. 2009. *School Choice: How Parents Negotiate the School Market in Australia*. NSW, Australia: Allen & Unwin.
Chetty, R., Friedman, J. N. and Rockoff, J. E. 2011. *The Long-Term Impacts of Teachers: Teacher Value-Added and Student Outcomes in Adulthood*. NBER Working Paper No. 17699.
Clinton, J. M., Anderson, M., Dawson, G., Dawson, A., Bolton, S. and Mason, R. 2016. *Systems, Frameworks and Measures of Teacher Effectiveness*. Melbourne, Australia: Centre for Program Evaluation.
Coleman, J. S., Campbell, E. Q., Hobson, C. J., McPartland, J., Mood, A. M., Weinfeld, F. D. and York, R. L. 1966. *Equality of Educational Opportunity*. Washington, DC: US Government Printing Office.
Connell, B., Ashenden, D. J., Kessler, S. and Dowsett, G. W. 1982. *Making the Difference: Schools, Families and Social Division*. Sydney: George Allen and Unwin.
Connell, R. 2013. The neoliberal cascade and education: An essay on the market agenda and its consequences. *Critical Studies in Education*, 54(2), 99–112.
Darling-Hammond, L., Amrein-Beardsley, A., Haertel, E. and Rothstein, J. 2012. Evaluating teacher evaluation. *Phi Delta Kappan*, 93(6), 8–15.
Espeland, W. N. and Stevens, M. L. 1998. Commensuration as a social process. *Annual Review of Sociology*, 24, 313–343. https://doi.org/10.1146/annurev.soc.24.1.313

Foucault, M. 1977. *Discipline and Punish: The Birth of the Prison*. London, UK: Penguin Books.
Foucault, M. 1997. *The Politics of Truth*. New York: Semiotext(e).
Foucault, M. 2008. *The Birth of Biopolitics*. Hampshire, UK: Palgrave Macmillan.
Gale, T. 2006. How did we ever arrive at the conclusion that teachers are the problem? A critical reading in the discourses of Australian schooling. In B. Doecke, M. Howie and W. Sawyer (Eds.), *'Only Connect . . .' English Teaching, Schooling and Democracy* (pp. 99–119). Kent Town: AATE & Wakefield Press.
Gearin, B. 2017. The mismeasure of monkeys: Education policy research and the evolution of social capital. *Journal of Education Policy*, 32(5), 604–627. https://doi.org/10.1080/02680939.2017.1309071
Giroux, H. A. 2011. *On Critical Pedagogy*. New York and London, UK: Continuum International Publishing Group.
Gottlieb, D. 2015. *Education Reform and the Concept of Good Teaching*. Hoboken, NJ: Routledge.
Hattie, J. 2003. *Teachers Make a Difference, What Is the Research Evidence?* ACER: Melbourne.
Hattie, J. 2009. *Visible Learning: A Synthesis of Over 800 Meta-analyses Relating to Achievement*. London, Routledge.
Hattie, J. 2012. *Visible Learning for Teachers: Maximizing Impact on Learning*. London, UK: Routledge.
Jones, K. and Thomson, P. 2008. Policy rhetoric and the renovation of English schooling: The case of creative partnerships. *Journal of Education Policy*, 23(6), 715–727.
Ladson-Billings, G. 2006. From the achievement gap to the education debt: Understanding achievement in U.S. schools. *Educational Researcher*, 35(7), 3–12.
Larsen, M. A. 2010. Troubling the discourse of teacher centrality: A comparative perspective. *Journal of Education Policy*, 25(2), 207–231.
Lewis, S. 2016. Governing schooling through "what works": The OECD's PISA for schools. *Journal of Education Policy*, 32(3), 281–302.
Lingard, B. 2000. Federalism in schooling since The Karmel Report (1973), *Schools in Australia*: From modernist hope to postmodernist performativity. *Australian Educational Researcher*, 27(2), 25–61.
Lingard, B., Hayes, D., Mills, M. and Christie, P. 2003. *Leading Learning: Making Hope Practical in Schools*. Philadelphia, PA: Open University Press.
Machin, S. and Vignoles, A. 2006. *Education Policy in the UK* (pp. 1–22). London, UK: Published by the London School of Economics.
Mausethagen, S., Prøitz, T. and Skedsmo, G. 2018. Teachers' use of knowledge sources in "result meetings": Thin data and thick data use. *Teachers and Teaching*, 24(1), 37–49. https://doi.org/10.1080/13540602.2017.1379986
Mockler, N. 2011. Beyond "what works": Understanding teacher identity as a practical and political tool. *Teachers and Teaching*, 17(5), 517–528. https://doi.org/10.1080/13540602.2011.602059
Morris, P. 2012. Pick "n" mix, select and project; policy borrowing and the quest for "world class" schooling: An analysis of the 2010 schools white paper. *Journal of Education Policy*, 27(1), 89–107. https://doi.org/10.1080/02680939.2011.596226
Muijs, D., Kyriakides, L., van der Werf, G., Creemers, B., Timperley, H. and Earl, L. 2014. State of the art teacher effectiveness and professional learning. *School Effectiveness and School Improvement: An International Journal of Research, Policy and Practice*, 25(2), 231–256.
Muijs, D. and Reynolds, D. 2005. *Effective Teaching: Evidence and Practice*. London: Sage Publications.
Naylor, R. and Sayed, Y. 2014. *Teacher Quality: Evidence Review*. Office of Development Effectiveness. Canberra, Australia: Department of Foreign Affairs and Trade.

Phillips, D. C. 2014. Research in the hard sciences, and in very hard "softer" domains. *Educational Researcher*, 43(1), 9–11.

Pianta, R. C. and Hamre, B. K. 2009. Conceptualization, measurement, and improvement of classroom processes: Standardized observation can leverage capacity. *Educational Researcher*, 38(2), 109–119.

Robinson, W. 2004. *Power to Teach*. London, UK: Woburn Press.

Rowe, K. 2003. *The Importance of Teacher Quality as a Key Determinant of Students' Experiences and Outcomes of Schooling*. ACER Research Conference, Melbourne, Australia, October 19–21.

Sachs, J. 2016. Teacher professionalism: Why are we still talking about it? *Teachers and Teaching*, 22(4), 413–425. https://doi.org/10.1080/13540602.2015.1082732

Seddon, T. 1991. Contradictions in the Australian teacher debate: Implications for policy and practice. *Journal of Education Policy*, 6(4), 359–369.

Sellar, S. 2015. A feel for numbers: Affect, data and education policy. *Critical Studies in Education*, 56(1), 131–146. https://doi.org/10.1080/17508487.2015.981198

Skourdoumbis, A. 2017. Assessing the productivity of schools through two "what works" inputs, *teacher quality* and *teacher effectiveness*. *Educational Research for Policy and Practice*, 16, 205. https://doi-org.ezproxy-f.deakin.edu.au/10.1007/s10671-016-9210-y

Totaro, P. and Ninno, D. 2016. Algorithms and the practical world. *Theory, Culture and Society*, 33(1), 139–152.

Triplett, J. and Bosworth, B. 2004. *Productivity in the U.S. Services Sector: New Sources of Economic Growth*. Washington, DC: Brookings Institution Press.

U.S. Department of Education. 1983. *A Nation at Risk. The Imperative for Educational Reform*. Retrieved from https://www.edreform.com/wp-content/uploads/2013/02/A_Nation_At_Risk_1983.pdf.

U.S. Department of Education. 2009. *Race to the Top Program: Executive Summary*. Retrieved from https://www2.ed.gov/programs/racetothetop/executive-summary.pdf

Zhao, Y. 2009. *Catching Up or Leading the Way: American Education in the Age of Globalization*. Alexandria, VA: ASCD.

3
REFORM

Introduction

In this chapter we deal with specific political and economic parameters that influence contemporary education in Australia and other Organization for Economic Co-Operation and Development (OECD) nations and will explain why education is involved in doing the work of the economic and political. It anchors the debate about TE and TQ and contemporary evaluations of pedagogy within these parameters. The chapter implies that accountability metrics such as TE and TQ are linked to a broader set of political and economic aspects of public education reform. As a result, the chapter will consider the modern policy prioritizations given to economic change and canvas the role that school education now has in this. The implicit facilitation of large-scale economic change occurs via the political process, and so the chapter will discuss the political imperative of economic transformation via market-driven approaches. It will introduce the mechanism of calculation borrowed from the field of economics that holds schools and public education to account – the education production function.

3.1 The political and economic question

The reformist interventions that infuse the current political and economic imaginary have their origin in the shifting tensions connected to the ever-present instabilities of capital. The Keynesian post-war settlements of state-administered capitalism have slowly loosened over time from the 1970s onwards. Streeck characterizes the loosening as a steady disintegration over time due to a series of economic crises.

> To be precise, three crises followed one another: the global inflation of the 1970s, the explosion of public debt in the 1980s, and rapidly rising private

indebtedness in the subsequent decade, resulting [more recently] in the collapse of financial markets.

(2016, p. 16)

While a period of relative economic stability under liberal capitalism has characterized "the West" for a number of decades post-World War Two, constant and growing economic uncertainty permeates the contemporary political terrain of the most advanced nations across the globe. The clear and structured relations of a once-settled mode of productive exchange – the economic boom years encompassing the late 1940s to the early/mid-1970s – now no longer dominates. The disorganized nodes of current-day capital are framed on a hegemonic and coercive neoliberal political and economic framework girded by globalization. Globalization is the change of scale in the 'formation of world systems' (Marginson 1991, p. 19) brought about through scientific and technological interconnections of the economic and political. Globalization incorporates 'finance and trade, communications and information technologies, migration and tourism, global societies, linguistic, cultural and ideological convergence and world systems of signs and images' (Marginson 1991, p. 19). Globalization is a complex phenomenon, and many factors (social, political, cultural, economic, historical) are involved in its genesis.

Neoliberalism conversely is viewed as a 'proliferating and increasingly taken-for-granted political settlement . . . built upon the diverse ideas and practices that presume the ascendancy of privatisation, marketization, corporatisation and competition' (Gerrard 2017, p. 59). Rowlands and Rawolle (2013) classify neoliberalism as the:

> rethinking of the way classical liberal theories should apply to political deliberations about government and individuals. These include the importance and security of private property, the rule of law, the importance of economic "maximisation" models to policy, the role of the state, the nature of obligations individuals hold to one another, the state (social and private contracts) and markets, choice and public decision making.
>
> *(p. 262)*

Neoliberalism 'means the agenda of economic and social transformation under the sign of the free market' (Connell 2013, p. 100). The neoliberal political and economic ethic is founded on an ideological commitment and belief in individual emancipation (i.e. the freedoms and choices that each self-guided individual can make). The active economic ingredient in neoliberalism is opportunity. In this sense it is no different from other forms of capital expansion, although a significant difference is its anti-statist drive.

> Neoliberalism seeks to make existing markets wider, and to create new markets where they did not exist before. Needs formerly met by public

agencies on a principle of citizen rights, or through personal relationships in communities and families, are now to be met by companies selling services in a market.

(Connell 2013, p. 100)

The neoliberal politico-economic project binds services such as education to the vagaries of the free market. This shift in administration is justified on the grounds that private enterprise is best suited to deliver on social services and that consumer choice will determine the type and level of service/s offered. The consequences for education in this type of political/economic set-up will be examined later in this chapter.

The 'disorganized neoliberal capitalism' (Fraser 2013, p. 220) of our current era is infused with a new "spirit" (see Boltanski and Chiapello 2005). The rigid and structured has given way to the devolved and shifting. Disorganization is most acute in the financial markets, resulting in the de-concentration of capital. Greater labour market flexibility embraces the seductive promise of self-capitalization. This means that each individual is immersed in a new ideological engagement, one that makes the life of each person a never-ending (continuous) working project. Teachers are centre stage here in preparing students for this new world of endless individual "re-badging" through education and/or training. We turn to this aspect again in Chapter 7.

Globalization and neoliberalism have shifted 'practices of governing', these being 'now less concerned with providing services for populations than in mobilizing those concerned to help themselves' (Edwards 2002, p. 354). This significant shift is one of structure and functionality de-coupling the individual from the vestiges of, as Rose (1996) terms, the 'territory of government in terms of community' (p. 333). Active and willing participation combined with an entrepreneurial capacity means that failure, if it occurs, is the responsibility of the self-governing individual. The individual transformation sought is of a 'government of conduct', an attitudinal attenuation of relations 'between the ways in which people are governed by others and the ways in which they are advised to govern themselves' (Rose 1996, p. 340). Social or career advancement is self-made, each accorded to their individual capacities. Risk, if it is to be experienced, is carried by the individual. Security is replaced by instability coupled with a political/economic precariousness with roots in the institutionalized dynamics of shifting virtual finance.

In addition to this and post the Global Financial Crisis (GFC) of 2007–2008 is, according to Emma Rowe, an attenuation of the neoliberal marked out not only by market instability but by a political and cultural/social shift. This shift is towards the "post-neoliberal" and contains a 'marked rise of alt-right politics' and a concomitant rise in 'bold progressive movements' (Rowe 2019, p. 272). It is also a period in which 'intangible capital – that is, capital that is made of "big data", valuable yet largely invisible data networks, software and "learning platforms'" (Rowe 2019, p. 273) makes a significant contribution to economic growth.

> The most valuable global companies are those that deal in the intangibles: branding, mathematical modelling, predictive software, algorithms. Companies such as Microsoft, Apple, Amazon, Facebook and Alphabet (which owns Google, and associated platforms such as YouTube, Google Maps and Google Chrome), are all companies which are driven by the intangible – digital net-works, education or training, software, branding and design, and human capital.
>
> *(Rowe 2019, p. 273)*

The rising importance of education to this mix is evidenced by what an OECD report (2013) suggests are the new drivers of economic growth, 'knowledge-based capital' backed by a strategy dependent on 'productivity-raising innovation' (p. 6).

3.2 Schooling and education in the new world

The purposes of schooling and the direction of education in this new world is a mix between exposure to basic literacy and numeracy, including the new emphasis on innovation, creativity, problem-solving and so on, and the inculcation of traditional values and norms that a society holds dear. Knowledge and the role of curriculum is central. Schooling in an age of information and increasing disorder means adapting to some major challenges these being new modes of work and the impact of technology and, the global widespread movement of large populations. Lyn Yates (2017) suggests that there are four key elements in thinking about the purposes of schooling and its direction when considering knowledge and the curriculum schools offer in these new times. These include thinking about schools as (1) sites for the development of knowledge and student capabilities; (2) as places that assist in forming people as future citizens; (3) as entities that serve individual purposes and (4) as institutions serving social and national purposes (pp. 86–87). The basic premise of these four elements is that schooling is about a process of immersion where young people are exposed to the kinds of knowledge needed for their successful transition into adulthood.

There is always contestation about the type of curriculum students are exposed to, and it is usually centred on 'what is chosen, by what processes, by whom, with what intent, and with what result' (Macdonald 2003, p. 140). In nations such as Australia, the U.S. and England, two themes on curriculum as school knowledge are evident. One is characterized by a values-based argument encompassing notions of choice with an emphasis on asserting individual and family rights. The other, as Yates (2017) points out, is 'concerned about the impact for the whole community and for the nation of the output of schools as a whole' (p. 88). This particular and secondary theme is about the outcomes of schooling and focuses on the traits considered relevant for community participation in the world of the 21st century and is comprised of an amalgam of 'skills, citizenship values (or alienation), and longer-term foundations for economic and social benefit' (Yates 2017, p. 88).

3.3 The impact of reform/s

Hargreaves and Goodson (2006) suggest that educational change occurs in distinctive phases and defined periods of time and is characterized usually by successive waves of reform based on economics and demographics. They identify three distinctive periods of educational change where a variety of reforms were implemented in public education, coinciding with the wave of politico-economic changes outlined earlier. The first incorporates the mid-20th century post-World War Two period extending into the 1970s, which they label a period of optimism and innovation. The second extends from the late 1970s and into the mid-1990s, which they label the period of complexity and contradiction, and the third extending from the mid-1990s onwards is the period of standardization and marketization. Each of the periods mentioned is influenced by identifiable elements.

The first period of optimism and innovation, often labelled the "Golden Age" (Hobsbawm 1994), was heavily influenced by the post-World War Two economic expansion of 'booming demographics and a buoyant economy' (Hargreaves and Goodson 2006, p. 29). State monetary investment was high, particularly in public education, leading to 'reforms and large-scale projects that emphasized teacher-generated innovation and student-centered forms of learning' (Hargreaves and Goodson 2006, p. 29). The optimism and innovation of the time aligned with teacher autonomy 'when professional commitment meant realizing the enthusiasms of youth' (Hargreaves and Goodson 2006, p. 29). The period of complexity and contradiction is also one of transition and contraction. The Keynesian political and economic framework by this stage had reached its high point, and the emerging ideological consensus agitated for a restructure of the state. The dynamics of the free market were championed, particularly by governments incorporating a 'managerialist, competitive performative state apparatus' (Lingard 2000, p. 24) concerned with efficiency and effectiveness and the outputs of education. The third (current) period of standardization and marketization is in many respects the new world of precariousness (see Standing 2011) that had its beginnings in the second period. It is delineated by the hallmarks of globalization that has shaped education via accepted orthodoxies, these being 'promoted by international financial organizations, where markets and standardization, accountability and performance targets, high-stakes testing and intrusive intervention are at the heart of almost all reform efforts' (Hargreaves and Goodson 2006, p. 30) in education.

3.4 Accountability

Talk of accountability is not complete without mention of performativity and performance, the latter of individuals and/or organizations. Accountability is about providing "an account of" through a legitimated 'discourse of power' (Lyotard 1984, p. 46) which first captures and then signifies the 'worth, quality or value of an individual or organisation within a field of judgement' (Ball 2003, p. 216). Ball (2003) defines performativity as 'a technology, a culture and a mode of regulation that employs judgements, comparisons and displays as means of incentive, control, attrition and change – based on rewards and sanctions (both material and symbolic)' (Ball 2003, p. 216). Accountability is about a regulated form of answerability which usually draws upon 'a set of standards for accountable actions and behaviours' (Baroutsis 2016, p. 570).

Teachers and education systems are subject to large-scale policy initiatives that involve high-stakes accountability mechanisms and processes. An Australian example is MySchool.[1] Initiatives such as MySchool are symptomatic of the new public management (NPM) 'corpus of managerial ideas' (Verger and Curran 2014, p. 254) that have propelled public sector reform over a series of decades post the 1980s. New public management is a form of public administration 'that employs knowledge and experiences acquired in business management and other disciplines to improve efficiency, effectiveness, and general performance of public services in modern bureaucracies' (Vigoda 2003, p. 813). NPM has legitimated the governance structures of devolved managerial administration that in school education favours school autonomy, payment by results, client choice and so on. The guiding force behind many of the NPM reforms instituted over time was budgetary austerity aligned with a policy-maker rationale favouring a public choice approach to social services.

There are behavioural connotations involved in NPM where data and evidence of performance channel control towards standards which govern the actions of school personnel. Standards reflect a maximum point of attainment and 'may be seen to be an opportunity for governments either to control education activity through the reporting requirements of student learning outcomes and teacher performance or to improve the provision and outcomes of schooling' (Sachs 2016, p. 417). The standards linked to teachers centre on their credentialing, their subsequent teaching practice/s once employed and their professionalism. Accountability effects often regularize the in-classroom actions of teachers by overtly focusing on surveillance of their work through heightened 'centralization, increased prescription of curricula and school self-management' (Sachs 2016, p. 418). The challenge for any accountability system is in adequately capturing and then reflecting the complexities connected to school education while ensuring that the needs of the public are met. This will become increasingly important in an era of new "globalizing educational accountabilities" where comparison, monitoring and management of 'education systems in connection with national economies' (Lingard, Martino, Rezai-Rashti and Sellar 2016, p. 3) utilizes the "big data" infrastructures of contemporary capitalism (see Lingard et al. 2016; Mayer-Schonberger and Cukier 2013, 2014).

3.5 New managerialism

The "new managerialism" (Clarke, Cochrane and McLaughlin 1994) connected to market models of management has devolved control of schools to the local level. This may seem desirable on the surface, although the state through its accountability mechanisms maintains rigid control, steering and/or governing things from a distance (see Marginson 1997). The focus on the outcomes of schooling is aligned with a vocabulary referencing 'customers, empowerment, charters, innovation and excellence' (Gale and Densmore 2003, p. 25). This represents an important development in school education as new managerialism feeds into the "enterprising self" ethos and neoliberal vision where school personnel (teachers) are encouraged to 'use their personal initiative to transform teaching and learning' (Gale and Densmore 2003, p. 25).

One of the central features of the new managerialism is that it elevates the status and role of the manager. Morley and Rassool (2000) explain how the glamorization of the manager towards transformational 'charismatic change agent and risk taker, associated with innovation, corporate culture and enterprise . . . has allowed public service managers the opportunity to demonstrate their connection to the business world with pressures and incentives operating at a number of levels' (p. 179). This means that the school principal is immersed in the compliance and performance processes of corporatism (i.e. administrative practices) 'characterised by market-style methods of competition, distribution and exchange, the measurement of outputs and efficiency, and the development of new techniques of "performance" monitoring and assessment' (Marginson 1992, p. 2). We say more about this and its concomitant effect on classroom teachers in Chapter 6 when we look at some of the major education policies and reports of the current era.

3.6 Choice

A distinctive feature of education reform since the 1990s is the 'rapid global expansion of public schooling dissolution' (Rowe 2017, p. 1) experienced more generally as devolution and choice. This global phenomenon is about the incorporation of consumer and consumption choices in schooling as an antidote to a "failing" public education system. "Choice" is now firmly entrenched as a school education policy motif, as are 'second-order effects' (Doherty, Rissman and Browning 2013, p. 122) of social division (see Doherty et al. 2013). These effects discriminate between various categories of class, race, wealth and opportunity. School choice is predicated on the belief that, as rational consumers, everyone within their means has a right to attend a school of their choice. See Rowe (2017) for more on the emblematic "free to choose" movement of the 1980s and beyond.

School choice operates at different levels. School choice has spurred new public education options: "academy schools" (England), "free schools" (Sweden), "schools of the future" (Australia), and "charter schools" (U.S.). The school choice "promise" is that high achievement is guaranteed through the transformational efforts of a highly motivated and innovative school leadership and teacher team. Choice can occur within or between school districts. It can be between public schools or between public and independent (private) schools.

School choice can base admission on equity grounds (i.e. be theoretically open to all) or enforce admission requirements where the school becomes the chooser. The school choice system means allowing for the opportunity to offer an educational service to all. In this respect school choice affirms individual agency and the freedom to assert the personal dynamics of culture, religion, beliefs and/or politics.

The discriminating element in school choice is that it 'changes the structure of the market for K-12 education' (Hoxby 2003, p. 3). Constraints, usually in the form of legislative regulations, are removed or diluted. Revenue can be and is generally tied to student enrolment. In pure economic terms school choice is reduced to understanding the relationship between market structure and how participants (schools and students) behave and perform. This particular relationship dismisses broader and relevant aspects which Hoxby labels 'superficial details – the transportation plan, the school buildings currently in use, and so on' (2003, p. 4). As an important element in the rise of new schooling options, marketization and the new governance arrangements that accompany it are often used to justify and explain higher levels of school effectiveness (see Chubb and Moe 1988). Others (Ball 1993) claim that marketization only leads to a more stratified and unequal school system.

Notwithstanding these and other arguments about the merits or otherwise of new forms of schooling, school choice and devolution connect to the increasing marketization and privatization of education (see Whitty and Power 2000). An example is the charter school initiative initially formed by American-based 'labor and social justice educators as the answer to class and race opportunity gaps' (Fabricant and Fine 2012, p. 2). This form of schooling option now backed by corporate interests (philanthropic organizations, hedge funds and real estate firms) is also favoured by pro-choice and privatization advocates. It trades heavily on a relentless critique of public education, portraying a system that is in crisis and suggesting that teachers in public schools simply don't measure up (see Fabricant and Fine 2012).

3.7 Privatization

Privatization in public education is now a widespread and accepted phenomenon. Ball and Youdell (2007) suggest that there are two forms of privatization in public education: endogenous and exogenous. Endogenous privatization in public education is about the 'importing of ideas, techniques and practices from the private sector in order to make the public sector more like businesses and more business-like' (Ball and Youdell 2007, p. 13). Exogenous privatization is about 'the opening up of public education services to private sector participation on a for-profit basis' (Ball and Youdell 2007, p. 13). Privatization in public education aligns with the political and economic ideology of minimalist government involvement in social and service provision. Rizvi (2016) suggests that with the global rise in demand for education as a universal right, full government funding of it is probably 'no longer a realistic option – especially in view of the inability or disinclination of most nation-states to fund educational expansion through taxes. Some degree and forms of privatization thus appear inevitable' (p. 2).

There are several reasons why privatization in public education is significant. Privatization alters how public education is 'organised . . . experienced by students and . . . thought about by policymakers, practitioners and families and the wider community' (Ball and Youdell 2007, p. 14). Privatization changes at a fundamental level the complex set of relationships inherent in public organizations, be they schools, technical colleges of advanced education or universities. It does this via a 'multiplicity of often minor processes' (Foucault 1977, p. 138) that reflect the 'general increase of business influence or ideology on government and policy or a process of pressure from the outside in' (Ball 2009, p. 93). The subtle and, in many cases, overt technologies of coercion that privatization brings to public education re-positions education policy narratives towards particular arrangements linked inextricably to modern economies. This means production of a new kind of workforce (managers, consultants, advisors, futurists) serving the interests of profit and product often supported by the invention of a utilitarian prudential rationalism.

3.8 The education production function

Efficacy, capacity and quality are the measures that count in proposals of public education reform. Quality is an elusive element to capture. Nonetheless, the economic model that reportedly captures efficacy and capacity is the production function. The production function is a mathematical construct used in the field of economics that relates the ratio of inputs to outputs. In industrial production maximum output or yield is a function of inputs (labour power, materials and relevant costs). The aim in industrial production is to maximize yield and minimize inputs, especially input costs. The well-known two-factor Cobb-Douglas production function is perhaps the most famous version. The Cobb-Douglas production function is a mathematical equation describing over time the relationship between manufacturing output (yield) and the two basic inputs of labour and capital, hence the name "two-factor". A Cobb-Douglas production function omits all other variables and assumes constancy in technological process (see Humphrey 1997). The usefulness of a production function is in the quantifiable determinations it provides connected to the fluctuations in the relationship over time between product (output) and labour and capital (inputs). A production function helps monitor and predict output based on numeric differences in inputs.

Humphrey (1997) suggests that the conceptual foundation of production functions dates back to the 18th century when a French physiocrat, A R. J. Turgot, used a variant of the method to describe product schedules. Other early exponents of production functions or versions thereof included Thomas Robert Malthus (1798) and David Ricardo (1817). Malthus did work on food production and its relationship to populations. Ricardo worked on various aspects of economic theory, including the labour theory of value, rent, comparative advantage and wages and profits.

The education production function operates on the same input-to-output principle as its industrial counterpart. The aim of the input-to-output model in education is to determine the relationship between the various inputs that will maximize the output of student achievement. The key determinant is a value-for-money argument linking resources to student achievement. Production functions and input-output analyses have an established history in education dating back more than 50 years (see López 2007). The work of Coleman et al. (1966) 'marks the start of the current era of research into relationships between schooling inputs and outputs, a period characterized by the increasingly sophisticated use of inferential statistics with large-scale data sets' (Hedges, Pigott, Polanin, Ryan, Tocci and Williams 2016, p. 144). The Coleman et al. (1966) study *Equality of Educational Opportunity* – the Coleman Report – was a school evaluation study. It tied together data about student background, school context and academic performance. The Coleman Report signified a major turning point in education research across the globe, as it shifted government focus towards efficiency rather than compensatory approaches in education policy. Defining equality of educational opportunity as the 'equality of results, given the same individual input' (Coleman et al. 1966, p. 14) the report used the input-output model to conclude that widespread racial segregation in the U.S. had a marked effect on achievement, as does social class, and that any noticeable school level effects on student achievement are minimal (see Gamoran and Long 2006). Criticisms of the report notwithstanding (Hanushek and Kain 1972), the Coleman et al. study has re-drawn the education policy and research landscape where production function analyses serve as the preferred model of choice in school and teacher evaluations justifying policy-maker appeals for major public education reform (see Alexander, Salmon and Alexander 2015).

Education production functions rely on regression analyses, a form of mathematical relationship between variables. Their conceptual basis specifies input variables of interest (i.e. numerical estimates of individual student ability, family, peers, finances, various school level inputs and so on). An education production function uses proxy measures for each of the inputs, as exact numeric values do not exist (see Alexander et al. 2015). Each input contains a variety of economic and demographic data. The family background input may contain measures of income level, socio-economic status, level of parental education attained, number of languages spoken in the home, the size and location of the home (urban, regional or rural), level of parental interest in education and so on. Some of the major input variables used in education production functions include family background, peer group influence/s, specific school level inputs, and individual student characteristics.

While education production functions are useful tools of analysis in education, they are not proof of causal inferences between the variety of inputs chosen and tested for and student outcomes. In addition, some education production function studies statistically control for a particular input while others do not. A difficulty with education production functions is in quantifying teacher and student level inputs, especially when the student is represented as both an input and an output. Similarly, the education production function assumes perfect linearity between inputs and outputs, an absent aspect from industrial production function models (see Alexander et al. 2015).

Alexander et al. (2015) have catalogued some of the major problems connected to education production functions. The problem of foremost concern is methodological, as education production functions rely on a perfect equilibrium between the input and output side of any measurable relationship. An underlying pedagogic and/or theory of learning is often absent, leaving the nature of the school inputs and their exact relationship on achievement undecided. The expected heterogeneity of student experiences is rarely catalogued nor can an education production function accurately and validly account for the interaction and sequence of inputs and their associated effect/s on achievement.

3.9 Conclusion

Education is firmly ensconced within a political and economic locus of control manifest in nation-state productive capacity. The response of classroom teachers, including their teaching practice/s to new forms and ways of engaging with current economic and political change (neoliberalism), necessitates constant checking. The 'intensifications of governmentality' through heightened performance measures expose individuals to 'different and multiple organizational and subjectivity becomings' (Taylor Webb 2011, p. 379). The expectation on classroom teachers results in a tailoring of their teaching practice/s to an accommodation of policy considerations espousing performance and improvement. Evidence of performance hinges on an accountability framework based on continuous evaluation, the teacher-subject constantly under formation through system implementation of compliance and measurement techniques (see Perryman 2006).

The pre-eminent measurement technique in the field of education is the production function. The production function partitions student achievement into two distinctive linear parts: inputs with a causal or quasi-causal effect on output. Absent in this breaking apart of student achievement is the "chain of events" that forms the whole. This important limitation sidesteps relevant "non-linear" features, which are the agentic interactions and system-based conditions prevalent in complex fields such as education (see Jacobson, Levin and Kapur 2019).

Note

1 MySchool is an Australian government website providing a range of publicly available data on all schools in Australia. MySchool was first introduced in early 2010 by the Labour government of Prime Minister Julia Gillard (2010–2013). It contains the ICSEA (Index of Community and Socio-Economic Advantage) score devised by the Australian

Curriculum Assessment and Reporting Authority (ACARA), which is a measure of socio-economic level. The ICSEA score is calculated on a range of measures, including parental level of education, occupation, language background, Aboriginality and rurality.

References

Alexander, K., Salmon, R. G. and Alexander, F. K. 2015. *Financing Public Schools: Theory, Policy and Practice*. New York: Routledge.

Ball, S. J. 1993. Education markets, choice and social class: The market as a class strategy in the UK and the USA. *British Journal of Sociology of Education*, 14(1), 3–19.

Ball, S. J. 2003. The teacher's soul and the terrors of performativity. *Journal of Education Policy*, 18(2), 215–228.

Ball, S. J. 2009. Privatising education, privatising education policy, privatising educational research: Network governance and the "competition state". *Journal of Education Policy*, 24(1), 83–99. https://doi.org/10.1080/02680930802419474

Ball, S. J. and Youdell, D. 2007. *Hidden Privatization in Public Education*. Retrieved from http://pages.eiie.org/quadrennialreport/2007/upload/content_trsl_images/630/Hidden_privatisation-EN.pdf

Baroutsis, A. 2016. Media accounts of school performance: Reinforcing dominant practices of accountability. *Journal of Education Policy*, 31(5), 567–582.

Boltanski, L. and Chiapello, E. 2005. *The New Spirit of Capitalism*. London: Verso Books.

Chubb, J. E. and Moe, T. M. 1988. Politics, markets, and the organization of schools. *The American Political Science Review*, 82(4), 1065–1087.

Clarke, J., Cochrane, A. and McLaughlin, E. (eds). 1994. *Managing Social Policy*. London: Sage.

Coleman, J. S., Campbell, E. Q., Hobson, C. J., McPartland, F., Mood, A. M., Weinfeld, F. D. and York, R. L. 1966. *Equality of Educational Opportunity*. Washington, DC: U.S. Government Printing Office. Retrieved from http://files.eric.ed.gov/fulltext/ED012275.pdf

Connell, R. 2013. The neoliberal cascade and education: An essay on the market agenda and its consequences. *Critical Studies in Education*, 54(2), 99–112.

Doherty, C., Rissman, B. and Browning, B. 2013. Educational markets in space: Gamekeeping professionals across Australian communities. *Journal of Education Policy*, 28(1), 121–152.

Edwards, R. 2002. Mobilizing lifelong learning: Governmentality in educational practices. *Journal of Education Policy*, 17(3), 353–365.

Fabricant, M. and Fine, M. 2012. *Charter Schools and the Corporate Makeover of Public Education: What's at Stake?* New York and London, UK: Teachers College, Columbia University.

Foucault, M. 1977. *Discipline and Punish*. London, UK: Penguin Books.

Fraser, N. 2013. *Fortunes of Feminism. From State-Managed Capitalism to Neoliberal Crisis*. London: Verso Books.

Gale, T. and Densmore, K. 2003. *Engaging Teachers: Towards a Radical Agenda For Schooling*. Maidenhead, UK: Open University Press.

Gamoran, A. and Long, D. 2006. *"Equality of Educational Opportunity": A 40-year Retrospective*. WCER Working Paper No. 2006–9. Madison, WI: Wisconsin Center for Educational Research.

Gerrard, G. 2017. The state of public schooling in *Educating Australia*. In T. Bentley and G. Savage (Eds.), *Challenges for the Decade Ahead* (pp. 55–68). Melbourne, Australia: Melbourne University Press.

Hanushek, E. A. and Kain, J. F. 1972. On the value of equality of educational opportunity as a guide to public policy. In F. Mosteller and D. P. Moynihan (Eds.), *On Equality of Educational Opportunity* (pp. 118–146). New York: Random House.

Hargreaves, A. and Goodson, I. 2006. Educational change over time? The sustainability and nonsustainability of three decades of secondary school change and continuity. *Education Administration Quarterly*, 42(1), 3–41.

Hedges, Larry V., Pigott, Terri D., Polanin, Joshua R., Ryan, Ann Marie, Tocci, Charles and Williams, Ryan T. 2016. The question of school resources and student achievement: A history and reconsideration. *Review of Research in Education*, 40(1), 143–168.

Hobsbawm, E. 1994. *The Age of Extremes: 1914–1991*. London, UK: Abacus.

Hoxby, C. M. (Ed.). 2003. *The Economics of School Choice* (pp. 1–23). Chicago, IL and London, UK: The University of Chicago Press.

Humphrey, T. M. 1997. Algebraic production functions and their uses before Coll-Douglas. *Economic Quarterly*, 83(1), 51–83.

Jacobson, M. J., Levin, J. A. and Kapur, M. 2019. Education as a complex system: Conceptual and methodological implications. *Educational Researcher*, 48(2), 112–119. https://doi.org/10.3102/0013189X19826958

Lingard, B. 2000. Federalism in schooling since The Karmel Report (1973), *Schools In Australia*: From modernist hope to postmodernist performativity. *Australian Educational Researcher*, 27(2), 25–61.

Lingard, B., Martino, W., Rezai-Rashti, G. and Sellar, S. 2016. *Globalizing Educational Accountabilities: Education in Global Context*. New York and London, UK: Routledge.

Lyotard, J.-F. 1984. *The Postmodern Condition: A Report on Knowledge* (Vol. 10). Manchester: Manchester University Press.

López, O. S. 2007. Classroom diversification: A strategic view of educational productivity. *Review of Educational Research*, 77(1), 28–80.

Macdonald, D. 2003. Curriculum change and the post-modern world: Is the school curriculum-reform movement an anachronism? *Journal of Curriculum Studies*, 35(2), 139–149.

Marginson, S. 1991. After globalization: Emerging politics of education. *Journal of Education Policy*, 14(1), 19–31.

Marginson, S. 1992. Education as a branch of economics: The universal claims of economic rationalism. *Melbourne Studies in Education*, 33(1), 1–14.

Marginson, S. 1997. Steering from a distance: Power relations in Australian higher education. *Higher Education*, 34(1), 63–80.

Mayer-Schonberger, V. and Cukier, K. N. 2013. *A Revolution that Will Transform How We Live, Work and Think*. Boston, MA: Eamon Dolan/Houghton Mifflin Harcourt.

Mayer-Schonberger, V. and Cukier, K. N. 2014. *Learning with Big Data: The Future of Education*. Boston, MA: Houghton Mifflin Harcourt.

Morley, L. and Rassool, N. 2000. School effectiveness: New managerialism, quality and the Japanization of education. *Journal of Education Policy*, 15(2), 169–183.

OECD. 2013. *New Sources of Growth: Knowledge-based Capital: Key Analyses and Policy Conclusions: Synthesis Report*. Retrieved from www.oecd.org/sti/inno/knowledge-based-capital-synthesis.pdf

Perryman, J. 2006. Panoptic performativity and school inspection regimes: Disciplinary mechanisms and life under special measures. *Journal of Education Policy*, 21(2), 147–161. https://doi.org/10.1080/02680930500500138

Rizvi, F. 2016. Privatization in education: Trends and consequences. *Education Research and Foresight Series*, No. 18. Paris: UNESCO. Retrieved from https://en.unesco.org/node/262287

Rose, N. 1996. The death of the social? Re-figuring the territory of government. *Economy and Society*, 25(3), 327–356.

Rowe, E. E. 2017. *Middle-Class School Choice in Urban Spaces: The Economics of Public Schooling and Globalized Education Reform*. London, UK and New York: Routledge.

Rowe, E. E. 2019. Capitalism without capital: The intangible economy of education reform. *Discourse: Studies in the Cultural Politics of Education*, 40(2), 271–279. https://doi.org/10.1080/01596306.2019.1569883

Rowlands, J. and Rawolle, S. 2013. Neoliberalism is not a theory of everything: A Bourdieuian analysis of illusio in educational research. *Critical Studies in Education*, 54(3), 260–272.

Sachs, J. 2016. Teacher professionalism: Why are we still talking about it? *Teachers and Teaching*, 22(4), 413–425.

Standing, G. 2011. *The Precariat: The New Dangerous Class*. London, UK: Bloomsbury.

Streeck, W. 2016. *How Will Capitalism End?* London, UK: Verso.

Taylor Webb, P. 2011. The evolution of accountability. *Journal of Education Policy*, 26(6), 735–756. https://doi.org/10.1080/02680939.2011.587539

Verger, A. and Curran, M. 2014. New public management as a global education policy: Its adoption and re-contextualization in a Southern European setting. *Critical Studies in Education*, 55(3), 253–271.

Vigoda, E. 2003. New public management. In J. Rabin (Ed.), *Encyclopedia of Public Administration and Public Policy* (Vol. 2). New York: Marcel Dekker.

Whitty, G., Power, S. 2000. Marketization and privatization in mass education systems. *International Journal of Educational Development*, 20, 93–107.

Yates, L. 2017. Curriculum: The challenges and the devil in the details. In T. Bentley and G. Savage (Eds.), *Educating Australia: Challenges for the Decade Ahead* (pp. 85–100). Melbourne, Australia: Melbourne University Press.

4
IMPROVE OR ELSE!

Introduction

In this chapter we canvas what we suggest is the "new normal" in school education. The rise of a knowledge-based economy (KBE) driven by a new sense of economic competition and enterprise has re-framed ambitions for public schooling. Responsibility for student achievement has been individualized downwards to classroom teachers, and public education has been characterized as in need of improvement through particular transformational structures. These include large-scale international comparisons and the need for development of new student skills, amongst others. The chapter traverses specific "pressure points" that maintain the focus on classroom teachers and their teaching as the knot that binds them to student performance.

4.1 The knowledge-based economy

We live in times where the contemporary education and training agenda is infused with a repeated mantra 'that economic competitiveness and national well-being depend crucially on the skills, adaptability and motivation of the workforce' (Payne 2000, p. 353). Several factors, according to Payne, contribute to this. The first involves the dominance of new service industries 'coupled with the growth of employment in professional, technical and administrative occupations' (Payne 2000, p. 354). Employees in these new industries require 'relational skills to effect face-to-face or voice-to-voice interaction with customer and clients' (Payne 2000, p. 354). Secondly, new post-Fordist organizational structures promote new ways of working, with an emphasis on 'advanced analytical and interactional skills such as communication, problem-solving, team working and creativity' (Payne 2000, p. 354). Workers with these skills are thought to provide contemporary firms with the necessary 'comparative advantage in high quality, high value-added product markets' (Payne 2000, p. 354). Thirdly, policy-maker concern around high youth unemployment from the mid-1970s has elevated the importance of the employability of young job seekers. Individual and firm adaptability in an age of uncertainty is vital and further developed via the 'acquisition of skills, knowledge and personal qualities' (Payne 2000, p. 354) that changing labour markets need.

The creation and management of information holds especial significance in the new world of a knowledge-based economy (KBE), as does an identification with adding value by and to knowledge. A KBE differs from earlier traditional economic imaginaries in that it is marked by an 'economics of abundance, the annihilation of distance, the de-territorialization of the state, the importance of local knowledge and the investment in human capital' (Peters 2001, p. 7). The large-scale change connected to the reorientation of national economies towards an interconnected world market has also expanded concern about what is deemed economically relevant. Education is central to this concern being considered now a 'directly economic factor' as it 'bears directly and ever more critically on economic competitiveness' (Jessop 2008, p. 29). The KBE necessitates a skilled labour force 'with the capacity to learn and adapt by continually producing and engaging with codified knowledge, particularly through information and communication technologies' (Gibb and Walker 2011, p. 383). This means that lifelong education and training is a given in the KBE with employees constantly updating their skill level/s.

4.2 The skills students need

Schools have responded to the era of skills and a KBE via the curriculum they provide. A skill set of a specific type is needed. This involves core skill levels in literacy and numeracy as well as a heightened proficiency in using technology as a major feature in learning. The need for creativity, innovation and resourcefulness in problem-solving is an expectation reinforcing the accepted belief in the technological demands of globalization. This is also representative of a new series of complex and global 21st-century environmental and social pressures requiring remedy into the future. The knowledge and "know-how" of the future is founded on a study of the major disciplines skewed more perhaps towards the sciences, technology, engineering and mathematics – the (STEM) disciplines. This is consistent with what are the accepted discourses of the KBE, which assumes that the jobs of the future will 'involve the generation of ideas and ingenuity' (Gibb and Walker 2011, p. 383).

The development of particular skill sets and the instability accompanying the liquid-modern world is an education that 'must be continuous and indeed lifelong' (Bauman 2009, p. 188). Bauman asserts that:

> No other kind of education or learning is conceivable, the "formation" of selves or personalities is unthinkable in any other fashion but that of an ongoing perpetually unfinished, open-ended reformation.
>
> *(2009, p. 188)*

His reasons for saying so are obvious to discern. Economic/political trends and specific policy reform strategies based on a change and improvement rationale form the contemporary and dominant "life-long learning" discourse.

> We are in a new age – the age of information and of global competition. Familiar certainties and old ways of doing things are disappearing. The types of jobs we do have changed as have the industries in which we work and the skills they need. At the same time, new opportunities are opening up and we see the potential of new technologies to change our lives for the better. We have no choice but to prepare for this new age in which the key to success will be the continuous education and development of the human mind and imagination.
>
> *(Department for Education and Employment 1998, p. 9)*

This type of policy discourse, particularly that of "competitiveness" (an aspect to which the chapter will return), shapes modern power relations where a 'manufactured uncertainty' (Bauman 2009, p. 189) is ever present.

The idea of life-long education and learning originated in the 1970s and was first linked to the provision of formal education courses for adults, particularly those who, for whatever reasons, discontinued their initial primary/secondary education (see OECD 1996). By the 1990s, the idea of life-long education and learning had been co-opted to signify all purposeful learning 'from cradle to grave, that aims to improve knowledge and competencies for all individuals who wish to participate in learning activities' (OECD 1996, p. 2). The life-long education policy rationale supports descriptions of a new emerging world of information and heightened global competition. National and personal prosperity depend upon a KBE, and the only investment worth making is in the form of human capital. Empowerment then comes in the form of a capacity and willingness to compete and take action based on the new skill sets needed. The 'fundamental purpose of education for the 21st century . . . is not so much the transmission of particular bodies of knowledge, skill and understanding as facilitating the development of the capacity and the confidence to engage in life-long learning' (Carr and Claxton 2002, p. 9). The cultivation then of a personal predisposition to continuously learn is crucial and is something that we return to in Chapter 7.

4.3 The seduction of comparison/s

Comparison in education, as in most social sciences, is about the "total analytical picture" that takes the particular in similarities and differences and extrapolates them to the universal. The epistemological foundations of the comparative model involves description, interpretation, juxtaposition and comparison (see Adick 2018) so that a valid comparative analysis can be claimed. This means that comparison is about categorization and the setting of boundaries, the latter often assigned without much consideration of 'ontological validity' (Pomeroy 2018, p. 6).

In education International Large-Scale Assessments (ILSAs) are the comparative measures of choice for governments. Their advantages include their alleged independent, unbiased nature, the knowledge and understanding gained of a nation's progress as measured against another, and an awareness of what is possible in terms of achievement gains (see Gorur 2017). The ILSA is a marker of performance in achievement for students, teachers and education systems. It dispenses with the messiness of subjective assessments of student performance, particularly by teachers often claiming that any large-scale policy reform be made through evidence-based/informed research. Nonetheless, a teacher in our research had other views about ILSAs.

> Look, I teach in secondary school. I cannot as an individual teacher account for – and neither can the school as far as I'm concerned – about student results when I've got them in year nine and their maths skills . . . I mean, like, how the hell does that work out? I mean, somebody else has taught them or not taught them for the previous seven years so how – how can NAPLAN [a standardized test] scores or whatever be attributed to the contribution of an individual teacher?
>
> *(Aaron)*

The case against ILSAs is framed on a narrowness in scope argument. Individual national context is often discounted, if not ignored altogether, for comparability purposes, as is consideration of the likelihood that students are exposed to different classroom teachers over their educational journey, the latter point made clear by one of our teacher participants, Aaron. Critics generally 'worry that ILSAs are shaping the policy discourse by colonizing the policy imagination with their simplistic and singular vision, and that this curtails pedagogic and policy innovation' (Gorur 2017, p. 344). Comparability has gained in added significance in an era dominated by 'the widespread contemporary imagination of education as a global "race" for economic competitiveness' (Sellar and Lingard 2013, p. 717). Major international bodies such as the OECD, amongst others, have re-positioned how we think about the performative aspects of education so that it stacks up as an instrumental sub-stratum of a nation's economy. The OECD in particular 'has been involved in helping to specify the skills and competencies that give contemporary human capital its value and has become a prominent actor in education policy globally due to its measurement and comparison of skills within nations' (Sellar and Lingard 2013, p. 718).

4.4 De-centring responsibility

De Lissovoy categorizes the contemporary political and economic era of which skill development is part as one of 'pervasive anxiety produced by contemporary processes of precarity and fragmentation' (2018, p. 187). The self-reliant aspects of an able and entrepreneurial individual is part of a 'politics of the subject' (De Lissovoy 2018, p. 188) that willingly accepts total responsibility for a livelihood earned through the application and acceptance of new flexible work structures. Risk and how it is managed features heavily in the choices that individuals and indeed governments make in this new era. Skills development as part of an education and training system aligned to national economic needs is used as a form of responsibilization. Responsibilization in this sense means possessing the requisite obligation and motivation needed in enterprising action to ensure the well-being of self. Responsibilization is then a re-organization of self and mindset so that we 'understand ourselves on the basis of principles of individual responsibility, autonomy, competition, and calculation' (De Lissovoy 2018, p. 188).

This aspect of modern living conceptualizes the notion of skills development as a form of "self-care". The reconstruction of self is guided by an active governmentality and governmentalization which are the series of 'power techniques and forms of knowledge' (Lemke 2001, p. 191) that govern. The entrepreneurial form underpins this reconstruction, which for the individual proceeds from 'an appraisal of subjective-voluntarist calculations' (Lemke 2001, p. 199). Human capital in this sense is then 'not capital like other forms, for the ability, skill and knowledge cannot be separated from the person who possesses them' (Lemke 2001, p. 199). There are two sides to the human capital spoken about here. The 'innate . . . acquired elements' (Foucault 2008, p. 227) representing individual genetics that are hereditary and the 'entirety of skills' (Lemke 2001 p. 199) encompassing the 'educational investments' (Foucault 2008, p. 229) amassed in life, not only via formal schooling and training but through upbringing.

4.5 Competitiveness and educationalization

An important characteristic connected to the new auto-reliant self is the co-option of an ideological credo (i.e. that competition and/or the development of a competitive self-starting ethos fixes everything). The emphasis more and more in education is of competition and the competitive spirit – schools, teachers and students competing against each other. We can see this in the various school education policy doctrines of nation states and non-government agencies such as the OECD where large-scale test result data are invariably set up as the competitive marker of national/international success.

The foundation of this development is based on what we contend is an evolving aspect of modernization connected to the normalization that occurs as part of the education reform process. The tendency is towards installing an ideological acceptance of education as the mechanism through which particular social and economic problems are treated. This also extends to addressing social inequalities of class, race, sex and so on. The action undertaken is a moulding of self through the "educationalization" occurring in the orientation of the individual to ways of learning that foster participation in a competitive society along with what passes for 'socially desirable behavior' (Depaepe and Smeyers 2008, p. 380).

4.6 A new form of leadership

The advent of heightened competitiveness in school education is not achieved without a guiding influence. School leadership is the hook upon which delivery of school education reform, particularly at the micro/local school level, is enacted. The policy commitment to school education reform in the pursuit of higher education standards, excellence and overall school quality and effectiveness can only be actualized through people. School education policy invests this accomplishment upon head teachers and school principals. We can see this over time and across various government jurisdictions, both nationally here in Australia and internationally in some of the following government and stakeholder statements. For example:

> The quality of the head often makes the difference between the success or failure of a school.
>
> *(DfEE 1997, p. 46)*

> The £19 billion is a substantial commitment on our part to do what we can . . . investment for reform, for change and for pursuit of higher standards and excellence . . . to bring this about there is no group of people more important than headteachers.
>
> *(Blair 1998)*

> Excellent leaders create excellent schools. Secondary schools need strong leaders at all levels, enabling them to provide a rich and diverse curriculum taught by professionals committed to success for every learner.
>
> *(Clarke 2004, p. 25)*

> School leadership that focuses primarily on improving teaching quality has the greatest impact on learner outcomes. Developing the capacity to lead teaching and learning effectively is crucial to the future success of any school leader.
>
> *(AITSL 2018, para 1)*

> High-quality school leadership is pivotal to delivering the best outcomes for young Australians. School leaders make the greatest impact on the progress and achievement of learners by using their educational expertise and management skills to focus the efforts of everyone in the school on improving the quality of teaching and learning. They do this in fast-changing and increasingly complex circumstances, understanding that the strong foundations of a great education are critical for preparing today's learners for the world of tomorrow. Regardless of the setting, these leaders know that teachers need the expertise to understand how their students learn and how to help them make the next steps in their learning.
>
> *(AITSL 2018, para 1)*

Leadership in school education matters and is now about an established manner of working in a purposeful way manifest in the 'power to do' (Gunter 2012, p. 77) by channelling the efforts of all school teaching personnel towards one end: effectiveness.

The extant research literature on school leadership is varied (see Gumus and Bellibas 2016), although it has a results orientation and is about a strong sense of purpose and direction geared towards student success. The strong and focused school leader is forever monitoring and improving teaching and learning. They set high expectations for all, acknowledging that leadership in the school sector is tantamount to any other sector where the focus is on success through achievement. In writing about this form of school leadership favoured by the new education initiatives of governments such as the British New Labour government of the late 1990s, Gunter states:

> In developing this approach, primacy was given to private-sector leadership models to secure leader responsibility and accountability, provide the language, processes and legitimacy for delegating work, and command commitment through followership.
>
> *(Gunter 2012, p. 20)*

This aspect of school leadership interconnects with the devolution of governance structure prevalent at the time that continues today. The aim to continuously demonstrate school improvement through student outcomes promotes a change management agenda of school leadership. School leaders carry the school modernizing anthem and are given greater responsibility over workforce decisions regarding school improvement. Sustained school-based change cannot simply work based on school leadership models which celebrate the 'solo, heroic, charismatic leaders' (Torrance and Humes 2015, p. 793) of the past. New forms of school leadership are 'deliberately given prominence within the policy context to assist the process of workforce reform through enhanced expectations placed on teachers' (Torrance and Humes 2015, p. 793).

4.7 Inspection

The key element in the performance regimes across school education systems is their normalizing effect/s. Normalization processes are evident across all layers of the school education system, including the teacher workforce, student achievement, the curriculum and assessment. While the emphasis is upon heightened performance against an externally benchmarked series of norms, the disciplinary mechanisms utilized are the harbingers of lasting change, particularly with respect to the autonomy of teachers. Gleeson and Gunter (2001) have chartered teacher autonomy over time. Three distinctive phases of teacher autonomy have been identified since the 1960s. The first period encompassing the 1960s to mid-1980s is characterized by Gleeson and Gunter as a period of "relative autonomy" for teachers. Teachers were 'accountable to themselves through informal reflection and peer review' (Perryman 2006, p. 148). National curricula were not yet established, and teachers worked within the innovations adopted through the neo-progressive era of the late 1960s and early 1970s such as 'school-based curricula, activity methods and "open education"' (Barcan 2010, p. 1). This had all changed by the early 1980s with the 'emerging economic rationalist, neo-liberal ideas [which] favoured devolution of administrative responsibilities to schools ("the entrepreneurial school"), central control of the curriculum, and an emphasis on vocational training' (Barcan 2010, p. 1). Relative autonomy gave way to "controlled autonomy", a period that began from the 1980s and lasted to the later stages of the 1990s. Teachers in this period were 'accountable to themselves through formal review' (Perryman 2006, p. 148). School leadership took on greater responsibility for schooling outcomes and was given authority over the incorporation of strong line management systems. Target setting aligned to professional development/learning, and the practical delivery of results was prioritized, as was a stronger emphasis on surveillance and mandatory school and individual teacher appraisal. Gleeson and Gunter suggest that we are now in a period of "productive autonomy". This period is characterized by the formalized audits of teacher performance linked directly to student learning outcomes. National curricula control what is taught, and there is an overt "system" enunciation of best teaching practice/s for maximizing results. All aspects of school functions are calculable based on formal evaluative systems that have been found "to work" through an established and rigorous evidence base.

Inspection and the normalization that stems from it must be grounded in a particular discourse. Boundaries are set which reflect imposed reforms. While performativity is about 'performing the normal within a particular discourse' (Perryman 2006, p. 150), panoptic performativity is the regime and system adopted to enforce, guide and ultimately gauge performance. Bentham's panopticon, the design exemplar for monitoring inmates, provides a 'metaphorical disciplinary mechanism' (Perryman 2006, p. 154) through which evaluative discourses and modes of judgement operate. Bentham's panopticon, a central tower comprised of individual cells, is about a permanent "gaze", managed through the use of backlighting, where the supervisor could watch the inmate without the inmate knowing that they were being watched.

> The panoptic mechanism arranges spatial unities that make it possible to see constantly and to recognize immediately. . . . Visibility is a trap. . . . Hence the major effect of the Panopticon: to induce in the inmate a state of conscious and permanent visibility that assures the automatic functioning of power.
>
> *(Foucault 1977, pp. 200–201)*

Power, though seemingly invisible, is exerted over teachers and students by institutional supervision that is ever present, through the verification mechanisms of large-scale standardized testing data sets. These 'special measures' (Perryman 2006, p. 154) of surveillance include 'continuous observation . . . inspection as not just constant but all-seeing . . . [and] increasing conformity to perceived expectations' (Perryman 2006, pp. 154–155). Page has referred to aspects of this new form of inspection/surveillance as an 'assemblage of strategies' encompassing 'learning walks, parental networks, student voice and management information systems' (2017, p. 1).

4.8 Parents

The research literature has tended to cast the relationship between parents and teachers as fraught at the best of times (Stacey 2016; Nespor and Hicks 2010; Cutler 2000). Quite often adversarial characterizations of parent-teacher interaction single out power differentials between teachers and parents (Crozier 1998). The "concerted cultivation" (Lareau 2011) experienced by the children of the middle classes, for example, not only affords their children a sense of rightful existence and entitlement in the schooling experience, but middle-class parents themselves are generally not threatened by it. The middle-class child-adult social milieu involves a 'steady diet of adult organized activities' (Lareau 2011, p. 3) immersing children into organized sporting and cultural lessons/enterprises geared towards development of key skills and attributes with a focus on strengthening particular talents. Conversely working-class or poorer parent groups are generally thought to be less inclined to interfere in the "work" of the school. Annette Lareau suggests that working-class groups prefer 'clear boundaries between adults and children', with working-class and poor children exerting 'more control over the character of their leisure activities' (2011, p. 3). This means that for these groups of children 'parents and guardians facilitate the *accomplishment of natural growth*' (Lareau 2011, p. 3, emphasis in original). Middle-class parents align their interactions 'with central institutions in the society, such as schools, which firmly and decisively promote strategies of concerted cultivation in child rearing' (Lareau 2011, p. 3). On the other hand, for working-class parents 'the cultural logic of child rearing at home is out of synch with the standards of institutions' (Lareau 2011, p. 3). In work on parental engagement and schooling carried out by Diane Reay, working-class and poorer parents often feel a sense of inadequacy in dealing with teachers and school authorities and are anxious about raising matters of educational importance with them (Reay 1998, 2017). This is generally as a result of working-class and poorer parents' negative schooling experiences, although it is not solely limited to this. Reay's sociological portrayal of the complexities involved in the broader 'web of social relationships, including those of life style, educational experiences and patterns of residence' (2017, p. 2) work to structure school outcomes.

> Material resources, educational knowledge, parents' own educational experiences and the amount of domestic and educational support parents,

> and in particular mothers, had access to, add up to an important class difference that impacted on their relationship to their children's education and the texture of their involvement in schooling. And it is important to point out . . . that it is mainly mothers who undertake the work of educating children.
>
> *(Reay 2017, p. 72)*

A further point made by Reay is that there are now significant material differences in terms of how state schooling 'increasingly relies on learning outside of school, at a time when resources to enable this are very unequally distributed across the social classes' (2017, p. 72).

Recent work by Sue Saltmarsh (2015) reinforces the extent to which education policy advocates for increased parental involvement in children's education. Shared responsibility is promoted in which parents 'are seen as critical to children's educational success' (Saltmarsh 2015, p. 43). Parents are increasingly characterized as major 'partners, stakeholders and collaborators in the education of children, as monitors of teacher and school accountability, and also as consumers driving demand for efficiency and excellence in an education market place' (Saltmarsh 2015, p. 43). This means that education policy deliberately constitutes parents 'as a policy lever through which the accountability of teachers and schools is demanded' (Saltmarsh 2015, p. 44). In an education policy environment that pushes for 'parents as consumers and choosers of schooling' (Saltmarsh 2015, p. 47) an effect of which is to centralize their role in the education equation, pressures them further into believing that they alone must guarantee the success of their children. This is a responsibility that 'weighs heavily' (Saltmarsh 2015, p. 46) on some parents, particularly those with children experiencing difficulties at school.

> The desire for children to do well, coupled with the expectation that schools now have an articulated responsibility to communicate effectively with and willingly involve parents, also gives rise to a broad range of cultural practices through which parents continually monitor not only their own and teachers' performance, but also the extent to which schools within their region are actively engaging with parents.
>
> *(Saltmarsh 2015, pp. 46–47)*

"Parental voice" (Saltmarsh 2015), manifest as a form of parental empowerment, is then a factor in how parents can exert control over teachers and their performance.

Parental empowerment, according to Gofen and Blomqvist, 'refers both to collective and individual involvement' (2014, p. 551) in the schooling of children. An example of collective parent involvement is advocacy through school council participation, while one-on-one parent-teacher communication is an example of individual parent involvement (see Gofen and Blomqvist 2014).

Empowerment of parents may involve questioning the unofficial status quo in the school; nevertheless, it complies with formal policy which attempts to increase parental involvement through various policy tools.

(Gofen and Blomqvist 2014, pp. 551–552)

While empowerment denotes a particular form of proactive expression and assertiveness through direct-action advocacy, parental involvement has multiple meanings. Parents, and in most cases usually mothers (see work on this by Landeros 2011), can be variously involved in the education of their children as teachers, learning supporters, resource providers, socializers, advocates, decision-makers and/or as partners in school management (see Gofen and Blomqvist 2014). Parental involvement in schooling can imply the narrow promotion of one's own child's needs and outcomes while also referring to an engagement in the broader aspects of education as a public good and resource vital to a community's well-being. The nature of parental involvement notwithstanding, school/teacher/parent partnerships have long been tempered by an education policy ethos 'whereby parents are encouraged to voice concerns and make demands' (Crozier 1998, pp. 126–127). In a competitive market-oriented society where parents are pressured to "play into the game" of the marketization of schools, new parental responsibilities have emerged. Parental responsibilities and schooling extend to matters of school choice, committing to the values of a particular school and its community, provision and maintenance of appropriate resources (school uniform and stationery), monitoring homework and so on. While parental empowerment has provided parents a greater opportunity to immerse themselves in schooling matters, it has nonetheless had an effect on teachers' professionalism. Many of the educational reforms outlined in some of the preceding chapters of this book position parents as consumers of education and teachers as producers. This means that parents are in a position to affect teachers' professionalism by perhaps questioning their professional judgement and also unsettling the teacher/parent dynamic (see Crozier 1998; Landeros 2011) through heightened surveillance and scrutiny, the latter being blamed for introducing a degree of uncertainty into the daily work of teachers (see Gofen and Blomqvist 2014).

4.9 Student voice

The notion of student voice is characterized in the research literature as the opportunity students have to contribute to 'decisions impacting their lives in and out of schools' (Rodgers 2018, p. 89). While student voice research began at the level of the classroom on matters that have an effect on student learning, work done by Dana Mitra (2008) suggests that it also can be regarded as 'the ways in which young people can work with teachers and administrators to co-create the path of reform' (p. 7) in education more broadly. This form of student involvement, which can otherwise be referenced as "student participation", "active citizenship", "youth leadership", "youth empowerment" and "pupil voice" (see Mitra

2008) is about young people expressing their perceptions of schooling in general, and teaching and learning more particularly.

> This process can enable youth to meet their own developmental needs and can strengthen student ownership of the educational reform process.
> *(Mitra 2008, p. 7)*

In this way, students can feel empowered and have some control over their 'experiences as learners and their right to have a say in those experiences' (Rodgers 2018, p. 89).

In work completed on student voice and effective teaching, Egeberg and McConney suggest that 'students' thoughts, beliefs and feelings are often portrayed as overlapping and interchangeable' (2018, p. 196) when considering their perceptions of learning situations, including of their individual teachers. This means that students often have strong views about what constitutes effective teaching, particularly as it relates to classroom management and broader issues of individual learning and behaviour. In addition, organizations such as the OECD and the Gates Foundation have advocated for the addition of student voice in driving school improvement efforts. The OECD suggests that students should be 'listened to and their voice used to drive whole school improvement' (OECD 2006, p. 25). Whereas, from the Gates Foundation Measures of Effective Teaching (MET) Project:

> No one has a bigger stake in teaching effectiveness than students. Nor are there any better experts on how teaching is experienced by its intended beneficiaries. But only recently have many policymakers and practitioners come to recognize that – when asked the right questions, in the right ways – students can be an important source of information on the quality of teaching and the learning environment in individual classrooms.
> *(MET Project 2012, p. 1)*

Student voice is then one of a series of strategies, such as those outlined by Page earlier, used as a 'means of managing the risks of school life, driven forward by neoliberal notions of quality and competition' (Page 2017, p. 1).

4.10 Individualizing the teacher subject

Stephen Ball (2003) identifies markets, managerialism and performativity as the three pillars of reform that currently govern the teacher subject. The new teacher subject is a reconstituted worker made over by the accountability and standards benchmarks of 'technologies of reform' (Holloway and Brass 2018, p. 361). These reform technologies are grounded in the individualization of specific evaluative practices where the work of classroom teachers, which is constantly on display and auditable, is reduced to the exactness afforded the singular numeric score.

Value is deemed a fixed calculable entity realized and visible through student achievement gains. The professionalism and restricted autonomy that accompanies reform technologies are legitimized by the adoption of prescribed classroom practices found to work. This form of 'professional compliance' (Hall and McGinity 2015, p. 3) is about alignment of teacher work with the standards agenda. By restricting the professional autonomy of teachers through national curricula and new organizational school structures, the re-engineered teacher subject is forced to grapple with the new purposes of education. A consequence of this development is the constant and heightened level of individual teacher comparison 'against their peers and former selves' (Holloway and Brass 2018, p. 363). Collegiality suffers in this scenario where the only teacherly disposition that matters is oriented towards tallied performance statistics.

The evaluative formations that performance statistics typify reflect the "New Taylorism" (see Au 2011) controlling teacher labour. With a history rooted in the "scientific" approach to education and curriculum design popularized by John Franklin Bobbitt, the quantification ruling teacher work is about a streamlined process of pedagogy. The symbolic enumerated uptake in which teachers and students become enmeshed represents an imposed orthodoxy which produces an accepted representation of the educational state of play. Through the accountability structures used where a series of itemized statistical analyses take place, the teacher subject is isolated, the dissemination of their performance rationalized against the productivity indicators of school and teacher effectiveness research.

4.11 Conclusion

Chapter 4 has canvassed what we say and label as "pressure points", some of which include: the non-negotiable imperatives of a KBE, new student skill sets, constant comparison, heightened economic competitiveness and so on. Each of these "pressure points" fingers classroom teachers and the work that they do as the link in the school system chain that is crucial in fostering educational achievement. This particular "making the difference" conceptualization of teachers' work focuses predominantly on the classroom teacher and their teaching practices as in need of improvement. This acute and invasive TE and TQ focus not only expects classroom teachers to make a difference in the lives of students, but they in many respects are "the difference". Schools are then positioned to act as the social conduit through which students are exposed to new economic objectives.

References

Adick, C. 2018. Bereday and Hilker: Origins of the "four steps of comparison" model. *Comparative Education*, 54(1), 35–48. https://doi.org/10.1080/03050068.2017.1396088

Au, W. 2011. Teaching under the new Taylorism: High-stakes testing and the standardization of the 21st century curriculum. *Journal of Curriculum Studies*, 43(1), 25–45, https://doi.org/10.1080/00220272.2010.521261

Australian Institute for Teaching and School Leadership. 2018. *Leading for Impact.* Canberra, Australia: Australian Guidelines for School Leadership Development. Retrieved 2 April 2018 from www.aitsl.edu.au/lead-develop/build-leadership-in-Australian-schools/leading-for-impact-online

Barcan, A. 2010. Public schools in Australia from the late 1970s to the late 1980s: The seeds of change. [online]. *Education Research and Perspectives*, 37(2), 1–37.

Ball, Stephen J. 2003. The teacher's soul and the terrors of performativity. *Journal of Education Policy*, 18(2), 215–228, https://doi.org/10.1080/0268093022000043065.

Bauman, Z. 2009. *Does Ethics Have a Chance in a World of Consumers?* Cambridge, MA: Harvard University Press.

Blair, T. 1998. *Speech to the New Heads Conference*. London, UK: DfEE.

Carr, M. and Claxton, G. 2002. Tracking the development of learning dispositions. *Assessment in Education: Principles, Policy & Practice*, 9(1), 9–37.

Clarke, C. 2004. *Transforming Secondary Education*. London, UK: DfES.

Crozier, G. 1998. Parents and schools: Partnership or surveillance? *Journal of Education Policy*, 13(1), 125–136. https://doi.org/10.1080/0268093980130108

Cutler, W. 2000. *Parents and Schools*. Chicago, IL: The University of Chicago Press.

De Lissovoy, N. 2018. Pedagogy of the anxious: Rethinking critical pedagogy in the context of neoliberal autonomy and responsibilization. *Journal of Education Policy*, 33(2), 187–205. https://doi.org/10.1080/02680939.2017.1352031

Depaepe, M. and Smeyers, P. 2008. Educationalization as an ongoing modernization process. *Educational Theory*, 58(4), 579–589.

DfEE (Department for Education and Employment). 1997. *Excellence in Schools.* Cm 3681. London, UK: DfEE.

DfEE (Department for Education and Employment). 1998. *The Learning Age: A Renaissance for a New Britain*. London, UK: Stationery Office.

Egeberg, H. and McConney, A. 2018. What do students believe about effective classroom management? A mixed-methods investigation in Western Australian high schools. *Australian Educational Researcher*, 45, 195–216.

Foucault, M. 1977. *Discipline and Punish: The Birth of the Prison*. London, UK: Penguin Books.

Foucault, M. 2008. *The Birth of Biopolitics: Lectures at the College De France*. Hampshire, UK: Palgrave Macmillan.

Gibb, T. and Walker, J. 2011. Educating for a high skills society? The landscape of federal employment, training and lifelong learning policy in Canada. *Journal of Education Policy*, 26(3), 381–398. https://doi.org/10.1080/02680939.2010.520744

Gleeson, D. and Gunter, H. 2001. The performing school and the modernisation of teachers. In D. Gleeson and C. Husbands (Eds.), *The Performing School: Managing, Teaching and Learning in a Performance Culture* (pp. 139–158). London: RoutledgeFalmer.

Gofen, A. and Blomqvist, P. 2014. Parental entrepreneurship in public education: A social force or a policy problem? *Journal of Education Policy*, 29(4), 546–569. https://doi.org/10.1080/02680939.2013.858275

Gorur, R. 2017. Towards productive critique of large-scale comparisons in education. *Critical Studies in Education*, 58(3), 341–355. https://doi.org/10.1080/17508487.2017.1327876

Gumus, E. and Bellibas, M. 2016. The effects of professional development activities on principals' perceived instructional leadership practices. *Educational Studies*, 42(3), 287–301.

Gunter, H. M. 2012. *Leadership and the Reform of Education*. London, UK and New York: Routledge.

Hall, D. and McGinity, R. 2015. Conceptualizing teacher professional identity in neoliberal times: Resistance, compliance and reform. *Education Policy Analysis Archives*, 23(88). http://doi.org/10.14507/epaa.v23.2092.

Holloway, J. and Brass, J. 2018. Making accountable teachers: The terrors and pleasures of performativity. *Journal of Education Policy*, 33(3), 361–382. https://doi.org/10.1080/02680939.2017.1372636

Jessop, B. 2008. A cultural political economy of competitiveness and its implications for higher education. In B. Jessop, N. Fairclough and R. Wodak (Eds.), *Education and the Knowledge-based Economy in Europe* (pp. 13–39). Rotterdam, The Netherlands: Sense Publishers.

Landeros, M. 2011. Defining the "good mother" and the "professional teacher": Parent–teacher relationships in an affluent school district. *Gender and Education*, 23(3), 247–262. https://doi.org/10.1080/09540253.2010.491789

Lareau, A. 2011. *Unequal Childhoods: Class, Race and Family Life* (2nd ed.). Berkeley, CA: University of California Press.

Lemke, T. 2001. "The birth of bio-politics": Michel Foucault's lecture at the Collège de France on neo-liberal governmentality. *Economy and Society*, 30(2), 190–207.

MET Project. 2012. *Asking Students About Teaching: Student Perception Surveys and Their Implementation* (Policy and Practice Brief). Seattle, WA: Bill and Melinda Gates Foundation. Retrieved from http://k12education.gatesfoundation.org/wp-content/uploads/2015/12/Asking_Students_Summary_Doc.pdf.

Mitra, D. 2008. *Student Voice in School Reform: Building Youth-Adult Partnerships that Strengthen Schools and Empower Youth*. New York: New York City Press.

Nespor, J. and Hicks, D. 2010. Wizards and witches: Parent advocates and contention in special education in the USA. *Journal of Education Policy*, 25(3), 309–334. https://doi.org/10.1080/02680931003671954

OECD. 1996. *Lifelong Learning for All*. Paris: Organization for Economic Cooperation and Development.

OECD. 2006. *Schooling for Tomorrow: Personalising Education*. Paris: Organization for Economic Cooperation and Development. Retrieved from http://www.oecd.org/innovation/research/personalisingeducation.htm

Page, D. 2017. The surveillance of teachers and the simulation of teaching. *Journal of Education Policy*, 32(1), 1–13. https://doi.org/10.1080/02680939.2016.1209566

Payne, J. 2000. The unbearable lightness of skill: The changing meaning of skill in UK policy discourses and some implications for education and training. *Journal of Education Policy*, 15(3), 353–369. https://doi.org/10.1080/02680930050030473

Perryman, J. 2006. Panoptic performativity and school inspection regimes: Disciplinary mechanisms and life under special measures. *Journal of Education Policy*, 21(2), 147–161. https://doi.org/10.1080/02680930500500138

Peters, M. 2001. National education policy constructions of the "knowledge economy": Towards a critique. *Journal of Educational Inquiry*, 2(1), 1–22.

Pomeroy, D. 2018. Educational equity policy as human taxonomy: Who do we compare and why does it matter? *Critical Studies in Education*. https://doi.org/10.1080/17508487.2018.1440615

Reay, D. 1998. *Class Work: Mothers Involvement in their Children's Primary Schooling*. London, UK: UCL Press.

Reay, D. 2017. *Miseducation: Inequality, Education and the Working Classes*. Bristol, UK: Policy Press.

Rodgers, D. 2018. Descriptive feedback: Student voice in K-5 classrooms. *Australian Educational Researcher*, 45, 87–102.

Saltmarsh, S. 2015. Michel de Certeau, everyday life and policy cultures: The case of parent engagement in education policy. *Critical Studies in Education*, 56(1), 38–54. https://doi.org/10.1080/17508487.2015.961166

Sellar, S., and Lingard, B. 2013. The OECD and global governance in education. *Journal of Education Policy*, 285, 710–725.

Stacey, M. 2016. Middle-class parents' educational work in an academically selective public high school. *Critical Studies in Education*, 57(2), 209–223. https://doi.org/10.1080/17508487.2015.1043312

Torrance, D. and Humes, W. 2015. The shifting discourses of educational leadership: International trends and Scotland's response. *Educational Management Administration & Leadership*, 43(5), 792–810.

5
THE CASE OF TEACHER EFFECTIVENESS RESEARCH

Introduction

Chapter 5 brings together a toolkit drawn from the writings of Michel Foucault and Pierre Bourdieu to critically reflect on the field of teacher effectiveness research (TER). The chapter traverses the specific techniques of measurement/surveillance used in TER and the regularizing discourse that accompanies it. It also explores some of the assumptions of TER using Bourdieu's notion of "doxa" to argue that the field of education policy incorporates some questionable beliefs about teaching and learning. The chapter also draws on some empirical qualitative data (teacher participant interviews) which detail how notions of "what works", effectiveness and quality play out in classroom contexts. The taken-for-granted positivist "logics of practice" are the conceptual drivers of TER, and so the chapter will discuss these to characterize them as symbolic orders of control that influence evaluations of teacher performance.

5.1 Models and algorithms

Teacher effectiveness research (TER) is about identifying the behaviours and practices of classroom teachers thought to make the most positive difference to student learning and achievement. Student progress in TER is believed to be solely determined by 'effective teacher guidance and instruction in the classroom' (Kyriakides, Campbell and Christofidou 2002, p. 292) rather than any other contextual influences (e.g. school level variables or socio-economic background). A typical regression (straight line) equation in TER used to evaluate teacher performance taken from some recent work by Torres (2018) can be written in this way:

$$A_{ijkzmt} = \beta 0 + \beta 1 A_{izt\_1} + \beta 2 S_m + \beta 3 C_{jm} + \beta 4 X_i + T_k + \mu_{ijkmt}.$$

The expression A*ijkzmt* is the achievement level of a random student *i* for a chosen standardized test in subject *z* attending class *j* taught by teacher *k* in school *m* at time *t*. Variables S, C and X are vectors (numeric indicators) of school, classroom and individual student characteristics respectively, while T is the average teacher effect on all students of teacher k; μ is the random error assigned a mean of zero (see Torres 2018). This collection of variables bundled together and expressed as an equation is typical of TER and is expected to encapsulate all of the situational variables at work in schools and classrooms, although it should be noted that it misses depicting any broader social, economic, political and historical influences.

An equation of the form presented earlier incorporates some assumptions and also potentially highlights some problems. Firstly, it suggests that the attained student test score is a complete reflection of the variables nominated in the equation. This means that the information contained in the equation and only this information is responsible for the student test score. Secondly, the data used in the equation regarding, for example, vectors of school, classroom and individual student characteristics are generally aggregated "average" measures. These measures typically generalize across groups and/or categories, for example, class, race, gender and so on. The problem here then about these measures regards their calculation. In brief what type of information and what statistical applications were used to derive them? An obvious issue regards the discounting of individual context. A third problem relates to something we mentioned in Chapter 2, the notion of "holding constant". Quite often in multiple regression analyses researchers seek to study the expected change in a particular variable against a unit of change in a corresponding variable while other variables are "held constant". "Holding constant" in statistical analysis is an arithmetical manipulation (see Berk 2004). In other words, the notion of "holding constant" is an artificial intervention into the manipulation of data. Berk points out that if 'one decides to interpret those manipulations as if some confounder were actually being fixed [in nature], a very cooperative empirical world is required' (2004, p. 115). This is an important point and aligns with something that Chad, one of our teacher participants, alluded to about students and their uniqueness as human beings.

> [A] very simple model exists at present; that you teach a child, you pre-test them . . . you sprinkle . . . it is like a plant . . . you put the plant in, you sprinkle fertiliser all over them and then they . . . all grow at the same rate and you've got your plants . . . whereas human beings all grow at different rates.
> *(Chad)*

Chad is saying here that student development doesn't necessarily adhere to some pre-fixed or pre-calculated idea of what ought to be the case. People (human beings) are all different as are particular classroom situations and contexts. Chad went on to outline in basic terms his approach to teaching and learning, which seems at odds with an absolutist or totalizing view of how people learn, which is what a typical regression equation in TER hopes to accomplish. The teaching and learning experience for Chad begins by using 'a variety of teaching approaches and techniques' (Chad) to assist students tease out what they know about a topic or issue. This occurs over a series of initial lessons and incorporates a series of brainstorming activities, usually performed by small groups of students working together followed by open-ended questioning and visual aids (videos on the topic and so on) before then settling on some in-depth reading. There is a sequential build-up over time leading to some formal assessment, usually culminating in a student presentation (perhaps group presentation) of their work and of what has been learnt.

> The important part is about the content knowledge and skills. We are using the knowledge and developing skills.
>
> *(Chad)*

Whereas for Heather, another of our teacher participants, the uniqueness of the learning experience is connected to creativity and the potentialities inherent in education.

> I suppose because I've had such a long time teaching in the arts my whole premise is around creativity and – and lateral thinking and the fact that students when they come into class are an untapped resource and they don't know what they can achieve until the teacher brings that out in them.
>
> *(Heather)*

Studies using TER often gloss over 'what the child brings to the school experience' suggesting that 'the teacher contributes more than any other factor to student achievement' (Griffin 2014, p. 101). Studies into effective teaching are founded on experimental pre-figured models where the focus of study is the scrutiny of particular classroom teacher characteristics and behaviours considered important in enhancing achievement (see Gage 1972). Nicholas Gage's study *Teacher Effectiveness and Teacher Education* (1972) has been influential in proposing a scientific approach to understanding the nature of teaching practice and the relationship to student learning, and his work led subsequently to some of the more important early studies in the area (e.g. Berliner 1979; Evertson 1982; Good and Brophy 1986; Stallings 1985). The behaviours and/or characteristics of teachers and classroom observation/s of teaching practice/s were the basis of examination in many of the early studies into teacher effectiveness.

The design rationale in TER is predicated on a process-product model of teaching and learning, the aim being identification of association/s between processes of teaching practices and the product of student learning (see Anderson, Evertson and Brophy 1979; Konstantopoulos and Sun 2014; Muijs et al. 2014). TER often uses a statistical correlational approach to analyze and evaluate links between classroom teaching practice and learning. Comparative measures based on the identification of key input variables (or factors) of different teachers found to contribute to student achievement are often used to distinguish between highly effective/effective teachers and effective/non-effective teachers. The particular input variables can include opportunity to learn and time on task, the form of academic instruction/interaction given in classrooms, classroom climate meaning the specific contribution/s of the teacher to establishing/creating a meaningful classroom learning situation, and teacher expectation/s (see Muijs et al. 2014). It is worth noting that TER often uses terms such as instruction rather than pedagogy and factors as opposed to variables when making reference to classroom experiences.

While quantitative attributions regarding how teachers affect student achievement should not be under-estimated, the complexity connected to how students learn in classroom situations is often just as much a result of multiple influences, most of which are extraneous to the classroom. Chad is seemingly making reference to this in his earlier comments. Recent work in this area has noted that classrooms are:

> messy, unpredictable contexts. Daily, educators teach students who come from different backgrounds, cultures, and life experiences; who have diverse interests and motivations; and who have varying levels of language proficiency, skills, and abilities.
>
> *(Parsons et al. 2018, p. 206)*

Vicki, one of our teacher participants, referred to this when talking about maintaining student engagement during lessons and how students can be easily distracted by a variety of things, including, as she put it, 'If it is not computer games stuff then it's some family thing or whatever'. Vicki continues by highlighting the varying daily dynamics on display in classrooms that teachers must deal with constantly – which TER never documents:

> you know, Freddy won't talk to Jane or Jane won't talk to someone and they've been excluded from parties and that then has an impact on school because then they don't want to sit in that row and so on. All of this makes things just that bit more complicated for the classroom teacher.
>
> *(Vicki)*

Recent developments in TER draw upon large-scale studies and surveys of teaching in order to gauge more precise estimations of teaching effects on student achievement (see Seidel and Shavelson 2007). This work has tended to rely on specific processes of learning in subject domains centring on the particular teaching practices used rather than an emphasis purely on the application of statistical models to large-scale survey data on student outcomes and instructional practices seeking changes in student learning over time (see Seidel and Shavelson

2007). A further significant development in TER includes value-added modelling (see Imig and Imig 2006; McCaffrey, Lockwood, Koretz and Hamilton 2004) and contextual value-added models. Value-added modelling is a form of TER based on establishing a causal connection between the teaching practice/s of teachers and student achievement while holding other variables (e.g. socio-economic status) constant. Any achievement gained is the teacher effect or the value-added component (see Sass, Semykina and Harris 2013). Contextual value-added (CVA) modelling as a form of TER accounts for contextual influences (e.g. gender and family circumstances) (UK Department for Education 2012). It is worth noting that value-added TER is often critiqued for the assumptions that it makes (e.g. the notion of "holding constant") with questions surrounding technical validity and implementation (see Darling-Hammond 2015).

Value-added (VA) and contextual value-added (CVA) teacher effectiveness research are both quantitative growth model designs. They numerically assign effectiveness by attributing educational gains made by a student solely to the individual teaching practice/s of a classroom teacher. The basis for the attribution is student pre- and post-test scores (see Schmidt, Houang and McKnight 2005) that are then compared against the expected gains to be made (see Lissitz 2006). CVA as distinct from VA research measures 'how well a school does with its pupil population compared to pupils with similar characteristics nationally' (DfE 2010, p. 68). While VA and CVA research grabs policy-maker interest for known reasons, including identifying "added value", simplicity and so on (see (Lissitz, Doran, Schafer and Willhoft 2006), there are problematic aspects attached to both. Some of the problematic aspects of VA research include establishing the interactive effects of prior achievement for teachers and education programs, demographic influences and so on (see Lissitz et al. 2006). A problematic element of CVA research is that it expects 'different levels of progress from different groups of pupils on the basis of their ethnic background, or family circumstances' which policy-makers believe is 'wrong in principle' (DfE 2010, p. 68) as it already "defines" an individual in deficit terms based on race or family circumstances. The characterization of aggregated student score that then proxies for school and/or teacher performance is about an exclusive focus on the single "one-off" measurement. Broadly speaking, VA and CVA research align with the belief that a period of school learning 'is synonymous with change' (Lissitz et al. 2006, p. 7) and so by implication any change is measurable.

5.2 A tapered view

A myriad of influences and complex interactions act on learning and student achievement (see Darling Hammond 2015). Heather, one of our teacher participants on this, suggests that for her 'I suppose – when I'm teaching I'm looking at the – development over each week of the child and the changes that I'm looking for, how they are developing their work . . . what they are actually producing'. Aaron, another of our teacher participants, on the other hand, points out, 'it's not about a number. It's not about – it's not about snapshots. It's about a teacher's experience – broad experience'. The plethora of "gold standard", large-scale, randomized control trial (RCT) studies and the allure of a scientific algorithmic logic favouring statistical predictive modelling have not only legitimated a specific form of research, but also it has privileged a form of thinking about education that dispenses with the complex. Trevor Gale makes the point that the RCT is about developing a particular "narrative" universalizing the 'reality of the physical world across the social world' so that 'certain knowledge outcomes (e.g. related to "interventions")' (Gale 2018, p. 211) is what matters. Specific model signifiers act as algorithmic substitutes for classroom interactions which by implication partition the messiness of the 'lived and enacted' (Bourdieu 1990, p. 104) sense of experience and practice in classrooms. The end result is often a distorted interpretation of the supposed predictability and calculation that accompany the 'state of pure appearance' (Bourdieu 1990, p. 104) afforded TER.

This means that the 'methodological objectivism' (Bourdieu 2004, p. 72) inferred by regression analysis – remember this means drawing a straight line between student achievement and teacher performance – is based on an artificial adjustment of collected data. The 'statistical regularity or algebraic structure' (Bourdieu 2004, p. 72) in TER, which relies on a "predictive model", distorts the classroom work of teachers so that we view education in absolutist and mechanical terms. This absolutist thinking about teaching and learning has resulted in what a teacher research participant in our research termed the 'medical model' (Chad). Chad moves on to say that in this model the student:

> presents as sick and the doctor (teacher) attempts to diagnose the sickness . . . after diagnosis the teacher works out a strategy to make the patient (student) well. We are treating students as though they're our patients and we need a diagnosis, so we do that through pre-testing and [then] implement a strategy.
> *(Chad)*

When asked what he thought of a model such as this in terms of education, Chad replied:

> No! . . . Because students aren't sick! They're not patients! They're individuals learning at their own level and pace . . . we're human beings . . . not controllable variables such as on a production line.
> *(Chad)*

Vicki and Heather on the same point:

> So standardized testing, all those things, are really – they're – they're faulty to start with. . . . I mean the standardized test assumes that we all learn the

same, learn all the same things at the same time . . . every teacher teaches the same . . . in the same way . . . what rubbish!!

(Vicki)

Standardized testing is not the sum of a child . . . none of these standardized tests are.

(Heather)

Heather is increasingly concerned about the contemporary emphasis in education on a standardized single score depicting achievement. She believes a single standardized test score doesn't reflect true or meaningful learning, nor does it respect the needs of what she terms is the 'creative thinker'. As she says:

we have to actually do something about creativity . . . what about the creative thinker? What about the creative child?

(Heather)

Heather has touched on an important aspect here. As an art teacher with a long and established record in teaching, she is very concerned at the narrow curricula and testing emphasis of the contemporary education system where, in her view, the artistic and creative student is marginalized through the stifling of creativity and imagination.

And – and this is the madness. As an Art teacher, I'm being asked to grade kids' work, right . . . but you cannot – you can't test for creativity or give it some score.

(Heather)

She continues by saying,

And, you know, a – a creative person and how you establish that has such huge benefits and we've – I believe . . . what they haven't tapped into is how much the arts make a difference to how and what students learn.

(Heather)

5.3 An economizing "doxic" discourse

TER formalizes teaching practices by incorporating pre-defined conceptions of pedagogy into the mechanisms of its research design. Judgements of effective and quality teaching are made against system criteria. Numerical comparisons are favoured where models of effective teaching deputize for the 'practical (social and material) world' (Yakhlef 2010, p. 409) of the classroom context, distorting the complex medium of learning and knowing. A set of practice-based "teaching universals" are substituted instead, for example, the creation of a 'businesslike, task-oriented environment' where students 'spend classroom time on academic activities rather than on socialising, free time, etc.' (Muijs and Reynolds 2000, p. 274). In researching school and teacher effectiveness in mathematics classrooms Muijs and Reynolds (2000) contend that:

> research has found that pupils learn more in classes where they spend most of their time being taught or supervised by their teachers, rather than working on their own. In these classes teachers spend most of their time presenting information through lecture or demonstration. Teacher-led discussion as opposed to individual seatwork dominates. The teacher carries the content personally to the student, as opposed to relying on textbooks or maths schemes to do this.
>
> *(p. 274)*

This form of teacher-led instruction is process-product oriented where the operationalization of effectiveness dominates the pedagogic relationship between teacher and student.

The regularizing practices inherent in TER reinforce an objectivist account of education where teaching and learning are reduced to a set of statistical co-variates, confounding factors, "teacher effects" and data (see Lomax and Kuenzi 2012). In seeking to extract the principles of effective and quality teaching practice which it then constitutes as norms, TER imposes a stringent 'logic of practice' (Bourdieu 2004, p. 19) to capture classroom action. In this way the imposition of an orthodox set of guiding structures (teaching practices/methods/strategies, teacher expectations, classroom organization and learning environment, and utilization of classroom resources) form the symbolic heart of what TER recognizes as important in pedagogic action. This is by no means accidental. The economizing logic of TER is about the inculcation of "rules" and a *putting into practice* of a 'repertoire of devices or techniques' (Bourdieu 2004, p. 20, emphasis in original) that presuppose and predefine effective teaching. An objectifying performance-oriented discourse is an example of this where effective teaching is generated through specific classroom-based actions vis-a-vis:

> Maximizing learning time, Grouping strategies, Benchmarking against best practice, and Adapting practice to student needs.
>
> *(Reynolds et al. 2014, p. 210)*

The implicit aim here is to regulate and recommend, prescribe and orient teaching practice/s so that they align with system-induced externally set benchmarks.

Pierre Bourdieu uses the term "doxa" when referring to the set of presuppositions operating in a field. Doxa is about an established self-evident order and taken-for-granted sense of action. The objective sense of TER often found in statistical correlations is about believing and accepting the set of presuppositions that define it as a research field. Some of these presuppositions include (1) the teacher "makes the difference", (2) context is not as important or as decisive in student achievement as are the practice/s of classroom teachers, (3) the "teacher effect" on student achievement can be isolated from other "effects" and (4) adherence to pre-defined behaviours and "standards" of classroom practice will enhance student achievement and learning in all classrooms and in all schools. This imposed universalist story is about the application of objective fundamentals that act as representations of what is possible. A doxa can only operate by way of 'misrecognition' (Bourdieu 1977). Belief in a particular set of fundamentals usually means overlooking, downplaying or misrecognizing the conditions that form a different set of representations.

> Schemes of thought and perception can produce the objectivity that they do produce only by producing misrecognition of the limits of the cognition that they make possible, thereby founding immediate adherence, in the doxic mode, to the world of tradition experienced as a 'natural world' and taken for granted.
>
> *(Bourdieu 1977, p. 164)*

"Scientistic" accounts of teaching practice do exactly what Bourdieu is referring to in the previous quote (i.e. they misrecognize the limits of their own view of observable action). TER breaks apart the multi-faceted compositions of classroom teaching and learning, partitioning the actions of teachers from the interplay of broader influences. This can only be done if there is a belief in a pure rationality and order that is found in specific regularities of inquiry and practice. The doxic logic of TER is about establishing an orthodoxy of practice (common sense) on classroom teaching that is not only expressed in the particular behaviours of teachers but is also found in the organized representations of curriculum and assessment practice/s.

Earlier in this chapter we used the work of Trevor Gale to highlight how particular forms of research (RCTs) which TER often draws upon are geared towards specific knowledge outcomes and interventions. An important interventionist element of TER is linked to its use in school improvement and effectiveness analyses. To this end the data logics of TER display an effective/affective double where what counts and what is expected fits an accountability-driven school effectiveness/improvement agenda. Lewis and Holloway (2018) have recently touched on this by showing that "datafication" (Lycett 2013) and the overuse of 'standardised modes of teacher evaluation and student assessment' (Lewis and Holloway 2018, p. 1) have redefined the teaching profession where the "effective" sense of self that teachers feel aligns with data-driven school and system-level expectations. Lewis and Holloway's research shows that effectiveness and quality for some teachers incorporates a 'data-driven disposition' (Lewis and Holloway 2018, p. 11), meaning that these teachers embrace judgement through data. Vicki, a teacher participant, made some reference to this aspect when discussing standardized testing and how it can distort perceptions of teacher effectiveness and quality:

> I suppose the general comment would be that most teachers are not effective as seen by the [standardized system] data.

Heather conversely made reference to this point when discussing a new school-based assessment and reporting initiative that her school had recently implemented:

> As an art teacher I should be able to encourage the students, not just in the classroom, but in say how we offer Art Club every week at lunchtime. But, also I have, at the end of every year, a big art and technology exhibition which all of us in the Art and Tech faculty are part of. Now . . . what I can see happening, depending on our dates for reporting, is that we're being pushed to the limit in that in the back of my mind now it's, When's the next assessment? When's the next assessment? I mean I am made to only think about 'the test' after a topic and not be broader in my thinking about teaching Art to kids.
>
> *(Heather)*

Heather continues to outline her antipathy towards the intensification experienced in schools regarding the collection of data for reporting and evaluation purposes:

> I think for me in – being my area of teaching (Art) . . . student achievement has to show growth in the student from where they are when they come in, for example, a Year 7 class, to where they end up after six months with me. And, one of the things I find difficult about this collecting of data, as I've spoken to another colleague about, in Art a child is not data, their artwork is not data.
>
> *(Heather)*

Education reform discourses shape the contexts and conditions in which teachers work. They also affect aspects of professional agency and teacher identity. The emphasis on measurable performance and individual teacher responsibility for student success is about the redefinition of 'teachers' self-concepts' (Buchanan 2015, p. 700). Teacher self-concept refers to professional identity and agency and is connected to the 'unique mix of personal and professional experiences and commitments' (Buchanan 2015, p. 701) that teachers bring to their work. Heather, for example, is committed to the teaching of art as an experience that students have, hence her commitment to the organization and display of student artwork. An aspect often overlooked or dismissed in TER is the complexity inherent in the number of interactions involved in pedagogic relationships. Morwenna Griffiths makes the point that relationships 'are not only complex, [they're] contingent on circumstance' (2014, p. 119). She then goes on to say that this 'aspect of teaching is often overlooked [where] the teacher remains oddly disembodied, ageless and displaced from any specific social or political context' (2014, p. 119).

The constant 'need to *perform* performance' (Lewis and Holloway 2018, p. 4, emphasis in original) excises the contingency of time from teaching and the pedagogic relationship. Heather refers to this aspect when talking about assessing student work in the current education policy environment of high stakes testing: 'Each child has an individual growth pattern. . . . I suppose growth . . . you cannot say is data because creative growth happens over time'. She continues:

> And, for me, I'm finding it difficult at the moment to give work a percentage; we're required to give student work percentages. I would rather give student work descriptive grades because a grade, to me, is a bit more friendly and it respects students as individuals and human beings. . . . So, A, B, C, D is better than saying 'Your artwork is 46 out of . . . 46 out of 100'.
> *(Heather)*

Similarly, Vicki, in talking about assessment in her science classes, states:

> What about the need to experience curiosity, ask questions . . . explore . . . before just narrow recall of scientific facts?
> *(Vicki)*

While we know that relationships are complex and contingent on circumstances, 'neither the complexity nor the contingency has been well represented in current research and theory' (Griffiths 2014, p. 118). We re-visit the notions of teacher agency and identity again in Chapter 7.

5.4 Symbolic orders of control

Teacher effectiveness and quality are often subsumed by a broader debate about teacher performance and development. This debate is usually expressed in the economic challenges and opportunities found in the knowledge economy of the 21st century. The Ministerial Council on Education, Employment, Training and Youth Affairs (MCEETYA), for instance, outlines how as a nation Australia must strive to be a world economic leader.

> In the 21st century Australia's capacity to provide a high quality of life for all will depend on the ability to compete in the global economy on knowledge and innovation. Education equips young people with the knowledge, understanding, skills and values to take advantage of opportunity and to face the challenges of this era with confidence.
> *(MCEETYA 2008, p. 5)*

A clear focus on improving teacher effectiveness has led to the creation of a performance and development culture in Australian schools (see AITSL 2012). There are two elements to a performance and development culture: improving teaching, which then should lead to enhanced student achievement. A performance and development culture is founded on aspects considered vital in sustaining successful schooling systems. The Australian Institute for Teaching and School Leadership (AITSL) considers these aspects to be: a focus on student outcomes, clear understanding of effective teaching, leadership, flexibility and coherence. These characteristics link to a performance and development cycle of reflection and goal setting, professional practice and learning and feedback and review (AITSL 2012, p. 3). Some of our teacher participants made reference to the new professional development/learning demands expected of teachers. Vicki, for example, suggests that 'It's all individual . . . and our PDs [professional development] have to be done in our time'. Heather, on the other hand, is thankful for her four days of professional development (PD) given to each teacher over the course of each year but suggests that due to time pressure issues in covering the curriculum adequately and also assessment intensification, she uses some of these days for correction and preparation: 'if we didn't have them and because we have so much to do we would be sliding under the table. So you can use your days for correction and preparation'.

The emphasis on teacher effectiveness and quality is set within measuring student progress against performance and development goals. Evidence of teaching practice/s found to be effective in enhancing student achievement forms the basis of review in evaluating effective teacher performance. The list of potential sources of evidence includes: evidence of the impact of teaching on student outcomes, direct observation of teaching, evidence of the teacher's impact on colleagues and the school as a whole, student feedback, parent feedback, peer/supervisor feedback, teacher self-assessment, evidence of participation in professional learning and teacher reflection on its impact (AITSL 2012). The AITSL (2012) points out that it is these sources of evidence which 'are most often cited in the international research on teacher effectiveness' (p. 6).

Teacher standards documents and their descriptors illustrate the knowledge and practice/s of effective teachers at the various career stages. Australia categorizes teacher standards around domains of professional knowledge, professional practice and professional engagement. In the U.S. teacher standards centre on five core propositions: Teachers are committed to students and their learning, teachers know the subjects they teach and how to teach those subjects to students, teachers are responsible for managing and monitoring student learning, teachers think systematically about their practice and learn from experience and teachers are members of learning communities (see National Board for Professional Teaching Standards 2018). The U.K. teacher standards are composed of two parts which encompass the categories of teaching (Part One) and personal and professional conduct (Part Two) (see Department for Education 2011). In the category of teaching, the standards outline a series of actions in which teachers engage, for example, teachers 'set high expectations which inspire, motivate and challenge pupils'. There are eight standards in total within the teaching category. In the category of personal and professional conduct, a series of behavioural and conduct statements outline how teachers are expected to 'demonstrate consistently high standards of personal and professional conduct' (Teachers' Standards 2011).

Standards prescriptively document the formal relationship between teacher and student. Quality assurance in teaching and learning, which teacher standards supposedly reflect, focuses on processes and specific outcomes which reinforce 'the technical-managerial approach' (Biesta 2004, p. 239) of audit systems. Education is then subsumed by targets and achievement levels and the effectiveness and efficiency of particular teaching practices and/or interventions. This new view of teacher and teaching quality has been discussed by Australian Sociologist Raewyn Connell. She suggests that the seasoned expertise of educators, usually acquired over time in classrooms, has been pushed aside 'in favour of generic managerial skills and practices, using technical measures of organizational efficiency and effectiveness' (Connell 2009, p. 217). In Connell's view, teacher effectiveness research 'treats schools and teachers as bearers of variables (attitudes, qualifications, strong leadership, etc.) to be correlated with pupil outcomes, measured on standardized tests' (Connell 2009, p. 217). The end-point to this form of managerialist logic is the identification and implementation of "best practices" that 'can be instituted and audited from above' (Connell 2009, p. 217). Some of the teachers in our research say something similar to what Connell is suggesting:

> The one size fits all. That's it!
>
> *(Heather)*

> but a teacher's job is much more complex because we're dealing with human beings . . . we're dealing with issues beyond our normal classroom duty . . . so to me it's very difficult to quantify the work of teachers and then say okay . . . we can then extrapolate this to all teachers and all schools. It's bigger and broader.
>
> *(Aaron)*

> They just load you up. You keep being loaded up as a teacher . . . and these accountability systems just paint you as some figure that is supposed to have all of these characteristics and behaviours . . . and somehow they come forth on the day everyday in classrooms.
>
> *(Chad)*

The central operating element at work in the controlling tendencies of teacher effectiveness research is the idea that only an "evidence-based approach" (Biesta 2007) homologous to the scientific tenets of the physical sciences and medicine provides useful and accurate knowledge about education, including teaching.

Educational decision-making is reduced to questions of 'effectivity and effectiveness' (Biesta 2007, p. 6). The professional action of teachers is then supposedly scrutinized in a framework of neutrality. Biesta though argues that the reference point of neutrality is a misrepresentation.

> Evidence-based practice conceives of professional action as intervention, and looks to research for evidence about the effectiveness of interventions.
> *(Biesta 2007, p. 7)*

While teacher effectiveness research as an evidence-based and interventionist approach to practice 'entails a *technological model of professional action*' (Biesta 2007, p. 8, emphasis in original), it favours a '*causal model of professional action*' (Biesta 2007, p. 7, emphasis in original). In other words, the effective intervention of particular teaching practices (the cause) will yield some form of result (effects) – good or bad.

5.5 Governing teaching work

The quantification of teaching practice and the latter's reduction to a single numeric value is about trust in the power of calculation. Scaling, calibrations, projections, estimates and moderations illustrate through numeric comparison an average amount of expected change over time. The numeric purpose involved in the calculation of teaching practice is to 'attach meaning to change (growth), usually at the student level' (Lissitz et al. 2006, p. 2) and compare any identified change to an expected and designated amount at the end of a specified period of educational time (school term/semester/year). While the aim here is education program or personnel (student and/or teacher) evaluation, it also legitimizes education policy decision-making.

Despite the current education policy interest in the evaluation of teaching practice, 'quantified understandings of teaching and teachers . . . is the latest manifestation of processes that have long been in train' (Lewis and Holloway 2018, p. 3). Lewis and Holloway characterize these processes as the general 'trust in numbers' (Porter 1995) phenomenon of quantifiable understandings of the social world that is also part of the broader and more significant movement towards an "audit society" and neoliberal governance arrangements.

> This includes a significant increase in data collection, analysis and use in education globally, with numbers relied upon to define, measure, compare and govern the performance of students, teachers, schools and schooling systems alike.
> *(Lewis and Holloway 2018, p. 3)*

The emphasis on numeric determinations of teacher performance and effectiveness ties aspects of the teacher competency model dominant in the 1960s and

1970s (particularly in the U.S.) with current assumptions about what constitutes good teaching (i.e. the particularizing of teaching practice/s into discrete segments). It is also used to engage teachers in a regime of daily administrative accountability, or what Vicki, a teacher participant, referred to as 'busywork'. When asked to elaborate on the notion of 'busywork', Vicki replied, 'Busywork is work that has no [educational] value but it keeps the person [teacher] busy and distracted from core work like planning and thinking about your students and what you know works best for them'. Vicki is making reference to the administrative load that teachers experience, which in her view 'has increased enormously' from the time when she first began teaching nearly 20 years ago. Heather, another of our teacher participants, makes reference to the notion of "busywork", although in more general terms.

> Well, my work day could start from reading all my emails in the morning to checking the daily organization sheet to see whether I have an extra [replacement class for an absent teacher], to replying to emails fairly promptly . . . emails from parents. Then it would be getting myself organised for the day, going straight to the classroom, getting organised before the actual classes, looking at my work schedule for the day and then deciding what my priorities are for the day in terms of getting work completed in the art room, doing maintenance work or what I would call preparation of materials. Cleaning is part of it because as the role of an art teacher we don't have an aide. So, we, as art teachers in the faculty, have to keep tools and materials up-to-date. We have to do ordering. We have to monitor our equipment and we have to make sure that everything is in order . . . then prioritizing our marking of work and collection of work from the students.
> *(Heather)*

This daily ensemble or 'to-do-list' (Chad) forms a major part of teacher work. The self-governing nature of the work implies that teachers have a degree of professional autonomy. While this is the case, it extends only insofar as a certain functionality is afforded the teacher so that particular administrative tasks are performed. The intrusion of "technology" has only, in the view of Chad, made this form of daily administrative ritual more onerous.

> There are more things to do. The whole idea that technology will make your job simpler is just a myth. It increases. . . . And we're drowning in bureaucracy . . . and whatever the latest fad is . . . which as you know comes with this idea of 'evidence'.
> *(Chad)*

While the modern teaching profession contains an element of self-steering and self-management as depicted by our teacher participants, the policy situation of accountability via standardized testing and its connection to teacher effectiveness and teacher quality directs the schooling experience towards specific ends. Stewart Ranson (2003) suggests that this 'preoccupation with specification, which accountability generates' stretches 'into the pedagogic core as well as the supporting services' (p. 466). This then is an example of one of the Foucauldian "technologies of power" – discipline – the other being biopolitics. Kelly (2003), in drawing on Foucault, notes that discipline 'is a technology which is concerned with individuals, the control of individual bodies . . . deployed to make individuals behave, to be efficient and productive workers' (p. 59), an element to which our teacher participants also make reference.

5.6 Conclusion

In this chapter we have used aspects of the theoretical frameworks of Foucault and Bourdieu to discuss the nature of TER and how it depicts teaching practice and student learning. We considered the application of an awkward and simplistic mathematical model for the evaluation of teaching practice and how it is supposed to report on the efficacy of a classroom teacher. A major part of this chapter was devoted to highlighting how the teacher effectiveness researcher's "tools of inquiry" are basically a collection of statistical representations which incorporate a series of assumptions.

The discursive composition and pragmatic mathematical logic of TER characterizes teaching practice as an activity that is technical and controllable. It favours behaviour modification in the form of control over individual teaching practice, and, secondly, it preferences observer intervention by imposing a dominant objective order shifting our gaze towards the tangible end points (outcomes) of schooling. All of this means that TER adheres to a positivist methodology screening the qualitative richness apparent in classrooms. Our teacher participants expressed some of this qualitative richness in their critical depictions of standardization, suggesting that measurement of student achievement is more than a "one-off" evaluation of learning. Participants provided us with an alternative practitioner-based understanding of how narrow connotations of effectiveness and quality work against broader holistic pedagogic approaches to learning and education that privilege the relational.

References

AITSL. 2012. *Australian Teacher Performance and Development Framework*. Victoria, Australia: Standing Council on School Education and Early Childhood.

Anderson, C., Evertson, C. and Brophy, J. 1979. An experimental study of effective teaching in first-grade reading groups. *Elementary School Journal*, 79(4), 193–223.

Berk, R. A. 2004. *Regression Analysis: A Constructive Critique*. Thousand Oaks, CA: Sage.

Berliner, D. C. 1979. Tempus educare. In P. Peterson and H. Walberg (Eds.), *Research in Teaching* (pp. 120–135). Berkeley, CA: McCutchan.

Biesta, G. J. J. 2004. Education, accountability, and the ethical demand: Can the democratic potential of accountability be regained? *Educational Theory*, 54(3), 232–250.

Biesta, G. J. J. 2007. Why "what works" won't work: Evidence-based practice and the democratic deficit in educational research. *Educational Theory*, 57(1), 1–22.
Bourdieu, P. 1977. *Outline of a Theory of Practice*. Cambridge, UK: Cambridge University Press.
Bourdieu, P. 1990. *The Logic of Practice*. London, UK: Polity Press.
Bourdieu, P. 2004. *Science of Science and Reflexivity*. Cambridge, UK: Polity Press.
Buchanan, R. 2015. Teacher identity and agency in an era of accountability. *Teachers and Teaching*, 21(6), 700–719. https://doi.org/10.1080/13540602.2015.1044329
Connell, R. 2009. Good teachers on dangerous ground: Towards a new view of teacher quality and professionalism. *Critical Studies in Education*, 50(3), 213–229. https://doi.org/10.1080/17508480902998421
Darling-Hammond, L. 2015. Can value-added add value to teacher evaluation? *Educational Researcher*, 44(2), 132–137.
DfE. 2010. *The Importance of Teaching: The Schools White Paper 2010*. London, UK: Department for Education.
DfE. 2011. *Teachers' Standards*. London, UK: Department for Education. Retrieved 8 April 2018 from https://assets.publishing.service.gov.uk/government/uploads/system/uploads/attachment_data/file/665522/Teachers_standard_information.pdf
Evertson, C. M. 1982. Differences in instructional activities in higher and lower achieving junior high English and math classes. *Elementary School Journal*, 82(4), 329–351.
Gage, N. L. 1972. *Teacher Effectiveness and Teacher Education: The Search for a Scientific Basis*. Palo Alto, CA: Pacific Book Publishers.
Gale, T. 2018. What's not to like about RCTs in education? In A. Childs and I. Menter (Eds.), *Mobilising Teacher Researchers: Challenging Educational Inequality* (pp. 207–223). London and New York: Routledge.
Good, T. L. and Brophy, J. E. 1986. School effects. In M. C. Wittrock (Ed.), *Handbook of Research on Teaching*. New York: Macmillan.
Griffin, D. 2014. *Education Reform: The Unwinding of Intelligence and Creativity*. Cham and Heidelberg: Springer.
Griffiths, M. 2014. Encouraging imagination and creativity in the teaching profession. *European Educational Research Journal*, 13(1), 117–129.
Imig, D. G. and Imig, S. R. 2006. The teacher effectiveness movement: How 80 years of essentialist control have shaped the teacher education profession. *Journal of Teacher Education*, 57(2), 167–180.
Kelly, M. G. E., 2003. Racism, nationalism and biopolitics: Foucault's society must be defended. *Contretemps*, 4(September), 58–70.
Konstantopoulos, S. and Sun, M. 2014. Are teacher effects larger in small classes? *School Effectiveness and School Improvement*, 25(3), 312–328.
Kyriakides, L., Campbell, R. J. and Christofidou, E. 2002. Generating criteria for measuring teacher effectiveness through a self-evaluation approach: A complementary way of measuring teacher effectiveness. *School Effectiveness and School Improvement*, 13(3), 291–325 http://doi.org/10.1076/sesi.13.3.291.3426
Lewis, S. and Holloway, J. 2018. Datafying the teaching "profession": Remaking the professional teacher in the image of data. *Cambridge Journal of Education*, 49(1), 35–51. https://doi.org/10.1080/0305764X.2018.1441373
Lissitz, R. W., Doran, H., Schafer, W. D. and Willhoft, J. 2006. Growth modelling, value added modelling and linking: An introduction. In R. W. Lissitz (Ed.), *Longitudinal and Value Added Models of Student Performance* (pp. 1–47). Maple Grove, MD: JAM Press.
Lomax, E. D. and Kuenzi, J. J. 2012. *Value-added Modeling for Teacher Effectiveness*. Washington, DC: Congressional Research Service.

Lycett, M. 2013. "Datafication": Making sense of (big) data in a complex world. *European Journal of Information Systems*, 22(4), 381–386.

McCaffrey, D., Lockwood, J. R., Koretz, D. M. and Hamilton, L. S. 2004. *Evaluating Value-added Models for Teacher Accountability*. Santa Monica, CA: RAND.

MCEETYA. 2008. *Melbourne Declaration on Educational Goals for Young Australians*. Melbourne, Australia: MCEETYA.

Muijs, D., Kyriakides, L., van der Werf, G., Creemers, B., Timperley, H. and Lorna, E. 2014. State of the art: Teacher effectiveness and professional learning. *School Effectiveness and School Improvement: An International Journal of Research, Policy and Practice*, 25(2), 231–256.

Muijs, D. and Reynolds, D. 2000. School effectiveness and teacher effectiveness in mathematics: Some preliminary findings from the evaluation of the mathematics enhancement programme (primary). *School Effectiveness and School Improvement*, 11(3), 273–303. http://doi.org/10.1076/0924-3453(200009)11:3;1-G;FT273

National Board for Professional Teaching Standards. 2018. *Five Core Propositions*. Retrieved 8 April 2018 from www.nbpts.org/standards-five-core-propositions/

Parsons, S. A., Vaughn, M., Scales, R. Q., Gallagher, M. A., Parsons, A. W., Davis, S. G., Piercynzki, M. and Allen, M. 2018. Teachers' instructional adaptations: A research synthesis. *Review of Educational Research*, 88(2), 243–285.

Porter, T. 1995. *Trust in Numbers: The Pursuit of Objectivity in Science and Public Life*. Princeton, NJ: Princeton University Press.

Reynolds, D., Sammons, P., De Fraine, B., Van Damme, J., Townsend, T., Teddlie, C. and Stringfield, S. 2014. Educational Effectiveness Research (EER): A state-of-the-art review. *School Effectiveness and School Improvement*, 25(2), 197–230. https://doi.org/10.1080/09243453.2014.885450

Sass, T. R., Semykina, A. and Harris, D. R. 2013. Value-added models and the measurement of teacher productivity. *Economic of Education Review*, 38, 9–23.

Schmidt, W. H., Houang, R. T. and McKnight, C. C. 2005. Value-added research: Right idea but wrong solution? In R. W. Lissitz (Ed.), *Value Added Models in Education: Theory and Applications* (pp. 145–166). Maple Grove, MN: JAM Press.

Seidel, T. and Shavelson, R. 2007. Teaching effectiveness research in the past decade: The role of theory and research design in disentangling meta-analysis results. *Review of Educational Research*, 77(4), 454–499.

Stallings, J. 1985. Effective elementary classroom practices. In M. J. Kyle (Ed.), *Reaching for Excellence: An Effective Schools Sourcebook*. Washington, DC: National Institute of Education.

Stewart, R. 2003. Public accountability in the age of neo-liberal governance. *Journal of Education Policy*, 18(5), 459–480. https://doi.org/10.1080/0268093032000124848

Torres, R. 2018. Tackling inequality? Teacher effects and the socioeconomic gap in educational achievement. Evidence from Chile. *School Effectiveness and School Improvement*, 29(3), 383–417. https://doi.org/10.1080/09243453.2018.1443143

UK Department for Education. 2012. *A Technical Guide to Contextual Value Added 2007 and 2008 Model*. Retrieved 2 July 2018 from www.education.gov.uk/performancetables/schools_08/s3.shtml

Yakhlef, A. 2010. The corporeality of practice-based learning. *Organization Studies*, 31, 409–430.

6

"MAKING THE DIFFERENCE" – SIDELINING THE CONTINGENT

Introduction

Chapter 6 makes use of data utilizing relevant document analysis. The chapter discusses the positioning of classroom teachers and their teaching practice/s within a dominant policy and major report-related narrative which frames teacher work in particular performance-oriented ways. Research reports to be analyzed include *Teachers matter: Attracting, developing and retaining effective teachers* (Organization for Economic Co-Operation and Development 2005) and Barber and Mourshed's (2007) *How the world's best-performing school systems come out on top*. These reports have been chosen because they both have had major global influence on the direction of school systems and the role of classroom teachers in enhancing student achievement in recent times (see Coffield 2012). Policy documents to be analyzed include the U.S. Department of Education's "No Child Left Behind" (2002) and "Race to the Top" (2009). Both of these major education policy initiatives emanating from within the U.S., with the former instituted as federal legislation, stand out for their articulation of accountability mechanisms and focus on the preparation and work of classroom teachers, standardization of curriculum content and pedagogy (see Hursh 2015). The chapter will critically engage with these documents to illustrate how major research reports and school education policy de-contextualizes school and teacher effects.

6.1 Master narratives – There Is No Alternative (TINA)

There is an implied "master narrative" (Alridge 2006; McAdams 1993; Lyotard 1984) that purports a given self-evident reality about schooling and teaching practice/s. Firstly, that there is a crisis in student performance that secondly requires reform so that schooling and the work of classroom teachers (i.e. their in-classroom teaching practice/s) "make the difference" to learning outcomes. In various major education policy, legislation and policy reports of recent decades (see U.S. Department of Education 1983, 2002, 2009; Department of Education and Employment 1997; Department for Education 2010; Australian Government 2013, 2016) master narratives often operate through a vital 'juxtaposition of an economic perspective and educational terms' (Fisher-Ari, Kavanagh and Martin 2017, p. 256). The master narratives of education policy discourse surrounding student learning are defined in particular performance-oriented ways so that accountability and the matching of grades attained to "standards" is the objective.

> Words and phrases, such as *student learning, achievement*, and *growth* enact a broad, comprehensive conceptual meaning, yet simultaneously enact a neoliberal action that redefines and limits these concepts as problems solvable by a free market.
> *(Fisher-Ari et al. 2017, p. 256, emphasis in original)*

Education policy discourse is comprised of power relations, and dominance is shown by the 'discursive contours' (Liasidou 2011, p. 889) set by particular meaning spheres of authority. The "who" and "what" of education policy discourse is determined by individuals (policy makers) and groups that develop and promote a particular form of it. In the case of education and student performance the "who" and "what" are in general the large supra-national organizations such as the Organization for Economic Co-operation and Development (OECD) that through its brand of economic and policy orthodoxy shapes 'global educational governance' including the 'constitution of a global education policy field' (Sellar and Lingard 2013, p. 710). Organizations such as the OECD promote large-scale testing as the means for verifying student and teacher performance.

We, in this book, view policy problems connected to the social world as discursive representations and not as detached absolutes (Edelman 1988; Bacchi 2000; Winton 2018). Discourse can define and differentiate as it provides the stipulations needed to name and describe (see Foucault 1977). It does so via 'a system of relations that might properly be called *discursive*' (Foucault 1977, p. 45, emphasis in original). Understanding the discursive aspects connected to discourse means recognizing the latter as the 'practices that systematically form the objects of which they speak' (Foucault 1977, p. 49).

An important feature of policy discourse is the 'range of rhetorical strategies' used by policy makers/actors 'to persuade others to interpret particular social practices in a particular way (i.e. as a policy problem)' (Winton 2018, p. 57). We know that the contemporary education policy context reinforces a 'social and political program' (De Lissovoy 2017, p. 2) of intense economic and political competitiveness via 'privatisation, competition, and accountability through testing' (Bøyum 2014, p. 857). This current political and economic imaginary meshes the economy and education so much so that 'education is accordingly seen as a part of economic policy' (Bøyum 2014, p. 857).

Rhetoric in policy making is about argument and it involves 'a process of shaping and creating a dynamic, a rationality, a logic of reasoning, a basis for decision making' (Gottweis 2006, p. 245). It needs a speaker, a writer and an audience. All the 'ways in which we attempt to persuade or influence in our discursive, textual, and gestural practice' (Edwards, Nicoll, Solomon and Usher 2004, p. 13) is rhetoric. This means that rhetoric is 'multifaceted' (Winton 2018, p. 57), made up of three elements: the context containing the rhetorical situation including exigence (the contextual need for a response to a particular situation) and audience, persuasive discourse/s, and the five canons of invention, disposition, style, memory and delivery (see Winton 2018, 2013; Leach 2000). The five rhetorical canons are variously concerned with the appeal, reason, emotion, confidence, organization, style, memory and delivery of argument (Winton 2013, 2018).

In the next section of this chapter we seek to analyze the "master narratives" involved in four major education policy-related documents: *Teachers matter: Attracting, developing and retaining effective teachers* (Organization for Economic Co-Operation and Development 2005), *How the world's best-performing school systems come out on top* (the McKinsey Report) (Barber and Mourshed 2007), "No Child Left Behind" (2002) and "Race to the Top" (2009). Two of these documents are major policy reports, the first of which was compiled by the OECD (*Teachers matter*), while the other was conceived by a major global consulting firm (the McKinsey Report). "No Child Left Behind" and "Race to the Top" are the stand-out legislative education policy proposals of the past 20 years emanating from the U.S. "No Child Left Behind" was enacted by the George W. Bush administration (2001–2009), while "Race to the Top" formed the Obama administration's (2009–2017) major education policy platform. We have chosen these four policy-related documents because each is an example of a dominant policy "master narrative" espousing de-contextualized and universal approaches to educational/schooling issues while also promoting particular "fixes" to a perceived student under-performance problem. The particular "fix" espoused centres on the work of classroom teachers, their teaching practice/s and a collection of performative elements and practices. The policy documents chosen outline the "master narratives" of increased school autonomy, heightened accountability and the privileging of a human capital (resource intensive) approach to, in particular, the education, preparation and professional learning of teachers. Destructive education policy discourses about student achievement and performance are taken as "truths" suggestive of 'no other ethical or practical alternative (TINA)' (Fisher-Ari et al. 2017, p. 257) to how school systems can work to enhance student achievement.

The set of school education policies/reports analyzed next flag a number of policy specifics. Some of these policy specifics relate to teacher shortages in key discipline areas (mathematics, science and languages), recruitment of the best and brightest into teaching and the development and enforcement of teacher/teaching standards. In addition to these particular policy specifics are others which focus on measuring teacher and teaching performance through accountability mechanisms, such as value-added models (VAMs) in "Race to the Top" and then others which detail changes to teacher education/preparation. Demonstrated student achievement gains forms the basis for the review of performance tied usually to an accountability framework of key national and student achievement indicators. The documents are also, in our view, examples of "fast policy" (Peck and Theodore 2015) 'emanating from the promotion of decontextualised best practices that can, so it is alleged, transcend the specific requirements of local contexts' (Lewis and Hogan 2019, p. 5). Fast policy is about 'policy shortcuts, or readymade examples of what works' (Lewis and Hogan 2019, p. 3). The fast policy phenomenon benefits from a combination of the '24-h news cycle and the technologically mediated compression of time and space' (Lewis and Hogan 2019, p. 3) evident in our contemporary world. In such an environment the 'policymaking process accelerates' and

> local policymaking increasingly begins with imported or borrowed designs. . . . This creates shortcut alternatives to more deliberative, developmental modes of policy formation, and tends to favour the kinds of technocratic strategies pushed by well-resourced multilateral agencies validated by evaluation science [data] over originally grown, endogenous approaches to policy innovation.
>
> *(Peck and Theodore 2015, pp. xxxi–xxxii)*

The documents presented earlier were chosen based on their purported significance, particularly in terms of school education policy reform and in determining the direction of school education, the preparation and professional learning of teachers and also enhancing student achievement. Each of the documents were read and catalogued in tabular form with specific attention given to sections within each document focusing directly on teachers and teaching. Key theme/s on teachers and teaching, particularly in terms of their preparation and classroom performance as set out in each of the documents, were then summarized in Table 6.1. The subsequent analysis is confined to an understanding of policy as 'textual interventions into practice' (Ball 1993, p. 12). This acknowledges that the text and discourse of policies 'do not normally tell you what to do; they create circumstances in which the range of options available in deciding what to do are narrowed or changed' (Ball 1993, p. 12). Policy is enacted as discourse in the 'way in which policy ensembles, collections of related policies, exercise power through a production of "truth" and "knowledge", as discourses' (Ball 1993, p. 14). In other words, policy discourses shape policy direction and they do so through the 'system of practices' and 'set of values and ethics' (Ball 1993, p. 14) they help enact.

TABLE 6.1

Data sources	Teacher/teaching related policy specific theme/s
Teachers matter: Attracting, developing and retaining effective teachers (Organization for Economic Co-Operation and Development 2005)	The importance of teachers (teachers matter); teacher policy concerns are intensifying. Major concerns include insufficient knowledge and skill base, poor/tenuous connection between teacher education/preparation, professional development and school needs, the poor image of teaching, maintaining a steady supply of appropriately qualified teachers, high rates of teacher attrition, particularly amongst early career teachers, impact of high workloads, increases in stress and poor working conditions, inequitable distribution of "quality teachers" amongst schools, retention of effective teachers. Key policy priority areas include making teaching an attractive career choice; developing teachers' knowledge and skills; recruiting, selecting and employing teachers; and retaining effective teachers in schools.
How the world's best-performing school systems come out on top (Barber and Mourshed 2007)	The identification of the world's best (top) performing school systems; getting the right people to become teachers, developing teachers into effective instructors, ensuring that the education system can deliver the best possible instruction for every child. Three key points about teaching: 1 The quality of an education system cannot exceed the quality of its teachers. 2 The only way to improve outcomes is to improve instruction. 3 High performance requires that every child succeed.
No Child Left Behind (NCLB) (2002)	Accountability; what works – scientifically proven teaching method/s; enhancing the quality of teachers and school principals; scientifically based professional development interventions/programs; correlating student achievement with teacher quality; whole school and district improvement plans; reporting on performance measures; mathematics and science based partnerships to improve student achievement in maths and science; new teacher recruitment programs (Troops to Teachers program; Transition to Teaching program – placing teachers in disadvantaged schools); new school based teaching initiatives (including the National Writing Project, Civic Education, the Teaching of Traditional American History); changes to teacher liability protection requirements; integration of technology resources in teacher education programs to better prepare pre-service teachers in using technology in classrooms to enhance student achievement.

(Continued)

TABLE 6.1 Continued

Data sources	Teacher/teaching related policy specific theme/s
Race to the Top (RTTT) (2009)	Investments only in innovative strategies likely to lead to enhanced student achievement; enhanced school and school system capacity; increased productivity and effectiveness; new standards and assessment/s in student preparation enabling them to compete in the global economy (school to college and beyond); formation of new data systems to measure student achievement/success and to provide information to teachers about student progress linked to classroom instruction; recruiting, developing, rewarding and retaining effective teachers and principals to work in disadvantaged schools; turning around under-performing schools; integration of Science, Technology, Engineering and Mathematics (STEM) content across classes and discipline areas; high-quality pathways for aspiring teachers and school leaders; improving teacher and principal effectiveness; equitable distribution of effective teachers and principals across school districts; improving the effectiveness of teacher and principal preparation programs; provision of effective support to teachers and principals.

6.2 Four education policy case studies

(Case study I) *Teachers matter*: attracting, developing and retaining effective teachers

The widespread education policy debate about teachers centres on specific concerns that the Organization for Economic Co-operation and Development (OECD) report *Teachers matter* (Organization for Economic Co-Operation and Development 2005) suggests relates to specific matters of interest. These are further developing teachers' knowledge and skills; the inadequate connection between teacher education, professional development and school needs; the persistent poor image of teachers; the high attrition rate of new teachers; inadequate recognition and reward; the continued and seemingly intractable problem of attracting the best teachers to the most disadvantaged schools and communities; and implementing a workforce strategy with the capacity to sack the most ineffective teachers. The report, while similar to many others on the topic of "teacher policy" (Organization for Economic Co-Operation and Development 2005), uses research on student learning to highlight the importance of the in-classroom work of teachers in enhancing learning outcomes:

> Research on student learning shows that the largest source of variation in student learning is attributable to differences in what students bring to school – their abilities and attitudes, and family and community background. Of those variables potentially open to policy influence, factors to do with teachers and teaching are the most important influences on student learning. In particular, the broad consensus is that 'teacher quality' is the single most important school variable influencing student achievement.
>
> *(Organization for Economic Co-Operation and Development 2005, p. 7)*

Implicit in these "evidence-based" findings is the basic 'assumption that social background and student abilities are *not* open to policy influence' (Connell 2009, p. 214, emphasis in original). The evidence derived representation of the classroom teacher in research of this type is as the variable that "matters most" in student learning, and it is 'excellence in teachers that make the greatest differences' (Hattie 2003, p. 4). The report highlights the inability of the teaching profession to attract what it deems are "high flyers", the implied message being that only those at the very top academically have what it takes to make the necessary difference as classroom teachers to enhance student achievement.

Construction of the "teachers matter" policy narrative involves a particular brand of field-specific distinction incorporating several policy-related objectives – further develop teacher competencies, allow for more flexible employment options and fully devolve responsibility for the employment (hiring/firing) of teachers to the local school level (see Organization for Economic Co-Operation and Development 2005). In addition, the adoption of certain elements connected to the work of classroom teachers constitutes their performance into an infrastructure of pedagogic practice. In *Teachers matter* (Organization for Economic Co-Operation and Development 2005), this infrastructure is listed as a series of performance-oriented behaviours or 'performative technologies' (Englund 2019, p. 502) that teachers should engage in to maximize student learning and includes the ability to: convey ideas in clear and convincing ways, create effective learning environments for different types of students, foster productive teacher-student relationships, be enthusiastic and creative and work effectively with colleagues and parents (p. 7). The ordering of pedagogic work in this way binds how we think about the in-classroom activity of teachers to a broader policy narrative involving the positioning of teachers and the 'increased expectations about their roles' (Organization for Economic Co-Operation and Development 2005, p. 7) in a changing economy. Accompanying this is the imposition of a duel set of policy operations: the surveillance of teachers through a "disciplining" process of active analysis (adherence to professional standards) and the alignment of their individual teaching practice/s to the progress of their students, and an accepted belief in and recognition of a widening gulf in student achievement (i.e. a burgeoning achievement gap between high- and low-performing students) (see Organization for Economic Co-Operation and Development 2005).

The report is also, in our view, an example of how major education policy popularized by large-scale intergovernmental organizations such as the OECD ignite general unease about societal supports such as education. The perceived need for action results in the production and promotion of 'research knowledge in order to influence policy production' which leads to 'simplified and definitive solutions of best practice' (Lewis and Hogan 2019, p. 2). A prominent reference in the report to 'Teacher Policy Concerns Are Intensifying' (Organization for Economic Co-Operation and Development 2005, p. 7) encourages the targeted urgency needed to redress educational under-performance. The report links the intensifying teacher policy concerns to changing economic and political/social dynamics:

- Teachers are facing increased expectations about their roles as economies and societies evolve. If the teaching profession is to retain the confidence of society it must adapt and act in a constructive manner within a fast-changing society.
- The teaching profession needs to have the skills, knowledge and training needed to cope with the many changes and challenges which lie ahead.
- Teachers themselves have concerns about the future of their profession: whether it is sufficiently attractive to talented new teachers and whether they are sufficiently rewarded and supported in their work.

(Organization for Economic Co-Operation and Development 2005, p. 7)

This form of discursive policy rhetoric is intended to highlight specific problems in education while offering clear solutions. For example, society and the economy are changing, necessitating a newly skilled teacher workforce to manage that change in a positive way for future generations.

(Case study II) *How the world's best-performing school systems come out on top* – the McKinsey Report

How the world's best-performing school systems come out on top by Michael Barber and Mona Mourshed (2007), also known as the McKinsey Report, was welcomed with widespread appeal amongst policy makers and elements of the broader educational community when it first appeared on the education policy scene (see Schleicher 2007). The report highlighted three key focal points of what it viewed successful school systems do. According to the report, successful school systems (a) attract the right type of people into teaching, (b) develop them into effective instructors and (c) ensure that systems deliver effective instruction. An interesting point to note is the use of terms such as "instructors" and "instruction". Both terms are widely used in North America. The report latches on to the "poor student achievement" mantra:

> Despite substantial increases in spending and many well-intentioned reform efforts, performance in a large number of school systems has barely improved in decades. Few of the most widely supported reform strategies (for instance, giving schools more autonomy, or reducing class sizes) have produced the results promised for them. Yet some school systems consistently perform better and improve faster than others.
> *(Barber and Mourshed 2007, p. 10)*

The one major reason, according to the McKinsey Report, as to why some school systems perform better than others is "teacher quality":

> The available evidence suggests that the main driver of the variation in student learning at school is the quality of the teachers.
> *(Barber and Mourshed 2007, p. 12)*

This particular aspect provides the foundational impetus to the report with it suggesting that school systems must focus on improving teacher and teaching quality/effectiveness and make workforce change a top priority by radically altering teacher selection mechanisms and ensuring higher starting salaries for graduate teachers. The report, as Coffield highlights, reduces 'a highly complex set of relations . . . to only one factor' (2012, p. 132) (i.e. the teacher).

The McKinsey Report claims that the top-performing school systems recognize that the 'only way to improve outcomes is to improve instruction' (Barber and Mourshed 2007, p. 29). Teaching practices/strategies and the instructional behaviour of teachers are the variables of most influence in learning, with the report claiming that 'to improve learning implies improving the quality of that interaction' (Barber and Mourshed 2007, p. 29) between students and teachers. The report also provides a universalist message about learning outcomes, suggesting that:

> The quality of the outcomes for any school system is essentially the sum of the quality of the instruction that its teachers deliver.
> *(Barber and Mourshed 2007, p. 29)*

This is an aspect of the report highlighting its absolutist discourse about teacher policy where, if only teachers could be "transformed", 'the performance of schools anywhere, irrespective of their culture or socio-economic status' (Coffield 2012, p. 131) will improve.

Classroom teachers, according to the report, have an essential role in improving learning outcomes by focusing on three things. Teachers will need to assess the various strengths and weaknesses of individual students, tailor instruction to meet identified student needs and then provide the requisite level of efficient and effective delivery of instruction. The type of effective "instruction" required needs definition, with the report (correctly, we add) suggesting that 'developing the curriculum and its associated pedagogies' (Barber and Mourshed 2007, p. 29) is challenging although important. The report suggests that:

> the challenge is broadly one of finding the best educators and giving them the space to debate and create a better curriculum and pedagogy.
> *(Barber and Mourshed 2007, p. 29)*

At a systems management level, the challenge is more about capacity building and 'giving thousands of teachers . . . the capacity and knowledge to deliver that great instruction reliably, every day, across thousands of schools, in circumstances that vary enormously from one classroom to the next – and all this with very little oversight' (Barber and Mourshed 2007, p. 29). In other words 'the belief in one right approach to teaching' (Coffield 2012, p. 140).

In addition to the changes outlined earlier, which the report claims are necessary but not sufficient, are further "teacher reforms". Fundamental change must also occur within classrooms at the level of instruction necessitating specific reform of the individual classroom teacher as a professional "worker". The report encapsulates the needed reforms in this way:

- Individual teachers need to become aware of specific weaknesses in their own practices. In most cases, this is not only building an awareness of what they do but the mindset underlying it.
- Individual teachers need to gain understanding of specific best practices. In general, this can only be achieved through the demonstration of such practices in an authentic setting.
- Individual teachers need to be motivated to make the necessary improvements. In general, this requires a deeper change in motivation that cannot be achieved through changing material incentives. Such changes come about when teachers have high expectations, a shared sense of purpose, and above all, a collective belief in their common belief to make a difference to the education of the children they serve.

(Barber and Mourshed 2007, p. 30)

Each of these points address characteristic qualities. The first quality pertains to inadequacy and a recognition that all teachers irrespective of experience are flawed in some way and that their classroom teaching practice will fall short on occasion if not always. This will mean that teachers must be continually immersed in regimes of professional learning and evaluation so as to "get the best out of themselves" always. The second quality addresses the idea of the singular process of "best practice" and only "what works" teaching. This quality implies that teaching work can be systematically captured and described and "technologically" managed/manipulated. We return to the notion of "best practice" in Chapter 9. The third quality connects more broadly to the "game" of school education committing to its 'presuppositions – doxa' (Bourdieu 1990, p. 66); teachers make the difference, socio-economic or other contextual influences have no effect on schooling outcomes and so on.

"Instructional leadership" is also a term used by the report to maintain the emphasis on in-classroom performance. The report draws on school leadership research from the National College in School Leadership (U.K.) which claims that 'school leadership is second only to classroom teaching as an influence on learning' (Barber and Mourshed 2007, p. 32). In a similar vein to the teacher recruitment emphasis mentioned earlier, the report focuses attention on recruiting the 'right teachers to become principals' (Barber and Mourshed 2007, p. 33), developing their instructional leadership skills and freeing them from excessive administrative demands so that they can spend more time on instructional leadership. This particular development accords with the pivotal connection between the role of school leaders in not only managing educational change and reform but leading it for school improvement and being duly held accountable 'through enhanced student test results' (Starr 2011, p. 646).

(Case study III) No Child Left Behind

"No Child Left Behind" (NCLB) was the signature education legislative agenda of U.S. President George W. Bush (2001–2009). The Elementary and Secondary Education Act (ESEA) of the U.S. was amended by George W. Bush in 2001, spawning NCLB (see Lavery 2016). NCLB initiated U.S. federal government involvement in standardized testing expanding government 'reach into public schools beyond anything previously known' (Hursh 2015, p. 12). NCLB is split into nine titles. The report in Title I Improving the Academic Achievement of the Disadvantaged begins by saying that 'all children have the opportunity to obtain a high-quality education and reach proficiency on challenging state academic standards and assessments' (U.S. Department of Education 2002, p. 13). The policy then highlights levels of student under-achievement, according to the National Assessment of Educational Progress (NAEP), before claiming that under Title I there will be provision of improved funding for a program that focuses on 'promoting schoolwide reform in high-poverty schools and ensuring students' access to scientifically based instructional strategies and challenging academic content' (U.S. Department of Education 2002, p. 13). Title I in NCLB refers to schools with high concentrations of disadvantaged students, and it focuses primarily upon basic educational programs, reading, literacy and prevention of school dropout. In addition, accountability and testing feature prominently throughout all of the titles that comprise NCLB:

> Title I provisions provide a mechanism for holding states, school districts and schools accountable for improving the academic achievement of all students and turning around low-performing schools while providing alternatives to students in such schools to enable those students to receive a high-quality education.
> *(U.S. Department of Education 2002, p. 13)*

NCLB required all American states to implement standardized testing. It also promotes federal solutions to under-achievement 'which may include converting publically funded schools into privately administered charter schools' (Hursh 2013, p. 576). Charter schools had their beginnings in the U.S. in 1991 (see Hursh 2017) largely through the advocacy of progressive teachers and union leaders 'as a mechanism for education reform in which new innovations might be piloted to address social justice issues, and where marginalized students might be offered opportunities more akin to those available in private schools' (Lefebvre and Thomas 2017, p. 358).

Lavery (2016) suggests that the policy logic of NCLB is founded upon several assumptions. Firstly, NCLB mandates standardized testing, believing that state-administered tests (by law) 'can accurately identify schools in need of improvement' (Lavery 2016, p. 346). Secondly, that school choice and other educational services 'such as tutoring, remediation, and enrichment activities will provide an opportunity for individual students to improve academic capacities' (Lavery 2016, p. 346). Thirdly, that coercive 'corrective action and restructuring' in core school functions, including changes to school leadership and staff, curriculum and so on, 'will greatly alter school culture and increase achievement' (Lavery 2016, p. 346). Finally, that only through state-enforced legal sanction will any worthwhile change 'for disadvantaged populations' be possible that ultimately 'will lead to improved academic outcomes for all' (Lavery 2016, p. 346).

The requirement of evaluation in connection with heightened forms of accountability is what NCLB is most known for (see Hursh 2015). The failure of schools to meet "Adequate Yearly Progress" (U.S. Department of Education 2002) resulted in 'a cascading increase in penalties, ranging from providing more professional development to replacing all the staff to closing the school and reopening it as a charter school' (Hursh 2015, p. 59). The landmark policy status of NCLB is best exemplified by the focus it has on four key elements: Accountability, Flexibility and Local Control, Enhanced Parental Choice and a focus on What Works. The recruitment, preparation and training of high-quality teachers and principals is an important feature of the policy. The policy specifics of this feature include: enhancing the quality of teachers and school principals; correlating student achievement with teacher quality; new teacher recruitment programs (including the Troops to Teachers program, and the Transition to Teaching program which involves placing teachers in disadvantaged schools); changes to teacher liability protection requirements; and the integration of technology resources in teacher education programs to better prepare pre-service teachers in using technology in classrooms to enhance student achievement (see U.S. Department of Education 2002).

The emphasis on evaluation and accountability at the individual teacher and school system level in NCLB aligned with a totalizing scientific "what works" approach to education. Under-achieving or designated "failing schools" were targeted for intervention based on the implementation of scientifically derived "proven" professional development strategies that "work". The 'scientifically proven strategies' (U.S. Department of Education 2002, p. 50) of teaching and learning grounded in 'scientifically based research' (U.S. Department of Education 2002, p. 50) were implemented as part of a general school improvement plan in NCLB with priority given to low-performing schools. Reporting against benchmarked standards in the areas of mathematics, literacy and science formed part of the school improvement plan.

(Case study IV) Race to the Top

The federal education policy program of the Obama administration (2009–2017) known as "Race to the Top" (RTTT) 'incentivized states to implement new and more rigid accountability frameworks', building upon NCLB initiatives such as 'standardized achievement tests, school "choice", and private sector vendors to reform curriculum and teaching through market pressures, privatization, and punitive measures tied to standardized test scores' (Holloway and Brass 2018, p. 364). RTTT developed common curriculum standards, including uniform assessments 'as well as teacher evaluation systems based on value-added measures (VAMs)' (Holloway and Brass 2018, p. 364). The competitive locus of RTTT provided federal government aid (approximately $4.35 billion from an education budget comprising $100 billion) to U.S. states interested in opting in to the RTTT program. David Hursh (2013) contends that U.S. states applying for RTTT funding usually did so due to their poor fiscal status as a result of the after-effects connected to the 2008 global financial crisis. An important aspect of the program involved tying teacher evaluations to student test scores and also 'increasing or removing the cap on the number of charter schools' (Hursh 2013, p. 582).

"Teacher policy" reforms in RTTT address important teacher effectiveness and quality aspects. The development and/or presence of alternative pathways into school education for aspiring teachers and principals; improvements in teacher and principal effectiveness based on performance measured by annual student achievement growth targets; and the equitable distribution of effective teachers and principals targeting schools in most need (U.S. Department of Education 2009) provide the basis for action. RTTT also uses descriptive markers for an effective/highly effective teacher/principal. An effective teacher/principal has 'students achieve acceptable rates (e.g. at least one grade level in an academic year) of student growth' and a highly effective teacher/principal has their 'students achieve high rates (e.g. one and one-half grade levels in an academic year) of student growth' (U.S. Department of Education 2009, p. 12). Hursh (2013) has illustrated the sleight of hand connected to these "effective/highly effective" performance descriptors in RTTT. Using the U.S. state of New York as an example, he points out that 'teachers are required to be rated on a bell curve, so that 10% of teachers, whether based on test scores, observation, or other locally created criteria, must be rated as "ineffective" and 40% as "developing"' (Hursh 2013, p. 583). In addition, Ravitch highlights the contradictory nature of RTTT. She uses U.S. President Obama's 2012 State of the Union plea that 'teachers should stop teaching to the test' (Obama 2012). Ravitch states:

> According to Race to the Top, states are required to evaluate teachers based in part on their students' test scores in order to compete for federal funding. When New York won $700 million from the Obama program, it pledged to do this. What the President has now urged ('stop teaching to the test') is directly contradicted by what his own policies make necessary (teach to the test or be rated ineffective and get fired).
> *(Ravitch 2012, no page)*

In our view there are two marked policy differences between NCLB and RTTT. NCLB espoused enhancing student achievement through the alleged certainties of "scientific evidence" and "what works" via strong accountability, standards, measurable results and changes in teaching practice/s. Federal government funding was subsequently issued based on school system implementation of the above. RTTT, on the other hand, embraced the evolving economic uncertainties of the times, advocating the need for "innovation" and privatization. While leaving many of the changes enacted under NCLB intact, RTTT also installed a competitive process for accessing federal funding where states competed for money based on the implementation of innovative reforms. This particular aspect of 'Obama's RTTT competition'

(Hursh 2013, p. 576) was based upon the fulfilment of several requirements, including development of a value-added teacher evaluation system, a significant rise in the number of charter schools and enhanced mayoral control over schools (see Hursh 2013). The particular "innovation" in RTTT is about holding teachers accountable 'using students' scores on state-wide standardized tests as 20% of teacher evaluations, and increasing or removing the cap on the number of charter schools' (Hursh 2013, p. 582). As Hursh has illustrated, some states (New York in particular) soon moved towards using 40% of a teacher's evaluation based on student test scores (see Hursh 2013).

6.3 Symbolic policy forms

The symbolic logic of education policy espousing teacher accountability generates meaning via the language that it uses to classify and group. Distinguishing between the "good/bad" teacher and "effective/in-effective" teaching is made possible through a symbolic policy system that follows a perceptual scheme which objectifies practice. Policy on teacher evaluation and accountability is conceived as a generator of categories with indicators that include and exclude based upon 'structuring structures' (Bourdieu 2014, p. 165) – teacher standards, standardized test results and so on – which purportedly should deliver on student learning outcomes. These symbolic policy forms act as 'constructions of social reality' (Bourdieu 2014, p. 165) subjecting in this case classroom teachers to arbitrary, yet seemingly rational (i.e. technical and methodological), orders of evaluation. To this end the symbolic policy message conveyed about teacher practice and student achievement from the policy reports and legislative agendas presented earlier is that an effective and quality classroom teacher is represented and recognized by a performative order that is definitive and constituted in super-rational compliance mechanisms.

While education policy on teacher effectiveness and quality typifies a political economy of symbolic power, it also mediates action through the standardization of teachers' work. This standardization reinforces a strategic set of pre-reflective actions on the part of classroom teachers geared towards satisfying evaluative effects, for example, value-added measurements in the form of school-level productivity gains. The symbolic policy interest of the documents outlined in Section 6.2 manifests as a form of investment where the problem of student under-achievement is rationalized, open to intervention via the 'policy technologies of market efficiency, business-managerialism and performativity' (O'Neill 2015, p. 832).

The axioms are then expressed by a symbolic policy order which captures classroom teacher performance and encompasses several underlying premises.

1   A purely rational positivist ethos which labels teacher work as either effective or ineffective and focuses towards that which is measurable.

2   The co-aptation of teachers into quantitative evaluation mechanisms so that they view the work they do in this way (i.e. in numeric and measurable ways).
3   The steady decoupling of the autonomous theoretical and academic disciplinary base of education from the work that teachers do so that it no longer concerns itself with broader considerations centred on questions of becoming human (see Biesta 2011).

In this way the policy symbolism connected to "master narratives" about teacher performance contributes to an authentication of the discursive dictates that report on it.

6.4 Conclusion

Chapter 6 has argued about the strategic value of education to national competitiveness and how classroom teachers are positioned by major education policy as key players in this mix. Concerned with how major education policy de-contextualizes school and teacher effects, the chapter has sought to show the discursive representations of global education policy discourse which assumes classroom teachers and their teaching practices play the most significant role in enhancing student performance and by implication advancing a nation's economic competitiveness. While we don't doubt the important role that classroom teachers have in contributing to overall national well-being, we do take issue with how major education policy tends to discount significant influences, be this in regard to achievement and/or national prosperity.

An important element in the analysis conducted in Chapter 6 involves how major 'agents and agencies . . . determine what is thinkable and doable' (Robertson 2016, p. 344). The language used by major education policy makes claims about teacher expertise, restructuring how we think about teacher labour. This has consequences not only for how we think about teachers' work but how we view the discipline of education in general. The change in education policy emphasis is towards a form of symbolic control and governance over teachers, be it in the form of how they work and of how we're to think about their contribution to society and the economy. Susan Robertson perhaps says it best:

> There is now an intense focus on learning and the learner, and linking this in a causal way to teachers and a specific kind of pedagogy, as the means for developing competitive national economies. Learning as individual development thus displaces education as development. Learning as development takes its logic, development trajectory, and forward momentum not from modernization theory – which assumed a teleology of development, but from neo-liberalism's rawer attention to the individual and their necessary engagement with competition as a means for development. The engine that keeps this governing system moving in a very dynamic, forward-going

way is competitive comparison – as it is constantly placing each player in hierarchical relation to the other. It is not a question of striving to reach a state of quality, as much as striving to move ahead of who is in front.

(2016, p. 357)

With this change in education policy emphasis centred on teachers and the classroom work that they do is also a change in the type of student learning favoured. Chapter 7 deals with some of the issues connected to the type of learning given priority by major education policy.

References

Alridge, D. 2006. The limits of master narratives in history textbooks: An analysis of representations of Martin Luther King, Jr. *Teachers College Record*, 108(4), 662–686.

Australian Government. 2013. *National Plan for School Improvement*. Canberra, Australia: The Treasury. Retrieved from https://archive.budget.gov.au/2013-14/glossy/glossy_NPSI.pdf

Australian Government. 2016. *Quality Schools, Quality Outcomes*. Canberra, Australia. Retrieved from https://docs.education.gov.au/system/files/doc/other/quality_schools_acc.pdf

Bacchi, C. 2000. Policy as discourse: What does it mean? Where does it get us? *Discourse: Studies in the Cultural Politics of Education*, 21(1), 45–57.

Ball, S. J. 1993. What is policy? Texts, trajectories and toolboxes. *Discourse: Studies in the Cultural Politics of Education*, 13(2), 10–17.

Barber, M. and Mourshed, M. 2007. *How the World's Best-Performing School Systems Come Out on Top*. McKinsey & Company. Retrieved from https://www.mckinsey.com/~/media/McKinsey/Industries/Social%20Sector/Our%20Insights/How%20the%20worlds%20best%20performing%20school%20systems%20come%20out%20on%20top/How_the_world_s_best-performing_school_systems_come_out_on_top.ashx

Biesta, G. 2011. Disciplines and theory in the academic study of education: A comparative analysis of the Anglo-American and Continental construction of the field. *Pedagogy, Culture & Society*, 19(2), 175–192.

Bourdieu, P. 1990. *The Logic of Practice*. Cambridge, UK: Polity Press.

Bourdieu, P. 2014. *On the State: Lectures at the Collège de France*. Cambridge, UK: Polity.

Bøyum, S. 2014. Fairness in education – A normative analysis of OECD policy documents. *Journal of Education Policy*, 29(6), 856–870. https://doi.org/10.1080/02680939.2014.899396

Coffield, F. 2012. Why the McKinsey reports will not improve school systems. *Journal of Education Policy*, 27(1), 131–149. https://doi.org/10.1080/02680939.2011.623243

Connell, R. 2009. Good teachers on dangerous ground: Towards a new view of teacher quality and professionalism. *Critical Studies in Education*, 50(3), 213–229. https://doi.org/n10.1080/17508480902998421

De Lissovoy, N. 2017. Pedagogy of the anxious: Rethinking critical pedagogy in the context of neoliberal autonomy and responsibilization. *Journal of Education Policy*. https://doi.org/10.1080/02680939.2017.1352031

Department for Education. 2010. *The Importance of Teaching: The Schools White Paper*. Retrieved from http://www.official-documents.gov.uk/

Department of Education and Employment. 1997. *White Paper: Excellence in Schools*. Retrieved from http://www.educationengland.org.uk/documents/wp1997/excellence-in-schools.html.

Edelman, M. 1988. *Constructing the Political Spectacle*. Chicago, IL: University of Chicago Press.

Edwards, R., Nicoll, K., Solomon, N. and Usher, R. 2004. *Rhetoric and Educational Discourse*. New York: RoutledgeFalmer.

Fisher-Ari, T., Kavanagh, K. M. and Martin, A. 2017. Sisyphean neoliberal reforms: The intractable mythology of student growth and achievement master narratives within the testing and TFA era. *Journal of Education Policy*, 32(3), 255–280. https://doi.org/10.1080/02680939.2016.1247466

Foucault, M. 1977. *The Archaeology of Knowledge and the Discourse on Language* (Translated from the French by A. M. Sheridan Smith). New York: Pantheon Books.

Gottweis, H. 2006. Rhetoric in policy-making: Between logos, ethos and pathos. In F. Fischer, G. J. Miller and M. S. Sidney (Eds.), *Handbook of Public Policy Analysis: Theory, Politics, and Methods* (pp. 237–250). Boca Raton, FL: CRC Press.

Hattie, J. 2003. *Teachers Make a Difference: What Is the Research Evidence?* Presentation for the Australian Council for Educational Research. Melbourne, Australia, October.

Holloway, J. and Brass, J. 2018. Making accountable teachers: The terrors and pleasures of performativity. *Journal of Education Policy*, 33(3), 361–382. https://doi.org/10.1080/02680939.2017.1372636

Hursh, D. W. 2013. Raising the stakes: High-stakes testing and the attack on public education in New York. *Journal of Education Policy*, 28(5), 574–588. https://doi.org/10.1080/02680939.2012.758829

Hursh, D. W. 2017. Review of *Charter School Report Card*. *Journal of Education Policy*, 32(4), 520–521. https://doi.org/10.1080/02680939.2017.1280271

Hursh, D. W. 2015. *The End of Public Schools: The Corporate Reform Agenda to Privatize Education*. New York and London, UK: Routledge.

Lavery, L. E. 2016. What parents still do not know about No Child Left Behind and why it matters. *Journal of Education Policy*, 31(3), 343–361. https://doi.org/10.1080/02680939.2015.1094576

Leach, J. 2000. Rhetorical analysis. In M. W. Bauer and G. Gaskell (Eds.), *Qualitative Researching with Text, Image and Sound* (Vol. 1 – Book 1 – Section, pp. 207–226). Thousand Oaks, CA: Sage.

Lefebvre, E. E. and Thomas, M. A. M. 2017. "Shit shows" or "like-minded schools": Charter schools and the neoliberal logic of Teach For America. *Journal of Education Policy*, 32(3), 357–371. https://doi.org/10.1080/02680939.2017.1280184

Lewis, S. and Hogan, A. 2019. Reform first and ask questions later? The implications of (fast) schooling policy and "silver bullet" solutions. *Critical Studies in Education*, 60(1), 1–18, 1–18. https://doi.org/10.1080/17508487.2016.1219961

Liasidou, A. 2011. Special education policymaking: A discursive analytic approach. *Educational Policy*, 25(6), 887–907. https://doi.org/10.1177/0895904810386587

Lyotard, J. F. 1984. *The Postmodern Condition: A Report on Knowledge*. Minneapolis, MN: University of Minnesota Press.

McAdams, D. P. 1993. *The Stories We Live By: Personal Myths and the Making of the Self*. New York: William Morrow.

O'Neill, A.-M. 2015. The New Zealand experiment: Assessment-driven curriculum – managing standards, competition and performance to strengthen governmentality. *Journal of Education Policy*, 30(6), 831–854. https://doi.org/10.1080/02680939.2015.1033766

Obama, B. 2012. *Remarks by the President in State of the Union Address*. Retrieved 1 August 2018 from https://obamawhitehouse.archives.gov/the-press-office/2012/01/24/remarks-president-state-union-address

Organization for Economic Co-Operation and Development. 2005. *Teachers Matter: Attracting, Developing and Retaining Effective Teachers.* Paris: OECD Publishing.

Peck, J. and Theodore, N. 2015. *Fast Policy: Experimental Statecraft at the Thresholds of Neoliberalism.* Minnesota, MN: University of Minnesota Press.

Ravitch, D. 2012. No student left untested. *New York Review Blog*, February 21. Retrieved from http://www.nybooks.com/blogs/nyrblog/2012/feb/21/no-student-left-untested/

Robertson, S. 2016. The global governance of teachers' work. In K. Mundy, A. Green, B. Lingard and A. Verger (Eds.), *The Handbook of Global Education Policy* (pp. 343–360). Chichester, West Sussex, UK: Wiley & Sons.

Schleicher, A. 2007. Foreword. In M. Barber and M. Mourshed (Eds.), *How the World's Best-Performing School Systems Come Out on Top.* London, UK: McKinsey & Company.

Sellar, S. and Lingard, B. 2013. The OECD and global governance in education. *Journal of Education Policy*, 28(5), 710–725. https://doi.org/10.1080/02680939.2013.779791

Starr, K. 2011. Principals and the politics of resistance to change. *Educational Management Administration & Leadership*, 39(6), 646–660.

U.S. Department of Education. 1983. *A Nation at Risk. The Imperative for Educational Reform.* Retrieved from https://www.edreform.com/wp-content/uploads/2013/02/A_Nation_At_Risk_1983.pdf

U.S. Department of Education. 2002. *No Child Left Behind.* Government of the U.S. Retrieved from https://www2.ed.gov/admins/lead/account/nclbreference/reference.pdf

U.S. Department of Education. 2009. *Race to the Top Program: Executive Summary.* Retrieved from https://www2.ed.gov/programs/racetothetop/executive-summary.pdf

Winton, S. 2013. Rhetorical analysis in critical policy research. *International Journal of Qualitative Studies in Education*, 26(2), 158–177. https://doi.org/10.1080/09518398.2012.666288

Winton, S. 2018. Challenging fundraising, challenging inequity: Contextual constraints on advocacy groups' policy influence. *Critical Studies in Education*, 59(1), 54–73. https://doi.org/10.1080/17508487.2016.1176062

7

INSTRUCTION, SKILLS OR PEDAGOGY – INVENTING THE NEW TEACHER

Introduction

Chapter 7 focuses on the relationship between standardized testing and "instruction", the latter term synonymous with TE and TQ. The chapter outlines how the term "instruction" as opposed to pedagogy is reductive in nature and is evident of the take-up of U.S. education policy language and particular "positivist" forms of research, particularly in regards to curriculum and how students learn. In addition, the chapter will discuss how the teacher's classroom role is configured differently now with an emphasis on developing students' skills and competencies so as to better align with the uncertainties connected to the prevailing job market. The discussion incorporates the contemporary importance of the teacher as learning facilitator with an increased responsibility for assisting students to self-regulate their learning in a world marked by displacement and deconstructed modes of working and learning.

7.1 Standards and outcomes

Testing is at the centre of most of the education reforms post the 1950s in the Anglo capitalist belt of nations. Testing programs, whether at local, national or international scales, are generally justified by claims about the utility of the data generated. The inherent promise in testing and measuring the outcomes of schooling is that both will help to improve efficiency and quality (for example at the system, school, teacher and student performance level) and that more and better data will give insights into the opaque world of the classroom. Regimes of testing aim to open the classroom to external scrutiny in order to putatively solve the problem of the unaccountable teacher through making them accountable to and for student performance.

The emphasis is on compliance with competencies rather than with thinking critically about practice; focusing on teaching rather than learning; doing rather than thinking; skills rather than values. This regime is maintained (and justified) by the regular production of local, national and international league tables that exert pressure to raise the stakes and raise the game at every opportunity.

(Maguire 2010, p. 61)

The issues that Maguire attests to in the previous quote resonate, often amongst the media, bureaucrats, parents, policy makers and politicians, but also amongst educational professionals themselves (see Lingard, Thompson and Sellar 2015).

The evaluative judgement involved in testing serves a plethora of purposes ranging from the basic about yearly student graduation progress to the more complex efficiency/effectiveness determinations of individual schools, teachers, districts, states and nations (see Clarke, Madaus, Horn and Ramos 2000). It also serves a governance aim through the 'datafication of schooling' (Lingard et al. 2015, p. 2). Clarke et al. (2000) note that the term "test" held sway in the education field during the 20th century, whereas "assessment" became the 'favoured term of the 1990s, either when used alone or when modified by one of the adjectives "authentic", "alternative" or "standards-based"' (p. 160). The rise of standardized testing and assessment in schooling coincides with the narrow "human capital" conception of education 'leading to what we might see as an "economisation" of education policy' (Lingard et al. 2015, p. 2).

The technological enterprise of testing and assessment has evolved over time, moving towards 'increased efficiency that has characterized standardized achievement testing for much of this century' (Clarke et al. 2000, p. 161). This has encompassed a firm belief in two things, a detached objectivity and the technological prowess of statistical reasoning (see Kanigel 1997). A consequence of an increasing use of testing, particularly as school enrolment figures grew over the 20th century across much of the developed world, was a shifting emphasis of blame where poor achievement levels were apportioned to not only the individual student but also the individual teacher. Tests and assessments of various kinds served a selection function most notably for the military and college admission (see Ocean and Skourdoumbis 2016). In more recent times standardized testing has enjoyed widespread appeal, particularly in an era marked by what Verger, Lubienski and Steiner-Khamsi label the global education industry (GEI), which has spawned the 'development of new market niches that are often outside of traditional state control, such as test preparation, edu-marketing, the provision of curriculum packages or school improvement services' (2016, p. 4). Clarke et al. (2000) nominate four reasons for the spread of standardized testing in the U.S. Their explanation begins by highlighting the general dissatisfaction felt in American society at the time about the state of the education system post the space-race 'Sputnik uproar of the 1950s' (Clarke et al. 2000, p. 164). This provided a context for a multitude of education reforms, including the basic skills movements of the 1970s and the release of seminal education reports and legislation in subsequent decades, including *A Nation at Risk* (U.S. Department of Education 1983) and *'Goals 2000: Educate America Act'* (U.S. Government 1994). The attention and influence that the Coleman Report (1966) provided in the latter half of the 1960s with its focus on "inputs and outputs", the effects of which are evident today in helping spawn the education effectiveness research literature more generally around the world, and the subsequent bureaucratization of schooling led to an argument for and use of standardized testing. Other nations (England, New Zealand, Australia and Canada) have followed the American lead on school and education reform regarding education performance evaluations. Standardized testing in Australia, for example, is encapsulated within 'an ensemble of policies that combine to produce the phenomenon of national testing in its broadest understanding' (Lingard et al. 2015, p. 4). This is not only about performance verification. The broader and well-established links of a 'data-infrastructure' (Lingard et al. 2015, p. 6) connects nations such as Australia to an international assessment regime of performance verification, which also works to shape and justify further education reforms, especially as they relate to standardization of teaching practice/s, curriculum and enhancing student achievement. This specific 'fear of falling behind regime . . . a new dominant configuration of discourses, political technologies, and practices' (Krejsler 2018, p. 393) affirms the risks involved in declining student achievement levels. A systematized standardized approach to the testing and ranking of schools ties 'the standards for student success and teacher effectiveness ever more closely to perceived national success and competitiveness' (Krejsler 2018. p. 396).

An important element of standardized testing with its emphasis on outcomes is its capacity for standardizing curricula. This in turn influences interactions between learners and teachers. What is more, the classroom enaction of curriculum has been found to exert an influence on teaching practices (Arbaugh, Lannin, Jones and Park-Rogers 2006; Tarr et al. 2008). A standards-based conception then of curriculum designates discipline-specific "content standards" 'defining what it is that students should be expected to know or do' (Schmidt, Wang and McKnight 2005, p. 526). A standardized curriculum has a prefigured and established answer to the two questions Michael Apple (2004) poses in *Ideology and curriculum*: what knowledge is of most worth? And whose knowledge is of most worth? Central to these two questions is a vying for dominance and the exertion of power and control. Schools and the education system are a primary source 'for preserving and producing a society's cultural tradition – i.e. what the society deems worthwhile knowledge – which means education is always a politically contested terrain' (Wheeler-Bell 2017, p. 563). However, the purpose of education and schooling more generally in an era of testing is more often than not about compliance and verification aligned against standardized outcomes.

In this way education has the capacity to discipline 'individuals both as objects and as instruments' (Foucault 1977, p. 170). Indeed, the work on "governmentality" by Michel Foucault illustrates how the field of education and the "disciplining tool" of standardized testing manages from afar, constructing 'governable persons' (Graham and New 2004, p. 295) via 'hierarchical observation, normalizing judgement and their combination in a procedure that is specific to it, the examination' (Foucault 1977, p. 170). Governmentality as Foucault has conceptualized it is about modes and actions of government in order to manage the behaviours of human beings. Policy captures the economy of a field having already considered its 'existence thinkable and calculable, and amenable to deliberated and planful initiatives' (Miller and Rose 1990, p. 3). Some of the specific "tools of governance" – measurement and statistical techniques – in education double as 'technologies of intervention: examination and assessment, training, propagation of forms' (Graham and Neu 2004, p. 299). The examination in the work of Foucault has especial significance in the management of people because only it combines the modalities and procedures of 'disciplinary power' (Foucault 1977, p. 170) (i.e. hierarchical observation and normalizing judgement).

> The examination combines the techniques of an observing hierarchy and those of a normalizing judgement. It is a normalizing gaze, a surveillance that makes it possible to qualify, to classify, and to punish. It establishes over individuals a visibility through which one differentiates them and judges them. That is why, in all the mechanisms of discipline, the examination is highly ritualized. In it are combined the ceremony of power and the form of the experiment, the deployment of force and the establishment of truth. At the heart of the procedure of discipline, it manifests the subjection of those who are perceived as objects and the objectification of those who are subjected.
> *(Foucault 1977, pp. 184–185)*

There are two reasons as to why Foucault attributes specific importance to examinations. Firstly, examinations impose a constant 'disciplinary gaze' (Foucault 1977, p. 174), their supervisory functions permanently 'enmeshing the examinees in particular relations of power' (Graham and Neu 2004, p. 300). Secondly, examinations provide 'documentary traces' (Graham and Neu 2004, p. 300), making 'each individual a "case" . . . which at one and the same time constitutes an object for a branch of knowledge and a hold for a branch of power' (Foucault 1977, p. 191). The examination is then a tool that individualizes and objectifies, rendering people governable. An effect of standardized testing is to govern not only how knowledge (curriculum) is experienced by students but also what form of knowledge is considered of most value and how that knowledge should be gained and/or taught.

7.2 Instruction versus pedagogy

A contemporary tension in school education is the attenuated approach taken to curriculum theorizing and pedagogy which over time 'has been reduced to questions about instructional content and classroom delivery' (Hamilton 1999, p. 136). The short-term pre-occupation with what students should know and be able to do and how best to facilitate these two elements of modern schooling has superseded issues of character, or, simply put, "what students should become". The pedagogical task 'conceived as a concern for the whole person of the student' (Biesta and Miedema 2002, p. 173) has narrowed to a concern about the instruction and delivery of content. David Hamilton suggests that the 'instructional turn' in schooling began with a divergence from the 'longstanding literature about upbringing' traversing a series of changes over time before settling on 'the notion of method (the delivery of instruction)' (1999, p. 138). This shift in emphasis in learning is also about a re-positioning of the education system 'towards a far greater external (governmental) control over the curriculum and a far greater emphasis on the measurable output and accountability, often related to tight systems of inspection' (Biesta and Miedema 2002, p. 174). According to Gert Biesta, 'under the current educational climate there is far too little attention given to the pedagogical dimensions of schooling' (2002, p. 174), some of these being related to the teaching of broader issues such as values, citizenship and so on.

The current dominant instrumentalist view of schooling which TER helps facilitate privileges instruction over broader forms of pedagogy by prioritizing the teaching of standardized knowledge and skills.

> In this context, the tendency to overload the curriculum, over-specify and micro-manage accountabilities can actually work against curriculum being enacted by teachers in ways that create educational value for their students.
>
> *(Yates 2017, p. 95)*

The polarization evident between instruction and pedagogy is seen in the concerns often expressed about what denotes knowledge and/or skills or capabilities. Lyn Yates makes the point 'that if curriculum is specified in terms of "knowledge", it sounds like memorising facts . . . but if it talks only skills and capabilities it does not contain enough substance about what students will actually be doing and developing during their twelve years in school' (2017, p. 94). The educational value of an enacted curriculum that Yates refers to is quite possibly accomplished by teachers attending to the purposes of an education, engaging critically with content and being mindful of the relationships that they want to establish as a result of their teaching. Whilst students require basic competences that only formal quality schooling can bestow, educational purpose beyond a narrow functionalism serves people in a multi-dimensional way, i.e. 'by equipping them with knowledge, skills and dispositions . . . but also . . . with the ways in which, through education, we become part of existing social, cultural and political practices and traditions' (Biesta 2017, p. 442).

An interest in the "scientific" facets of education meaning certitude, exactness and measurement aligns historically in the U.S. with the work of Edward

Thorndike (a psychologist) and the influence of the discipline of behavioural psychology. Gibboney (2006), for example, claims that the 'mechanistic view of learning espoused by Thorndike dominated the last half of the 20th Century in so-called school reform' (p. 170). Educational thinking in Europe and the U.S. up until the latter 19th and early 20th centuries concentrated on educational purposes and the implementation of teaching practices to help in enacting the aims and objectives of education. Specialization and an encroaching professionalization helped define the study of education as a discipline in the latter stages of the 19th and early 20th centuries, particularly in the U.S. Active at the time in the U.S. were two competing educational approaches: the Deweyan progressivist approach where education is about the nurture and incorporation of knowledge to help develop and realize "democracy" and "democratic community", and the instrumentalist/behaviourist approach favoured by Thorndike, deterministic in nature espousing "factual material" over and above discussion and exposition. Learning in this categorization of education is about stimuli/response framed by the differences bestowed by nature that characterize individual human beings.

Thorndike's foray into the field of education and educational research centred on work carried out on animal learning.

> Specifically, it should be noted that Thorndike believed that what was known about how animals learned was also applicable to how children learned. He did not offer experimental evidence for this foray into anthropomorphism. He applied this belief in his discovery of universal laws of learning applicable to all animal life in his subsequent works throughout his career. In spite of this unproved unscientific leap of faith, Thorndike's research quickly placed him at the center of major educational questions and controversies and gave him a reputation that has endured.
> (Johanningmeier and Richardson 2008, p. 253)

Thorndike's influence over the study of education and "pedagogy" soon displaced any Deweyan conception about how learning and schools not only could but should help engender open and holistic thinking. Reasons for this are as much about old-fashioned gender prejudices as they are about the reception a field such as education had in American academe at the time. Education being a highly feminized field lagged in prestige in comparison to the male-dominated fields of law, medicine and engineering, delaying its reception in many of the more esteemed American universities of the era such as Harvard and Columbia. A way forward in terms of academic acceptance was for a 'professional science of education' (Lagemann 2000, p. 64), which argued for the improvement of teaching through a professional knowledge base. The behaviourist Thorndike favoured identifying "laws of learning" clarifying the limits of and connections inherent in an education. This view aligned with dominant thinking at the time about the need for a professional scientific knowledge base of teaching and education. The three "educational" laws formulated by Thorndike include:

the law of readiness, the law of exercise and the law of effect. Readiness implies a preparedness to action on the part of the learner to engage in the learning of or about something. The law of exercise implies drill or practice – to learn something is to engage in it over time. The law of effect centres on the satisfaction gained by the learner in what has been learnt. Consolidation in learning is established via the satisfaction gained. The study of education and pedagogy, according to Thorndike, necessitated 'controlled experimentation and precise quantitative measurements' (Lagemann 2000, p. 59). Lagemann claims that Thorndike 'favored precise, numerical measurements of anything and everything relevant to education – mental capacities, changes in behaviour, and even the aims of education' (2000, p. 59). The pedagogy favoured by Thorndike, espoused in his *The Principles of Teaching,* singled "the teacher" out for particular attention. Teaching occupied a subordinate position in the educational hierarchy in Thorndike's view. While Thorndike viewed teaching as an occupation that required some basic level of technical expertise, he believed that 'education in general, and teaching in particular, could be improved by scientific knowledge, generated outside of schools and totally apart from the idiosyncratic circumstances of particular teachers, children and classrooms' (Lagemann 2000, p. 62). In this regard the teacher merely delivers content via a series of instructions where the 'education researcher was the searcher for truth' and the teacher practitioner 'merely the person concerned with application' (Lagemann 2000, p. 61). The purpose of schooling, including 'the curriculum was interpreted as the instruction and efficient organization of teaching resources' (Young 2013, p. 104). Teaching, in Thorndike's view, was about a 'process of instruction that is *delivered* to the learner' (Johanningmeier and Richardson 2008, p. 250, emphasis in original). Edward Thorndike and the influence of the field of education psychology more generally in the U.S. are both credited with shaping early thinking on education research and how people learn, including viewing teaching practice as a form of instruction that is performed on people (see Johanningmeier and Richardson 2008).

7.3 Skills and competencies

Skills and competencies, as with standards and outcomes, are about what students should learn at school and leave school with. The basic question of curriculum (what should be taught in school?) is also an epistemological question that is centred on three things: "knowing that", "knowing how" and "knowing what is right". Curriculum enaction in school is about the interdependence of two educational purposes: one involves the transmission of past knowledge, while the other is about using past knowledge in the creation of new knowledge (see Young 2013). The former emphasizes 'knowing things' while the latter is about 'being able to do things' (Yates and Collins 2010, p. 89). The former is also about valuing curriculum for the knowledge that is intrinsic to it; the latter has a utilitarian bias where what counts as knowledge is what is readily useful to an individual in the opportunities that it may bring them, which are usually employment related.

The current turn in curriculum is towards skills and competencies. It is a turn characterized by the 'global network of corporate and governmental influences that promotes competences suited to fit the future knowledge economy' (Hilt, Riese and Søreide 2019, p. 1). Hilt et al. have identified these skills and competencies as critical thinking, decision-making, problem-solving, communication, co-operation, responsibility and creativity (2018, p. 1). These terms over recent decades have populated the major education policies of many nation states and of international agencies such as the OECD, World Bank and International Monetary Fund, amongst a host of others. The terms carry an employability bent, skewing the curriculum away from the "theoretical knowledge" (Wheelahan 2015) that Michael Young (2013) suggests has characterized the European tradition, which was also infused by elements of the Confucian and Islamic traditions, the importance of which is evident in exposing all students and particularly the disadvantaged to the knowledge which is 'clearly differentiated from pupils' everyday experience' (p. 102). This is a view which holds that the curriculum is 'a source of the "sacred" which, since the 19th century, has been progressively secularized to form the familiar disciplines of the university and the subjects of the school with their increasingly global reach' (Young 2013, p. 102). While the skills/competencies turn is for many driven by the need for 'increased competitiveness in a global marketplace' it is also propelled (politically speaking) by an 'enhancing social justice' (Whitty 2010, p. 28) argument. This particular viewpoint stems from concerns about the large and quite disparate achievement gaps between low socio-economic and high socio-economic status students (Valant and Newark 2016; De Bortoli and Thomson 2010).

Curricular change in contemporary times carries with it all of the standpoint trademarks generally associated with economic globalization: rapid interconnected and global economic exchange girded by competitive participation 'in a much bigger world than in the past' (Meyer 2007, p. 264). This is a world of supposed individual empowerment where the 'individual student is not to be prepared for a fixed and limited place in a stably structured society' (Meyer 2007, p. 259). National and global progress now interlinked as never before depends upon the empowered, 'unconstrained capacities for growth and development' (Meyer 2007, p. 259) of the individual. The "static" canonical knowledge of the past is superseded by the development of a curriculum fostering 'generalized competence, general empowerment and all-purpose skills' (Meyer 2007, p. 265). This is about an outcome focused and "learner centred" education. While notions of "learning outcomes" and "competencies/competences" are used in different ways depending on nations and context (see Allais 2012), a basic commonality exists in how they are framed in terms of national qualifications frameworks and outcomes-based curriculum reforms. That framing is usually expressed around 'the importance of education to individuals and economies' and how outcomes-based frameworks empower 'learners to make good choices'

(Allais 2012, p. 258) around developing their skills to maximize their chances in gaining future employment.

This exercise in "normalization" (Foucault 1977) – a term used by Foucault to denote an unquestioned acceptance and way of acting – is about constructing the employable and 'competent learner worker' (Williams 2005, p. 33). The competent learner worker is 'expected to take responsibility for and manage their own learning and development over the course of their working lives' (Williams 2005, p. 34). This entails a change in human subjectivity. A substantive element of that change involves the development through education and/or training of an '"employable", but not necessarily "employed"' (Moore p. 28) self. Teachers have a role here in that education programs and curricula are needed which prepare students adequately. An important element of this preparation is about student self-management, particularly of a sort that Zygmunt Bauman suggests necessitates 'the skill of quick learning' (Bauman 2012, p. 18), meaning the ability to change direction in outlook as needed. This is especially important in a world defined now by difference and transience and the 'superfluity [of liquid] modernity' (Bauman 2012, p. 21) characterized by the flexible and temporary worker at the mercy of precarious global economic and vocational trends (see Petrella 1997). While no different for teachers, the increased expectation around what constitutes 'skillful teaching' (Gottlieb 2015, p. 84) pivots on how it should be enacted, measured and verified.

Furthermore the reach of corporate private sector influence in provision of core education services has re-defined notions of educational "good" (see Hogan, Sellar and Lingard 2016). The use of products and services developed and marketed by the private sector is now often linked in education to 'test development and preparation, data analysis and management, and remedial services' (Hogan 2016, p. 94). Edu-businesses (contractors, service providers, consultants and large corporations) not only contribute to education policy and research, but they are also active in classroom work, be it through espousing particular teaching approaches or the promotion of the development of generic skills and competencies. The large corporation Pearson, for example, in its vision statement, states that it aims to have a:

> direct relationship with millions of lifelong learners and to link education to the way people aspire to live and work every day. To do that, we'll collaborate with a wide group of partners to help shape the future of learning.
> *(Pearson 2019)*

Hogan, Sellar and Lingard have shown how Pearson, through its Efficacy Framework, contributes to the 'medicalization of educational research, drawing on the example of the pharmaceuticals industry. This is research for policy, located within the rise of a narrowly pragmatic ("what works") technoscientific reworking of knowledge production' (Hogan et al. 2016, p. 120). The Efficacy

Framework provides direct appraisal of targeted learner outcomes with the design and implementation of a Pearson educational product, be it some curricular learning module or assessment/verification exercise. While corporations such as Pearson have legitimate business interests in education, their influence now extends more broadly and deeply. Pearson is an active "policy player" in the field of education immersed in 'policy agenda setting, policy construction, implementation, and evaluation' (Hogan et al. 2016, p. 121), often sidelining the voice of teachers. Moreover, 'Pearson's involvement in testing encourages standardization of schooling with potential reductive effects on curriculum provision and the broader, democratically framed purposes of schooling in relation to opportunity and citizenship' (Hogan et al. 2016, p. 121).

7.4 The pedagogical encounter

An era of increasing complexity, uncertainty and plurality requires a learning environment that not only supports but helps develop student learning. Pádraig Hogan (2013) suggests that learning environments which develop student 'capabilities more than competencies' are needed and to this end he proposes the 'idea of venturesome environments of learning' (p. 238) as a way through a constricting education policy scene that seemingly favours formalist skills, effectiveness and rudimentary practical knowledge. There are several interconnected aspects involved in venturesome learning environments with the student situated at the centre. Safety and a preparedness on the part of the learner to 'venture his or her considered thoughts' (Hogan 2013, p. 238) on matters is the first aspect. The open possibility of free inquiry is to be encouraged, offering 'new perspectives on the matter under exploration, and new possibilities for learning' (Hogan 2013, p. 239). Secondly, venturesome learning environments respect what Hogan claims is the 'plurality of the human condition' (p. 239), embracing an educational outlook that invites the student learner into a learning "conversation". Hogan is here drawing upon Michael Oakeshott and a conceptualization of education that favours 'conversation in cultivating the intellectual and moral openness' over the embedded and 'acquired beliefs and convictions of individuals' (Williams and Williams 2017, p. 253). Thirdly, a venturesome learning environment contains an ethical component with links to the imaginative possibilities of 'fruitful experiences of learning' (Hogan 2013, p. 239). This means committing to the learning experience in order to experience 'progressively higher levels of accomplishment' (Hogan 2013, p. 239).

While this connotes a Deweyan progressivist vision of the educational experience, it nonetheless offers contemporary pedagogues a side of the pedagogical relationship that is beyond the de-personalized conditioning on offer in a sizeable portion of modern curricula. An instrumentalist approach to learning is unwelcome because the pedagogical relation, which Hogan splits into four domains, preferences an enriching form of educational engagement. The four domains of the pedagogical relation that Hogan has identified include:

(1) the teacher's relations with the subject or material being taught;
(2) the teacher's relations with his or her students;
(3) the teacher's relations with colleagues, parents, educational authorities, and a wider range of others; and
(4) the teacher's relation to him- or herself, within which the character and significance of the other three domains are decided.

(2013, p. 240)

Each of the domains listed are a platform to a reciprocal form of pedagogical exchange valuing our *'ways of being human*, and of relating to ideas and people' (Hogan 2013, p. 246, emphasis in original). Hogan's work mirrors that of Amartya Sen and Martha Nussbaum and their work on the capability approach. Nussbaum's work on capabilities focuses on human development via 'progressive cultivation of human capacities to think critically, to attend with discernment, to anticipate with circumspection, to act with moral insight and energy, and so on' (Hogan 2013, p. 237). Nussbaum on that account proposes a list of capabilities which she identifies, including (1) life, (2) bodily health, (3) bodily integrity, (4) sense, imagination and thought, (5) emotions, (6) practical reason, (7) affiliation, (8) other species, (9) play and (10) control over one's political and material environment (see Nussbaum 2006). Amartya Sen conversely refrains from naming particular capabilities per se, stressing instead an evaluative framework which acts 'as a critique of resources-and utility-based assessment of human well-being and disadvantage' (Gale and Molla 2015, p. 812). Sen eschews the purist's traditional utilitarian approach to resource evaluation (for example, Gross Domestic Product [GDP] or Gross National Product [GNP]). He pursues what Gale and Molla term 'a freedom-based approach to well-being, development and justice' (2015, p. 812), meaning that 'individual advantage is judged in the capability approach by a person's capability to do the things he or she has reason to value' (Sen 2009, p. 231).

The educational effectiveness and quality research literature persist with a fixed depiction of the 'perceived failings' (O'Donnell 2013, p. 265) of educational systems, focusing primarily on skills-based approaches to learning that promote and seek to measure competence. Understood in this way, effectiveness and quality are about 'imposing prescriptive modes of subjectification and socialization in pedagogy' (O'Donnell 2013, p. 265). Missing is an 'educative milieu' (O'Donnell 2013, p. 276) which gives precedence to a pedagogical relation emphasizing an outward-looking focus. The educative milieu heightens classroom teacher involvement through a respect for their 'singular judgment and pedagogical creativity in responding to opportunities and obstacles' (O'Donnell 2013, p. 267). This means being attuned to the 'simple act of noticing and seeing a sense of possibility' (O'Donnell 2013, p. 267). An educative milieu eschews 'speedy and tangible evidence of progress' (Dewey 1933, p. 65) via reductive performance objectives for system verification purposes. Avoiding a "mechanical" study of subjects, it respects the emancipatory tendencies of intellectual power, privileging teacher expertise to help guide and foster personal and individual student growth and well-being. The educative milieu is about the educative potential of a progressive pedagogy engaging students, it is to be hoped, through the 'shift in horizons' that comes with a 'changing of perspective, the provocation to think, and the opening of the mind' (O'Donnell 2013, p. 276). This, according to O'Donnell, is the authoritative barometer of effectiveness and quality founded and also 'bound to practice, creative responsiveness, and the judgment of the educator in concrete, singular pedagogical situations, rather than construed in terms of generic models of "best practice"' (O'Donnell 2013, p. 265).

7.5 Hardwiring perfection – role intensification

The work of classroom teachers in an era of high-stakes accountability has 'increased, intensified and expanded' where large-scale education policy reform demands of teachers that they 'relate to their students differently, enact pedagogies that are often at odds with their vision of best practice, and experience high levels of stress' (Valli and Buese 2007, p. 520). A policy context of heightened accountability has re-shaped the teacher role in and outside of the classroom. Teacher role is defined as a 'multidimensional, dynamic construct' (Valli and Buese 2007, p. 522) encompassing all of the tasks carried out by classroom teachers on a daily basis. While recent studies show that teachers are now working harder (Ballet, Kelchtermans and Loughran 2006; O'Day 2002) through increased work intensification and expansion, the particular conditions responsible for this development connect to dominant 'external plans and requirements such as prespecified lists of competencies and objectives, pretests and post tests for determining student skill level, and an increase of record keeping and evaluation' (Valli and Buese 2007, p. 524). Some of these elements were mentioned by our teacher participants in Chapters 2 and 5.

The demands of re-structured teacher work have elevated the practical in classroom practice, emphasizing the basics of literacy and numeracy yet also tying the teacher into a compliance regime where they are increasingly considered responsible and 'answerable for making demonstrable improvements in their students' learning' (Maguire 2010, p. 62). Role intensification is about reforming the classroom teacher so that they perform the simultaneous tasks of expert, professional classroom practitioner adept at managing high-quality calculable student learning at less cost in set time periods (see McWilliam 2008). This "ideal" 'reconstructed teacher is produced out of sets of recipes for action, systemic rules, technologies of performance and routine classroom actions that are designed (by others) to "deliver" quality and "assure" high standards' (Maguire 2010, p. 62).

An important, though understated, contributor to this state of affairs is policy-maker faith in teachers and an education system constantly creating and maintaining a vision of progress. Stillwaggon suggests two reasons why we preference progress in our educational thinking. Firstly, 'we tend to assume that education draws each student from a less to a more human state simply by virtue of each young person's greater engagement with the technologies of human traditions that make up its distinctively human discursive environment' (2017, p. 31). Secondly, there is the influence of institutional commitment to 'the narrative of progress' where children are schooled on a yearly basis, passing 'from one grade to the next toward a fantasy of mastery' (Stillwaggon 2017, p. 31) and some glorified evolving future of upward mobility. Recent work by Barker (2008) has highlighted how many of the education reforms of recent decades (choice and competition between schools, rigorous accountability, standardized testing, an emphasis on leadership and human resource management and reliance on evidence-based policy) have only resulted in 'a variety of tensions, issues and concerns that compromise progress' (p. 671). The effects of social disadvantage in education, for example, continue to prove 'stubbornly resistant to central and local action' (Barker 2008, p. 673) despite the transformations enacted by education policy reform.

> Choice and markets undermine the drive for equal opportunities and social inclusion. Tests and performance tables encourage schools to teach to the test and frustrate attempts to personalise learning and meet the diverse needs of our students. Productivity is celebrated, quality ignored.
>
> *(Barker 2008, p. 679)*

Progress is difficult to attain if founded on an effectiveness framework of disconnected rationalist concepts and assumptions that are charged with explaining complex educational processes with deep-seated social, cultural, political and economic roots (see Fielding 2000).

7.6 Conclusion

Teachers currently operate 'within a context of conditional trust' (Avis 2003, p. 329). A series of education policy reforms ranging from decentralization to marketization and their concomitant effect/s via efficiency and effectiveness have brought to the surface a reductive re-conceptualization of core teacher work. Standardized "teacher proof" (Maguire 2010) curricular and assessment has impeded if not dislodged teacher professional judgement, while teachers' practices – predominantly their teaching – is more closely directed and monitored. This 'on-going positioning process' involves a 'preprogrammed role for the teacher' (Luttenberg, Imants and van Veen 2013, p. 293) such that the instructional "skilling" of students and high-stakes tests proxy for learning. This represents a re-constructed school-based context that has professional connotations for classroom teachers.

One professional connotation ties a classroom teacher's pedagogic expertise and disciplinary knowledge to performance and development cycles where a teacher's contribution to student learning is under constant watch. Avis suggests that this form of systemic intervention will mean that classroom teachers are

> trusted to exercise some autonomy, innovation, and creativity, all of which will be informed by knowledge of pedagogic practice and their awareness of the findings of evidence-based research which will provide models of best practice to improve student learning. However, the trust won at this level will have been achieved through performance management and be subject to on-going review.
>
> *(2003, p. 329)*

The invented new classroom teacher is then simply the enabler of performance management objectives, the latter setting 'the terrain on which the teacher is to act' (Avis 2003, p. 329).

References

Allais, S. 2012. "Economics imperialism", education policy and educational theory. *Journal of Education Policy*, 27(2), 253–274. https://doi.org/10.1080/02680939.2011.602428

Apple, M. 2004. *Ideology and Curriculum*. London and New York: Routledge.

Arbaugh, F., Lannin, J., Jones, D. L. and Park-Rogers, M. 2006. Examining instructional practices of Core-Plus lessons: Implications for professional development. *Journal of Mathematics Teacher Education*, 9, 517–550.

Avis, J. 2003. Re-thinking trust in a performative culture: The case of education. *Journal of Education Policy*, 18(3), 315–332. https://doi.org/10.1080/02680930305577

Ballet, K., Kelchtermans, G. and Loughran, J. 2006. Beyond intensification towards a scholarship of practice: Analysing changes in teachers' work lives. *Teachers and Teaching: Theory and Practice*, 12(2), 209–229.

Barker, B. 2008. School reform policy in England since 1988: Relentless pursuit of the unattainable. *Journal of Education Policy*, 23(6), 669–683. https://doi.org/10.1080/02680930802212887

Bauman, Z. 2012. *On Education: Conversations with Riccardo Mazzeo*. Cambridge, UK: Polity Press.

Biesta, G. J. J. 2017. The future of teacher education: Evidence, competence or wisdom? In M. A. Peters, B. Cowie and I. Menter (Eds.), *A Companion to Research in Teacher Education* (pp. 435–453). Singapore: Springer.

Biesta, G. J. J. and Miedema, S. 2002. Instruction or pedagogy? The need for a transformative conception of education. *Teaching and Teacher Education*, 18, 173–181.

Clarke, M. M., Madaus, G. F., Horn, C. L. and Ramos, M. A. 2000. Retrospective on educational testing and assessment in the 20th century. *Journal of Curriculum Studies*, 32(2), 159–181. https://doi.org/10.1080/002202700182691

Coleman, J. S., Campbell, E. Q., Hobson, C. J., McPartland, J., Mood, A. M., Weinfeld, F. D. and York, R. L. 1966. *Equality of Educational Opportunity*. Washington, DC: US Government Printing Office.

De Bortoli, L. and Thomson, S. 2010. *Contextual Factors that Influence the Achievement of Australia's Indigenous Students: Results from PISA 2000–2006*. Camberwell, Victoria: Australian Council for Educational Research Press.

Dewey, J. 1933. *How We Think: A Restatement of the Relation of Reflective Thinking to the Educative Process*. Lexington, MA: D.C. Heath and Co.

Fielding, M. 2000. Community, philosophy and education policy: Against effectiveness ideology and the immiseration of contemporary schooling. *Journal of Education Policy*, 15(4), 397–415. https://doi.org/10.1080/026809300413419

Foucault, M. 1977. *Discipline and Punish: The Birth of the Prison*. London, UK: Penguin Books.

Gale, T. and Molla, T. 2015. Social justice intents in policy: An analysis of capability for and through education. *Journal of Education Policy*, 30(6), 810–830. https://doi.org/10.1080/02680939.2014.987828

Gibboney, R. A. 2006. Intelligence by design: Thorndike versus Dewey. *Phi Delta Kappan*, October, 170–172.

Gottlieb, D. 2015. *Education Reform and the Concept of Good Teaching*. New York: Routledge.

Graham, C. and Neu, D. 2004. Standardized testing and the construction of governable persons. *Journal of Curriculum Studies*, 36(3), 295–319. https://doi.org/10.1080/0022027032000167080

Hamilton, D. 1999. The pedagogic paradox (or why no didactics in England?). *Pedagogy, Culture and Society*, 7(1), 135–152. https://doi.org/10.1080/14681369900200048

Hilt, L. T., Riese, H. and Søreide, G. E. 2019. Narrow identity resources for future students: The 21st century skills movement encounters the Norwegian education policy context. *Journal of Curriculum Studies*, 51(3), 384–402. https://doi.org/10.1080/00220272.2018.1502356

Hogan, A. 2016. NAPLAN and the role of edu-business: New governance, new privatisations and new partnerships in Australian education policy. *Australian Educational Researcher*, 43, 93–110. https://doi.org/10.1007/s13384-014-0162-z

Hogan, A., Sellar, S. and Lingard, B. 2016. Corporate social responsibility and neo-social responsibility in education. The case of Pearson plc. In A. Verger, C. Lubienski and G. Steiner-Khamsi (Eds.), *World Yearbook of Education 2016: The Global Education Industry* (pp. 107–125). London: Routledge.

Hogan, P. 2013. Cultivating human capabilities in venturesome learning environments. *Educational Theory*, 63(3), 237–252.

Johanningmeier, E. V. and Richardson, T. 2008. *Educational Research, the National Agenda and, Educational Reform: A History*. Charlotte, NC: Information Age Publishing.

Kanigel, R. 1997. *The One Best Way: Frederick Winslow Taylor and the Enigma of Efficiency*. New York: Viking.

Krejsler, J. B. 2018. The "fear of falling behind regime" embraces school policy: State vs federal policy struggles in California and Texas. *International Journal of Qualitative Studies in Education*, 31(5), 393–408. https://doi.org/10.1080/09518398.2018.1449984

Lagemann, E. C. 2000. *An Elusive Science: The Troubling History of Education Research*. Chicago, IL and London, UK: The University of Chicago Press.

Lingard, B., Thompson, G. and Sellar, S. 2015. National testing from an Australian perspective. In B. Lingard, G. Thompson and S. Sellar (Eds.), *National Testing in Schools: An Australian Assessment* (pp. 1–18). London, UK and New York: Routledge.

Luttenberg, J., Imants, J. and van Veen, K. 2013. Reform as ongoing positioning process: The positioning of a teacher in the context of reform. *Teachers and Teaching*, 19(3), 293–310. https://doi.org/10.1080/13540602.2012.754161

Maguire, M. 2010. Towards a sociology of the global teacher. In M. W. Apple, S. J. Ball and L. A. Gandin (Eds.), *The Routledge International Handbook of the Sociology of Education* (pp. 58–68). London and New York: Routledge.

McWilliam, E. 2008. Making excellent teachers. In A. Phelan and J. Sumsion (Eds.), *Critical Readings in Teacher Education: Provoking Absences* (pp. 33–44). Rotterdam and Taipei: Sense Publishers.

Meyer, J. W. 2007. World models, national curricula, and the centrality of the individual. In A. Benavot and C. Braslavsky (Eds.), *School Knowledge in Comparative and Historical Perspective* (pp. 259–271). The Netherlands: Springer.

Miller, P. and Rose, N. 1990. Governing economic life. *Economy and Society*, 19(1), 1–31.

Moore, P. V. 2010. *The International Political Economy of Work and Employability*. Basingstoke, UK: Palgrave Macmillan.

Nussbaum, M. C. 2006. *Frontiers of Justice*. Cambridge, MA: Harvard University Press.

O'Day, J. 2002. Complexity, accountability, and school improvement. *Harvard Educational Review*, 72(3), 293–329.

O'Donnell, A. 2013. Unpredictability, transformation, and the pedagogical encounter: Reflections on "what is effective" in education. *Educational Theory*, 63(3), 265–282.

Ocean, J. and Skourdoumbis, A. 2016. Who's counting? Legitimating measurement in the audit culture. *Discourse: Studies in the Cultural Politics of Education*, 37(3), 442–456. https://doi.org/10.1080/01596306.2015.1061977

Pearson Foundation. *Pearson Foundation-Values*. Retrieved 19 April 2019 from www.pearson.com/corporate#our-strategy

Petrella, R. 1997. Une machine infernale. *Le Monde Diplomatique*, June.

Schmidt, W. H., Wang, H. C. and McKnight, C. C. 2005. Curriculum coherence: An examination of US mathematics and science content standards from an international perspective. *Journal of Curriculum Studies*, 37(5), 525–559. https://doi.org/10.1080/0022027042000294682

Sen, A. 2009. *The Idea of Justice*. Cambridge, MA: The Belknap Press of Harvard University Press.

Stillwaggon, J. 2017. On the unmourned losses of educational growth: An introduction. *Educational Theory*, 67(1), 31–36.

Tarr, E. J., Reys, R. E., Reys, B. J., Cha´vez, O., Shih, J. and Osterlind, S. J. 2008. The impact of middle-grades mathematics curricula and the classroom learning environment on student achievement. *Journal for Research in Mathematics Education*, 39(3), 247–280.

U.S. Department of Education. 1983. *A Nation at Risk. The Imperative for Educational Reform*. Retrieved from https://www.edreform.com/wp-content/uploads/2013/02/A_Nation_At_Risk_1983.pdf

U.S. Government. 1994. *Goals 2000: Educate America Act*. Retrieved from https://www2.ed.gov/legislation/GOALS2000/TheAct/index.html

Valant, J. and Newark, D. A. 2016. The politics of Achievement gaps: U.S. public opinion on race-based and wealth-based differences in test scores. *Educational Researcher*, 45(6), 331–346.

Valli, L. and Buese, D. 2007. The changing roles of teachers in an era of high stakes accountability. *American Educational Research Journal*, 44(3), 519–558.

Verger, A., Lubienski, C. and Steiner-Khamsi, G. 2016. The emergence and structuring of the global education industry. Towards an analytical framework. In A. Verger,

C. Lubienski and G. Steiner-Khamsi (Eds.), *World Yearbook of Education 2016: The Global Education Industry* (pp. 3–24). London: Routledge.

Wheelahan, L. 2015. Not just skills: What a focus on knowledge means for vocational education. *Journal of Curriculum Studies*, 47(6), 750–762. https://doi.org/10.1080/00220272.2015.1089942

Wheeler-Bell, Q. 2017. Standing in need of justification: Michael Apple, R.S. Peters and Jürgen Habermas. *Journal of Curriculum Studies*, 49(4), 561–578. https://doi.org/10.1080/00220272.2017.1279219

Whitty, G. 2010. Revisiting school knowledge: Some sociological perspectives on new school curricula. *European Journal of Education*, 45(1), 28–45.

Williams, C. 2005. The discursive construction of the "competent" learner-worker: From key competencies to "employability skills". *Studies in Continuing Education*, 27(1), 33–49. https://doi.org/10.1080/01580370500056422

Williams, K. and Williams, P. 2017. Lessons from a master: Montaigne's pedagogy of conversation. *Educational Philosophy and Theory*, 49(3), 253–263. https://doi.org/10.1080/00131857.2016.1214900

Yates, L. 2017. Curriculum: The challenges and the devil in the details. In T. Bentley and G. S. Savage (Eds.), *Educating Australia: Challenges for the Decade Ahead* (pp. 85–100). Melbourne, Australia: Melbourne University Press.

Yates, L. and Collins, C. 2010. The absence of knowledge in Australian curriculum reforms. *European Journal of Education*, 45(1), 89–102.

Young, M. 2013. Overcoming the crisis in curriculum theory: A knowledge-based approach. *Journal of Curriculum Studies*, 45(2), 101–118. https://doi.org/10.1080/00220272.2013.764505

8
PEDAGOGIC ADAPTABILITY

Introduction

Chapter 8 introduces the notion of pedagogic adaptability. The chapter suggests that contemporary school education policy assumes a false classroom context, this being a teacher faced with a single student. Group relations are then often overlooked. The tensions inherent in teachers constantly balancing the needs of the group versus the single student are explored. The chapter in effect is a discussion of pedagogical relations. It will outline in more detail important socio-economic/cultural contingencies that affect learning in classrooms and introduce "caring" as an absent relational characterization of the good and "effective" teacher in contemporary school education policy. The chapter provides a basis for recognizing some of the adaptations that teachers will need to make if the complexity and challenge of school education in the current period is to be more fully understood and acknowledged.

8.1 The relational

Our concern now is to situate our exploration of TE and TQ within a broader relational narrative, where the narratives are related to the fields where they are active. The reduction of TE and TQ to what we say are narrow statistical indices ignores some fundamental epistemological and, perhaps more importantly, ontological issues. To come back to the first chapter, part of the power that has been exercised through TE and TQ has been to exercise this power to reduce the complexity of things that are legitimate and knowable so as to largely ignore the real-world contexts of schools and classrooms. This has also systematically ignored the creative play and micro-decisions that accompany the everyday lives of teachers and principals in school, seeing in this expert practice only fluctuations to be tamed and controlled. These issues if considered provide a broader and expansive view of schooling and the work of teachers. Indeed, we argue that this kind of pedagogic adaptability is so central to teachers' practices that it ought to be considered a part of teacher capital. This more expansive view of schooling and the work of teachers is about providing what we say is a finer grained and more detailed account of the complexities linked to education and the effectiveness research that dominates and contributes to education policy. To establish this expansive view of schooling we begin by clarifying the nature of the schooling experience, including the artificial parameters that TE and TQ researchers use to document effectiveness and quality. Part of this requires robust exploration of the relationship between not only the researcher and the researched but of the school system itself.

The representation of schools and teachers in TE and TQ research omits the "storied" (Clandinin and Murphy 2009) experiences of people. While people 'shape their daily lives by stories of who they and others are' (Clandinin and Murphy 2009, p. 598), they do so as a result of their cultural, institutional and other experiences influenced by broader forces of interaction over which they have no tangible control. We are not suggesting that TE and TQ research ought to include a narrative-based component of inquiry (although we don't necessarily see why it shouldn't), we are, however, saying that ignoring the 'storied phenomenon' (Clandinin and Murphy 2009, p. 598) of schooling and the work of teachers misses the full picture of the educational experience. What we do argue is that the omission of these narratives follows a logic that is specific to the field of SESI, where the history of the field has been built on a self-imposed reduction of these narratives in order to focus on factors that are more amenable to measurement. There are consequences of these reductions as policy makers have drawn on SESI models in sometimes literal ways to inform teacher entry requirements, reporting requirements, and, increasingly assumptions about teachers. Teachers are reimagined to be the ideal agents represented by TE and TQ in SESI models, and standards build around these reductions as rational decision makers who draw on the insights of SESI models to inform their practice while ignoring models or research that is not amenable to these reductions or who problematize their implications. There are, therefore, cross-field effects of SESI models into fields of schooling. A more recent and noteworthy consequence in the acceptance of this logic is a shift in the burden of proof, where the assumption that students' learning is linked to specific teaching is no longer accepted but must be demonstrated, where teachers must provide evidence that supports particular teaching strategies and show how this links to student learning gains (AITSL 2018).

A documented researched account of TE and TQ should also consider how the phenomenon of schooling is being experienced by those in schools as a key feedback loop. Our "theory of experience" (Dewey 1938) following Dewey involves an 'emphasis on the social dimension of inquiry, temporality of knowledge generation and continuity that is not merely perceptual but ontological'

(Clandinin and Murphy 2009, p. 599). Reality, if it is to be researched and "captured", is then 'relational, temporal and continuous' (Clandinin and Murphy 2009, p. 599). The acknowledgment of individual experience respects the recognition, identity and agency of the "Other". There is no such thing as a 'disembodied and decontextualized' (Griffiths 2013, p. 221) pedagogy devoid of the heterogeneous and personal because the experience of schooling is bound up in the political, cultural and economic structures and events of the prevailing times. It is also found in the idiosyncratic identities of individual teachers and students.

8.2 Identity and agency

Teacher professional identity, as Mockler (2011) highlights, is 'formed and re-formed constantly over the course of a career mediated by a complex interplay of personal, professional and political dimensions of teachers' lives' (p. 518). This accords with Griffiths' (2013) notion of becoming an "excellent/good" teacher, which she attributes to the 'pedagogical relationships between teachers, students and subject matter' (p. 118).

Identity and agency of teachers interconnect and both are shaped by dominant 'macro level discourses and historical forces' (Buchanan 2015, p. 705). While accountability discourses currently dominate education policy "talk" with effects on teacher identity and agency, it does not totally re-define teachers' self-concepts.

> Teachers are more complex and multifaceted than that. Each individual teacher brings with him or her a unique mix of personal and professional experiences and commitments.
>
> *(Buchanan 2015, pp. 700–701)*

Teachers draw upon their professional agency to interpret, work with, learn from and negotiate their way through conditions and expectations at and of work. This means that the identity and agency of teachers not only develops over time, but also it is 'multifaceted and influenced by external contexts' (Buchanan 2015, p. 703). Day and Gu (2007) have found that teacher identity is significantly influenced by school context. Mockler (2011) contends that teacher identity is an evolving "project", 'ongoing, dynamic and shifting; influenced by personal, professional and political dimensions of teachers' lives and work which interplay in an overlapping and active way' (p. 526). While identity is about who teachers are, agency addresses the actions that teachers believe that they can enact. The actions of teachers, however, including their in-classroom actions, involve a set of options that can and usually 'are shaped by larger force relations' (Buchanan 2015, p. 704), some of which we will outline next in this chapter.

A critical understanding of teacher identity and agency points to the contemporary practice of modern schooling. The dominant instrumentalist tendencies of contemporary education mean that the work of teachers is often of a functionalist mode.

> Instrumentalist approaches to teachers and their work embedded in the discourses of 'what works' typically seek to subjugate these dimensions, which serve to highlight the complexity of the educational enterprise and the perils of providing simple 'answers' ('evidence-based', of course) to what are in fact highly complex 'questions'.
>
> *(Mockler 2011, p. 518)*

This means that the transformational possibilities of education as evinced by thinkers such as Dewey where teachers are 'engaged, not simply in the training of individuals, but in the formation of the proper social life' (Dewey 1897, p. 80) go unrealized. We also say that the importance of more meaningful aims of education transacted by teachers with an agentic professional identity as change agents is a missing element in contemporary schooling. The consequences for teacher identity and agency are such that we argue 'many teachers struggle to locate their work within deep consideration of the purposes of education' (Biesta, Priestley and Robinson 2015, p. 636).

8.3 Pedagogic adaptability

When we use the term "pedagogic adaptability", we are referring to "in-the-moment" in-classroom adaptations that are enacted by teachers to respond to and enhance learning. There is a given in schooling that Parsons et al. (2018) refer to:

> Classrooms are messy, unpredictable contexts. Daily, educators teach students who come from different backgrounds, cultures, and life experiences; who have diverse interests and motivations; and who have varying levels of language proficiency, skills and abilities.
>
> *(p. 206)*

This means that to effectively cater to student needs teachers 'must be flexible and creative in their approach' (Parsons et al. 2018, p. 206). Adaptability is about recognizing and acting upon student difference/s. It is founded upon a belief that educational development often requires of teachers a reflective course of action. Hoffman and Duffy (2016) define an "in-the-moment" adaptation as 'thoughtfully changing teaching strategies in response to students or situations' (p. 173). While the extant research literature acknowledges the importance of adaptability to effective teaching, 'there is no consensus on the language to describe this phenomenon' (Parsons et al. 2018, p. 205).

Classroom teachers teach groups of students, as they never solely and continuously direct their pedagogic attention to one student. The skilled classroom teacher practitioner is expected to engage and focus the attention of all students on the classroom activity chosen for a designated lesson. This means that the pedagogic approach adopted must be expansive enough to coalesce the interests of all students yet contain the flexibility to cater to individual student needs. Contextual influences on the pedagogic approach adopted are many and may involve what is accepted pedagogic practice in a particular school or extend to how students in a class relate to course content. They also involve the individual perceptions and views of teachers as they relate to curriculum, assessment and pedagogic/schooling beliefs.

An assumption of education policy is its supposed universal classroom applicability. Prescribed accountability systems and core educational/curriculum "standards" are designed for the whole student body, never for the discrete classroom located individual. The policy expectation "in theory" is that teachers, through their adopted pedagogic approach, cater to the educational needs of all students uniformly. In practice things are often different. Nonetheless, policy implementation in schooling is about the alignment of teaching with forms of assessment, curriculum, standards and professional development that contribute to improvements in student achievement. While this is the case presently in most school systems across the globe, research often finds that implementation and alignment vary. Some studies (Mintrop and Sunderman 2009; Au 2007; Herman 2004) have shown that in the U.S., for example, high stakes accountability policies have only marginally improved student achievement. In addition, schooling policies advocating stronger accountability implementation as an antidote to "underachievement" have unintended consequences.

> Among other things, policy influenced what teachers taught but failed to improve how they taught it, marginalized low-stakes subjects, delivered resources to students based on their likelihood of passing the test, and increased the time devoted to teaching test-taking skills as distinct from the context being tested.
> *(Coburn, Hill and Spillane 2016, p. 245)*

In effect, policy implementation varies and/or misaligns with intentions because quite often school personnel (teachers and school administrators) have their own 'constructed understandings of policy' (Coburn et al. 2016, p. 245) that influence their responses to it.

8.4 Adaptive teaching

Adaptive teaching is responsive to the contextual needs of students. Researchers in the field consider it the benchmark of exemplary in-classroom practice (Darling-Hammond and Bransford 1996). Studies often show that excellent teachers adapt their pedagogic practice/s to suit the needs of their pupils (see Parsons et al. 2018). In addition, national teacher standards documents often reference adaptive teaching strategies as a vital component of accepted professional teacher practice. For example Standard 3, "Plan for and implement effective teaching and learning", in the Australian Professional Standards for Teachers states that lead[1] teachers should 'work with colleagues to review, modify and expand their repertoire of teaching strategies to enable students to use knowledge, skills, problem solving and critical and creative thinking' (Australian Institute of Teaching and School Leadership 2014, p. 5). Similarly, England's Teachers' Standards under Teaching Standard 5 states that a teacher must 'adapt teaching to respond to the strengths and needs of all pupils' (Department for Education 2018, p. 11).

The recent work of Parsons et al. (2018) provides a comprehensive outline of the conceptualization of adaptive teaching in the extant research literature. Their work shows that the term is associated with a particular terminology that has varied over time (see Parsons et al. 2018, pp. 215–216). This terminology encapsulates a range of teaching approaches and teacher-led classroom actions, for example, teacher decision-making, adaptive instruction, reflective teaching, teacher metacognition, instructional design, improvisation, flexibility, mediated learning, differentiation and so on (see Parsons et al. 2018). Interestingly, Parsons et al. note that for the decade 2005–2014, the term "adaptive teaching" aligns with a number of studies into teacher effectiveness.

> This international focus on teacher effectiveness may also be related to the dramatic increase in the number of studies exploring adaptability during this decade as compared with previous decades.
>
> *(Parsons et al. 2018, p. 221)*

Teacher decision-making is the centrepiece of resolving classroom dilemmas in adaptive teaching situations. Teachers must constantly grapple with classroom dilemmas, often seeking 'optimal solutions to situations' (Jonasson, Mäkitalo and Nielsen 2015, p. 834). The unpredictable nature of teaching means that teachers actively create responses to classroom situations so that their students' learning continues unhindered. Several important stimuli which often precipitate in-classroom teacher decision-making centred on adaptive teaching involve observations of and responses to student learning, motivation and behaviour (see Parsons et al. 2018). The active role of the teacher in how they deal with these student issues hinges on their adaptive teaching capacity, which 'requires knowledge about different options and possible consequences, as well as a professional sense of the ethics of teaching' (Fransson and Grannäs 2013, p. 10).

Germane to the earlier discussion is what Parsons et al. (2018) term "teacher factors". These, broadly defined, incorporate the set of beliefs individual teachers have about schooling, teaching practice, curriculum, assessment, student welfare and so on. Bound up in teacher beliefs is teacher identity, the former having influence over the latter, 'both of which influence classroom practice' (Hamilton 2018, p. 153). Connections between 'pedagogical actions' and teacher practice, whilst influenced by teacher identity and beliefs, are also shaped by 'teaching context' (Hamilton 2018, p. 153).

The concept of context in education helps situate how the complexities involved in schooling exert influence over educational outcomes. Context is about recognizing 'school-specific factors which act as constraints, pressures and enablers' (Ball, Maguire and Braun 2012, p. 19), which then shape and influence school outcomes. Historically, context in studies of schools and education has been associated with student motivation (Anderman and Maehr 1994), student achievement (Eccles and Lord 1991), teaching practice (Russell 1993), school change (Boyd 1992) and student learning (Kilgore and Pendleton 1993). Recent work on context and schooling, however, focuses on 'contextual dimensions' (Ball et al. 2012, p. 19), which include the material conditions and resources in which schools are located and under which they operate. Ball et al. (2012) have developed an analytical framework that incorporates context in education policy development which encompasses a 'set of objective conditions in relation to a set of subjective "interpretational" dynamics' (p. 20). Their contextual framework comprises

> situated contexts (e.g. locale, school histories and intakes), professional cultures (e.g. values, teacher commitments and experiences and 'policy management' in schools), material contexts (e.g. staffing, budgets, buildings, technology, infrastructure), external contexts (e.g. degree and quality of LA support; pressures and expectations from broader policy context, such as Ofsted ratings, league table positions, legal requirements and responsibilities).
> *(Ball et al. 2012, p. 21)*

Ball et al. (2012) maintain that contexts are fluid with shifting and dynamic tendencies 'in and outside schools' (Singh, Heimans and Glasswell 2014, p. 827). The analytical framework Ball et al. (2012) have adopted is an attempt at re-inserting context into our understanding of how it can affect schooling and educational outcomes. Their argument is that they have disrupted the removal of context by particular forms of education research and education policy from the specific material, professional and other contingent challenges faced by those working in schools.

Terri Seddon (1993) has previously characterized the contemporary experiences of schooling as one seemingly of continual 'contextual change' (p. 6). This is in regards to what she terms the 'milieu, institutional matrix and medium of meaning within which educational practice occurs' (Seddon 1993, p. 6). The contextual change that Seddon (1993) refers to is

> a reality which impinges on the participants of schooling as a quite tangible force. It is experienced as new sets of constraints, and new opportunities. Context is no longer something simple and taken for granted, a backdrop to whatever is important. It is palpable and present. It is forced to the front of educators' attention and is central to their lived experiences.
> *(p. 6)*

In a general and broad sense, the research literature specifically on school context seems to describe the physical nature of a school, its resources, its population, its social makeup and the other extraneous influences that can act upon it. These are often linked to the particular education policies in operation at a particular point in time.

Gale and Densmore (2000) have characterized the contextual influences acting on individuals in schools through what they term 'systems of domination' (p. 64) that are ideological in nature. These dominating systems are in effect the ideas and practices that are manifest in the school through policy discourse and often extend to include a school's particular ethos, organizational and teaching practices, its policies and the ideas and beliefs held by its teachers and leaders. As a result, the contextual character of a school is framed by particular 'parameters of ideological domination' (Gale and Densmore 2000, p. 65) which in current times are defined by narrow interpretations of what an education should stand for and be about.

In work conducted by Mills and Gale (2010), school context was found to be an important consideration in determining student achievement. Their work illustrated the specific attention that is needed regarding incorporation of school context in analytical determinations of effectiveness and quality. The thoughtful and considered documentation of student achievement cannot be done without specific mention of context – social, political and economic – as these are the 'influences that adversely position students and schools' (Mills and Gale 2010, p. 29), especially the disadvantaged. The key issue here is of reduction where TE and TQ research eliminates broader sociological background effects, for example, class, and so the 'functions of the educational system [are reduced] to its technical function, that is, reducing the ensemble of relations between the educational system and the economic system to the "output" of the school' (Bourdieu and Passeron 2000, pp. 178–179). This produces a skewed view of teacher, student and school performance, condemning all to a series of abstract statistical comparisons devoid 'of the significance which the facts measured derive from their position in a particular structure, serving a particular system of functions' (Bourdieu and Passeron 2000, pp. 178–179). This particular point from Bourdieu and Passeron is missing from the contemporary debate about TE and TQ.

8.5 Power contingencies: socio-economic status and class

In suggesting that 'the sociological is everywhere in our lives' (Arrighi 2007, p. 15), Barbara Arrighi is plainly asserting the social, political and economic effects of class, culture, gender and race and how each separately and together affects our lives. There is no surprise in saying, as Diane Reay does, that the 'education system itself is one which valorizes middle- rather than working-class cultural capital' (2001, p. 334). The means to achieve this is by universally imposing

> the same demands without any concern for universally distributing the means for satisfying them, thus helping to legitimate the inequality that

one merely records and ratifies, while additionally exercising (first of all in the educational system) the symbolic violence associated with the effects of real inequality within formal equality.

(Bourdieu 2000, p. 76)

Class, in association with other social, political and economic elements, still correlates strongly with academic success and/or failure in countries such as England, the U.S. and Australia (Connell 1995; Apple 1996; Gale and Densmore 2000; Teese and Polesel 2003).

There is increasing evidence that inequality, especially income inequality, is on the rise in major Anglo-capitalist nations of the world (see Douglas 2018; Reay 2017; Piketty 2014). The industrial and labour certainties of the post-Second World War "Golden Years" (1950s, 60s and 70s) (Hobsbawm 1994) 'were a brief, positive surge in a more pessimistic current' (Reay 2017, p. 23). The education system, far from narrowing inequality gaps, is often implicated in their augmentation, as it is 'enmeshed in, and increasingly driven by, the economy' (Reay 2017, p. 11) rather than any pressing need for ameliorating disadvantage. The widening gap in income, general wealth and opportunity means growing economic uncertainty for many within a burgeoning 'precariat' (Standing 2011). While there is no single cause of the current uncertainty experienced by many, there is nonetheless a sense that the policy pre-occupation with "trickle-down", laissez faire, neoliberal economics, which valorizes hyper-competitive individualization discourses disempowers (Kennedy-Lewis 2014). This, in the education system, links with notions of individual merit and/or aspiration.

The work of Pierre Bourdieu has shown that the education system, through the actions and effects of schooling, reproduces 'all the more perfectly the structure of the distribution of cultural capital among classes' (Bourdieu 1973, p. 80). Indeed, the cultural and social reproduction at work in both the school and higher education systems makes social hierarchies and the 'reproduction of these hierarchies appear to be based upon the hierarchy of "gifts", merits, or skills' (Bourdieu 1973, p. 84). Scholastic attainment in this scenario is then about the deliberate actions of individuals to "get ahead" through their own hard work and/or intelligence. Those that either drop out, fall behind or simply don't "make it" are the authors of their own destructive predicaments, having either made poor decisions along the way or are lacking in that "special" something.

In setting about researching the social and scholastic variables at work in the inequalities connected to academic attainment, Bourdieu adopted a theoretical model which links the two systems of relations characterized by cultural capital and degree of selection (Bourdieu and Passeron 2000). He does this to illustrate the complex ways in which education can often mediate class background effects that operate via selective processes and categories with social class-based/structured origins. These selective class-based processes and categories operate at different levels and have varying effects throughout the academic journey. These effects, which are often found in the communicative resources bound up in language as a form of linguistic/cultural capital, are more pronounced in the early school years where the 'capacity to decipher and manipulate complex structures, whether logical or aesthetic, depends partly on the complexity of the language transmitted by the family' (Bourdieu and Passeron 2000, 73). Language is not 'simply an instrument of communication', as it also acts as a marker of what Bourdieu terms the 'educational mortality rate' which increases 'as one moves towards the classes most distant from scholarly language' (Bourdieu and Passeron 2000, 73). Nonetheless, academic performance appears less affected by these class-based processes and categories in the later academic years 'because the surviving lower-[socio-economic] class students represent a highly select sub-group' (Swartz 1997, 201). Academic success and/or failure is then about the interaction of influences at different levels of the educational continuum (see Swartz 1997) and highly dependent upon the level of selectiveness operating throughout the varying hierarchies of the education system.

Schools and universities are, for Bourdieu, institutional entities that through their varying and dominating 'differentiating and differentiated conditionings' (1984, pp. 470–471), which, in turn, are based upon systems of rules of assessment/verification, amongst other practices, fortify social divisions. These divisions are internalized in the least advantaged as limits. This form of cognitive representation and conceptualization (doxa) about one's sense of place and institutional belonging is manifestly (to them) self-evident.

> Dominated agents, who assess the value of their position and their characteristics by applying a system of schemes of perception and appreciation which is the embodiment of the objective laws whereby their value is objectively constituted, tend to attribute to themselves what the distribution attributes to them, refusing what they are refused ('That's not for the likes of us'), adjusting their expectations to their chances, defining themselves as the established defines them, reproducing in their verdict on themselves the verdict the economy pronounces on them, in a word condemning themselves to what is in any case their lot.
>
> *(Bourdieu 1984, 471)*

This means that economic and cultural inter-relationships enacted in schooling and/or higher education contribute to the sense of un/familiarity and alienation one feels and moreover, ability one possesses in navigating highly competitive and class-based social spaces (see Byrom and Lightfoot 2013; Watson 2013).

8.6 Caring

Fernandez makes the point that the underpinning element distinguishing teacher work from the work of many other professionals is a genuine need to care for students.

> Unlike other occupations where professionalism is characterized by detached and impartial treatment of clients, those who work in education have to care genuinely for their students.
>
> *(Fernandez 2000, p. 240)*

Caring in teaching can be understood in a myriad of ways (see Vogt 2002), the connecting thread being that teachers' work entails an emotional and personal dimension (O'Connor 2008). The importance of care and commitment is central to teachers' work (Barber 2002), reinforcing the view that 'caring is arguably one of the predominant and visible emotions that teachers demonstrate in their work' (O'Connor 2008, p. 121). Teachers, in the work carried out by O'Connor, engage in several forms of caring behaviour that she characterizes as performative, professional and philosophical/humanistic. The performative is mainly about the pedagogical, where teacher behaviours centre on caring that students reach designated learning and achievement goals. The professional aligns with the maintenance of appropriate student/teacher relationships commensurate with that expected of the teacher as a professional worker with duty-of-care responsibilities. The philosophical/humanistic involves a personal element where the teacher makes the decision to care based on her individual philosophical outlook or code of ethics (see O'Connor 2008). The caring behaviour that teachers engage in suggests that the work of teachers entails a considerable amount of emotional labour – a variable that TER refrains from adopting in its metrics – and that the demands of their professional role require the creation of an empathetic understanding (Hargreaves 2001). This 'capacity for connectedness' (Palmer 2017, p. 11) means that there is an inherent difficulty in reducing teaching to mere technique. Teaching incorporates an emotional side which distinguishes it as a relational activity ill-suited to the representations of standards, and, moreover, the caring that teachers engage in 'cannot be quantified by any objective means' (O'Connor 2008, p. 123).

The metrics of TE and TQ are devoid of any reference to and/or capacity for grappling with the emotional and personal nature of teaching. O'Connor (2008) makes the point in her work that policy makers find the intangible nature of the emotional and empathic qualities of teaching of no real value because they cannot be measured. Students conversely recognize and value the caring displayed towards them by teachers. Recent work by Luttrell (2013) shows how children value 'the emotion work that teachers do', (p. 298) and they recognize the complex aspects that comprise teachers' caregiving in classroom situations. This relational part of caring on the part of teachers has two sides in that it is characteristic of the '*joy*' often expressed by caring teachers towards their students but comes at the expense of the '*exhaustion* and tiredness that it may at the same time cause over time' (Aspfors and Bondas 2013, p. 255, emphasis in original).

8.7 Conclusion

In this chapter we have argued that classroom teaching is a complex activity. Teachers are expected to attend to the needs of a large group of people within a short time period (a classroom lesson). This calls for a level of adaptability. There is also an emotional labour side to teaching that is often unrecognized by TER and school education policy. This intangible part of teaching work is rarely emphasized in the research literature on TE and TQ. Technical competencies in the form of prescribed standards dominate while the ethical, moral and emotional work that teachers engage in daily is never documented.

Note

1 Lead teachers are recognized and respected by colleagues, parents and other community members as exemplary teachers. Lead teachers are often allocated substantive administrative responsibilities in conjunction with their teaching responsibilities.

References

Anderman, E. M. and Maehr, M. L. 1994. Motivation and schooling in the middle grades. *Review of Educational Research*, 64, 287–309.

Apple, M. 1996. *Cultural Politics and Education*. Buckingham, UK: Open University Press.

Arrighi, B. (Ed.). 2007. *Understanding Inequality: The Intersection of Race/Ethnicity, Class, and Gender*. Lanham, MD: Rowman & Littlefield Publishers Inc.

Aspfors, J. and Bondas, T. 2013. Caring about caring: Newly qualified teachers' experiences of their relationships within the school community. *Teachers and Teaching*, 19(3), 243–259. https://doi.org/10.1080/13540602.2012.754158

Au, W. 2007. High-stakes testing and curricular control: A qualitative metasynthesis. *Educational Researcher*, 36(5), 258–267.

Australian Institute of Teaching and School Leadership. 2014. *Australian Professional Standards for Teachers*. Retrieved 22 October 2018 from www.aitsl.edu.au/teach/standards

Ball, S., Maguire, M. and Braun, A. 2012. *How Schools Do Policy: Policy Enactments in Secondary Schools*. New York: Routledge.

Barber, T. 2002. A special duty of care: Exploring the narration and experience of teacher caring. *British Journal of Sociology of Education*, 23(3), 383–395.

Biesta, G., Priestley, M. and Robinson, S. 2015. The role of beliefs in teacher agency. *Teachers and Teaching*, 21(6), 624–640. https://doi.org/10.1080/13540602.2015.1044325

Bourdieu, P. 1973. Cultural reproduction and social reproduction. In Richard Brown (Ed.), *Knowledge, Education and Cultural Change*. London, UK: Tavistock Publications.

Bourdieu, P. 1984. *Distinction: A Social Critique of the Judgement of Taste*. Cambridge, MA: Harvard University Press.

Bourdieu, P. 2000. *Pascalian Meditations*. Cambridge, UK: Polity Press.

Bourdieu, P. and Passeron, J.-C. 2000. *Reproduction in Education, Society and Culture*. London, UK: Sage Publications.

Boyd, V. 1992. *School Context: Bridge or Barrier for Change?* Austin, TX: Southwest Educational Development Laboratory.

Buchanan, R. 2015. Teacher identity and agency in an era of accountability. *Teachers and Teaching*, 21(6), 700–719. https://doi.org/10.1080/13540602.2015.1044329

Byrom, T. and Lightfoot, N. 2013. Interrupted trajectories: The impact of academic failure on the social mobility of working-class students. *British Journal of Sociology of Education*, 34(5–6), 812–828.

Clandinin, D. J. and Murphy, M. S. 2009. Relational ontological commitments in narrative research. *Educational Researcher*, 38(8), 598–602.

Coburn, C. E., Hill, H. C. and Spillane, J. P. 2016. Alignment and accountability in policy design and implementation: The common core state standards and implementation research. *Educational Researcher*, 45(4), 243–251. https://doi.org/10.3102/0013189X16651080

Connell, R. 1995. *Masculinities*. Cambridge: Polity Press.

Darling-Hammond, L. and Bransford, J. (Eds). 1996. *Preparing Teachers for a Changing World: What Teachers Should Learn and Be Able to Do*. San Francisco, CA: Jossey-Bass.

Day, C. and Gu, Q. 2007. Variations in the conditions for teachers' professional learning and development: Sustaining commitment and effectiveness over a career. *Oxford Review of Education*, 33, 423–443.

Department for Education. 2018. *Teachers' Standards*. Retrieved 22 October 2018 from https://assets.publishing.service.gov.uk/government/uploads/system/uploads/attachment_data/file/665520/Teachers__Standards.pdf

Dewey, J. 1897. My pedagogic creed. *The School Journal*, LIV(3), 77–80.

Dewey, J. 1938. *Experience and Education*. New York: Touchstone Books.

Douglas, B. (Ed.). 2018. *A Fair Go For All Australians: Urgent Action Required*. Report of High Level Roundtable. Parliament House Canberra. Published by Australia 21 and The Australia Institute.

Eccles, J. S. and Lord, S. 1991. What are we doing to early adolescents? The impact of educational contexts on early adolescents. *American Journal of Education*, 99, 521–542.

Fernandez, A. 2000. Leadership in an era of change: breaking down the barriers of the culture of teaching. In C. Day, A. Fernandez, T. E. Hauge and J. Møller (Eds.), *The Life and Work of Teachers: International Perspectives in Changing Times* (pp. 235–250). London, UK: Falmer Press.

Fransson, G. and Grannäs, J. 2013. Dilemmatic spaces in educational contexts: Towards a conceptual framework for dilemmas in teachers work. *Teachers and Teaching*, 19(1), 4–17. https://doi.org/10.1080/13540602.2013.744195

Gale, T. and Densmore, K. 2000. *Just Schooling: Explorations in the Cultural Politics of Teaching*. Philadelphia, PA: Open University Press.

Griffiths, M. 2013. Critically adaptive pedagogical relations: The relevance for educational policy and practice. *Educational Theory*, 63(3), 221–236.

Hamilton, M. 2018. Pedagogical transitions among science teachers: How does context intersect with teacher beliefs? *Teachers and Teaching*, 24(2), 151–165. https://doi.org/10.1080/13540602.2017.1367658

Hargreaves, A. 2001. Emotional geographies of teaching. *Teachers College Record*, 103, 1056–1080.

Herman, J. L. 2004. The effects of testing on instruction. In S. H. Fuhrman and R. F. Elmore (Eds.), *Redesigning Accountability Systems for Education* (pp. 141–166). New York, NY: Teachers College Press.

Hobsbawn, E. 1994. *The Age of Extremes: 1914–1991*. London, UK: Abacus.

Hoffman, J. V. and Duffy, G. G. 2016. Does thoughtfully adaptive teaching actually exist? A challenge to teacher educators. *Theory Into Practice*, 55(3), 172–179. https://doi.org/10.1080/00405841.2016.1173999

Jonasson, C., Mäkitalo, Å. and Nielsen, K. 2015. Teachers' dilemmatic decision-making: Reconciling coexisting policies of increased student retention and performance. *Teachers and Teaching*, 21(7), 831–842. https://doi.org/10.1080/13540602.2014.995484

Kennedy-Lewis, B. L. 2014. Using critical policy analysis to examine competing discourses in zero tolerance legislation: Do we really want to leave no child behind? *Journal of Education Policy*, 29(2), 165–194. https://doi.org/10.1080/02680939.2013.800911

Kilgore, S. B. and Pendleton, W. W. 1993. The organizational context of learning: Framework for understanding the acquisition of knowledge. *Sociology of Education*, 66(1), 63–87.

Luttrell, W. 2013. Children's counter-narratives of care: Towards educational justice. *Children & Society*, 27, 295–308. https://doi.org/10.1111/chso.12033

Mills, C. and Gale, T. 2010. *Schooling in Disadvantaged Communities: Playing the Game from the Back of the Field*. Heidelberg: Springer Dordrecht.

Mintrop, H. and Sunderman, G. L. 2009. Predictable failure of federal sanctions-driven accountability from school improvement: And why we may retain it anyway. *Educational Researcher*, 38(5), 353–364.

Mockler, N. 2011. Beyond "what works": Understanding teacher identity as a practical and political tool. *Teachers and Teaching*, 17, 517–528.

O'Connor, K. E. 2008. "You choose to care": Teachers, emotions and professional identity. *Teaching and Teacher Education*, 24, 117–126.

Palmer, P. J. 2017. *The Courage to Teach: Exploring the Inner Landscape of a Teachers' Life*. San Francisco, CA: Jossey-Bass.

Parsons, S. A., Vaughn, M., Scales, R. Q., Gallagher, M. A., Parsons, A. W., Davis, S. G., Pierczynski, M. and Allen, M. 2018. Teachers' instructional adaptations: A research synthesis. *Review of Educational Research*, 88(2), 205–242.

Piketty, T. 2014. *Capital in the Twenty-First Century*. Cambridge, MA: The Belknap Press of Harvard University.

Reay, D. 2001. Finding or losing yourself?: Working-class relationships to education. *Journal of Education Policy*, 16(4), 333–346. https://doi.org/10.1080/02680930110054335

Reay, D. 2017. *Miseducation: Inequality, Education and the Working Classes*. Bristol, UK: Bristol University Press.

Russell, T. 1993. *A Teacher Educator Reflects on the Impact of Context on Teaching Practice: Seeking Voice in Teacher and Teacher Educator Research on Practice*. Paper presented at the Annual Meeting of the American Educational Research Association, Atlanta, GA, April 12–16.

Seddon, T. 1993. *Context and Beyond: Reframing the Theory and Practice of Education*. London, UK: The Falmer Press.

Singh, P., Heimans, S. and Glasswell, K. 2014. Policy enactment, context and performativity: Ontological politics and researching Australian National Partnership policies. *Journal of Education Policy*, 29(6), 826–844. https://doi.org/10.1080/02680939.2014.891763

Standing, G. 2011. *The Precariat: The New Dangerous Class*. London, UK: Bloomsbury Publishing.

Swartz, D. 1997. *Culture and Power: The Sociology of Pierre Bourdieu*. Chicago, IL: Chicago Press.

Teese, R. and Polesel, J. 2003. *Undemocratic Schooling: Equity and Quality in Mass Secondary Education in Australia*. Melbourne, Australia: Melbourne University Press.

Vogt, F. 2002. A caring teacher: Explorations into primary school teachers' professional identity and ethic of care. *Gender and Education*, 14(3), 251–264. https://doi.org/10.1080/0954025022000010712

Watson, J. 2013. Profitable portfolios: Capital that counts in higher education. *British Journal of Sociology of Education*, 34(3), 412–430. https://doi.org/10.1080/01425692.2012.710005

9
IMPLICATIONS

Introduction

In this chapter we draw on the Bourdieuian notion of habitus to suggest that contemporary education policy structures and categorizes classroom teaching in "performative" ways. Whilst interconnected with the economic reforms we have outlined in Chapters 3, 4 and 6, the "performative" in classroom teaching is also about the modifications needed in teacher preparation that align teachers' work with "standards". The "performative" then in classroom teaching is inscribed as a particular form of "conditioning". Teachers prepared in the "right" way are needed, which is achieved only if major education policy encapsulates the intra-active nuances of "best practice/s".

9.1 The performative habitus in teaching

The Bourdieuian notion of habitus (1977) is a theoretical representation of action and/or practice. Habitus are 'generative principles of distinct and distinctive practices' (Bourdieu 1998, p. 8) that condition and also structure.

> The habitus is both the generative principle of objectively classifiable judgements and the system of classification (*principium divisionis*) of these practices. It is in the relationship between the two capacities which define the habitus, the capacity to produce classifiable practices and works, and the capacity to differentiate and appreciate these practices and products (taste), that the represented social world, i.e., the space of life-styles, is constituted.
> *(Bourdieu 1984, p. 179, emphasis in original)*

Habitus in conjunction with capital/s and field/s are central to Bourdieuian social theory. All three concepts are used in the work of Bourdieu to elucidate a deeper articulation of the practices at work in particular social fields. The school "space" is composed of the particular social relations of agents, each of which brings with them unique dispositional characteristics – a habitus – framed upon an 'objective social structure and subjective personal experience' (Bourdieu 1984, p. 121). Habitus is about the embodied inscriptions manifest as cultural mannerisms and behavioural dispositions which are enacted by agents in daily life.

> The habitus is necessity internalized and converted into a disposition that generates meaningful practices and meaning-giving perceptions, it is a general, transposable disposition which carries out a systematic, universal application – beyond the limits of what has been directly learnt – of the necessity inherent in the learning conditions.
>
> *(Bourdieu 1984, p. 170)*

To better understand the contemporary teacher habitus is to focus on the cycles through which it is operationalized. This means there needs to be a focus on the distinctive framework of field-specific aspects upon which it is based. Key amongst these is an acute performance-oriented aspect reinforcing education policy and geared towards the "manufacture" of a particular type of classroom teacher.

In their work on initial teacher training/education in England, Stanfield and Cremin (2013) talk about a 'new emphasis on teachers' dispositions' (p. 21). The emphasis is about mobilizing 'a specific set of ideological practice in the classroom' (Stanfield and Cremin 2013, p. 30) and 'importing into education' (Stanfield and Cremin 2013, p. 32) a habitus orientated towards an 'ideal performativity' (Stanfield and Cremin 2013, p. 33). A particular type of teacher is sought to enact this ideal performativity, one that they say is typically the 'Elite Graduate, the High Flyer and the Ex-Soldier' (Stanfield and Cremin 2013, p. 21). These "ideal" teacher constructions best exemplify the 'specific cultural capitals that define the "ideals" – elite university education, success in the corporate world and military "service"' (Stanfield and Cremin 2013, p. 33). Belief in the meritocratic 'legitimation of imported expertize and practices that accompanies [sic] these "ideals" . . . not only shores up the "ideals" against exposure to professional and institutional habitus, but also gives them organizational authority within schools' (Stanfield and Cremin 2013, p. 34). This meritocratic confidence is expressed by the "ideal" achieving and effective teacher through a set of interpersonal interactions which are 'positive, active, decisive' dispositions that are 'in contrast with the current teachers who are passive, indecisive and unable to effect change' (Stanfield and Cremin 2013, p. 34) (i.e. are ineffective).

Dispositions in the work of Bourdieu have especial significance, as they contribute to the habitus which in turn is the mechanism through which our daily decisions and actions are regulated. While the 'conditionings associated with a particular class of conditions of existence produce *habitus*', the 'systems of durable, transposable dispositions, structured structures predisposed to function as structuring structures, that is, as principles which generate and organize practices' (Bourdieu 1990, p. 53, emphasis in original) guide conduct. Dispositions, as David Swartz suggests, reflect a 'capability and reliability' (2002, p. 635) that moulds action in time. This means that there is a temporal aspect connected to dispositions and habitus. The dynamics of dispositions means that they can exert spontaneous reaction beneath 'the level of calculation and even consciousness, beneath discourse and representation' (Bourdieu and Wacquant 1992, p. 128).

This then has some contemporary salience in the field of teacher education and for teacher preparation. With the advent of radical reforms in recent times, the plethora of "Teach For" (see Wiseman Adhikary, Lingard and Hardy 2018) organizations as simply one example, more education policy-focused attention is brought to bear on the type of teacher now needed. Stanfield and Cremin have already alluded to this (i.e. a teacher not interested in resisting), 'the veracity of the "meritocracy"' (Stanfield and Cremin 2013, p. 35). This "new" teacher type accepts the educational "game" as it is currently played. Performance is internalized by these teachers as modes of conduct 'in the form of personal tendencies, preferences, actions and inactions' (Mills et al. 2017, p. 857). In returning again to Stanfield and Cremin (2013), the '*illusio* of the "ideals" is enabled . . . by an ontological complicity', specifically, belief in the "game" of education, 'which emphasizes meritocratic possibility over structural inequality, national identity over class division' (p. 34, emphasis in original). This, alongside an orientation to performance, represents the new operationalized (performative) habitus in teaching.

The belief expressed by those in the of field of education and by education policy-makers in particular sustains the dominant doxa inherent in the presuppositions of economic rationalizations; for instance, that student learning outcomes solely depend on effective teaching practice/s or that the education system is so configured that those who strive and work hard succeed, or indeed that only particular types of teaching practices "work". Teachers and the "new" contemporary teacher education is both playing the neoliberal game evinced by "fast capitalism" (Shacklock 1998) and demonstrating the belief that it is a game worth playing. This practical education/teacher education policy belief "illusio" or "state of mind" is being expressed by a policy discourse of effectiveness, quality and excellence. Enacted by a reductive discursive doxa claiming declining academic performance in both school students and pre-service teachers, it reinforces a systematic response via key education policy priorities founded on "best practice/s", "continuous school improvement" and what is coming to be known as "evidence-based innovation".

9.2 A new teacher education: "best practice/s"

Cochran-Smith (2005) claims that a "new teacher education" is emerging framed on three distinctive yet interrelated reform components: (1) that it is a policy problem and (2) it must be research driven and (3) outcomes based. Three major agendas are thought to influence current teacher education reforms linked in various ways to professionalization, deregulation and social justice (see Zeichner 2009). Reform agendas notwithstanding, a major strategic commitment in the current direction of teacher education is adherence to fundamental quality assurance principles. Specific priorities centre around the importance of continuous improvement personified as a 'permanent disposition' (Bourdieu 1990, p. 70) which functions as a form of self-regulation. Competing field interests set about re-defining how players in teacher education think about quality and effectiveness. Impact is what counts, which is made possible through settling on key policy drivers (or "best practice/s") centred on enhancing the quality of initial teacher education, aligning theory and practice, ensuring classroom prowess and developing innovative programs of delivery (see Teacher Education Ministerial Advisory Group 2015). Best practice in teacher education can be understood as a 'normative activity' (Lenglet 2011, p. 46) shaping the field in such a way that it narrows action towards adherence to a series of benchmarks and/or practical skills (see Maguire 2014). There is a time element embedded in these benchmarks where calculable (tangible) results are needed quickly. Their intervention in teacher education/preparation slices the extant body of work inherent in the field accumulated over time so that only "visible" bits grounded in quantitative models of pedagogy and "practical skills" bordered by performance indicators are valued. We can see evidence of this in some of the more recent teacher education reforms enacted within Australia and England (see Rowe and Skourdoumbis 2019; Mockler 2018; Maguire 2014).

Osburn, Caruso and Wolfensberger (2011) claim that the concept of "best practice" is best understood both as a term and idea. "Best practice" implies a single uniform "one best way" of doing something or thinking about something, for example, the best form of teaching practice to enhance student achievement. As an abstract concept, "best practice" has Taylorist connotations where its industrial conceptualization is centred on improvements to the productive capacity and efficiency of manufacturing firms (see Kanigel 1997). The crossover in use of the term and concept into the field of education and teacher education stems from a business and financial management appropriation of pedagogic imperatives. Part of the reconceptualized contemporary approach to education involves a political program of strategic control over the processes of schooling and the preparation, training and education of teachers (see Menter, Peters and Cowie 2017). This is generally justified through market-based mechanisms of efficiency, effectiveness and quality. The common points of policy concern are the preparation of "effective and quality teachers" and overcoming the perceived disconnect between theory and practice which often manifests in the minds of pre-service teachers as an unpreparedness in dealing with contemporary classroom demands across a variety of teaching contexts (see Churchward and Willis 2019). While "best practice" is a term now often used to convey the priorities of market-based management in education, its application to the work of teachers implies a form of preference. "Best practice" as a global idea in teaching is about communicating something unique and simple about teachers which invariably is that the 'preferred teacher' (Smyth and Shacklock 1998, p. 107) has particular qualities that are organizational and pedagogic givens universally expected and accepted. Teacher education has the responsibility to ensure that teachers of the right "type" not only move into teaching but also that they are comprehensively prepared in a way where they accept and enact political and economic priorities.

The struggle over teacher education and how pre-service teachers (PSTs) should be prepared has a long history (Trippestad, Swennen and Werler 2017: Ellis and McNicholl 2015). Fixed positions are adopted by the various players in the field about the nature of schooling and the practice of teaching and what effective and quality teaching looks like and should accomplish. A contemporary education policy reference point about teacher education is how suitable it is in developing teachers with requisite skills 'capable of helping students to acquire the competencies needed to evolve in today's societies and labour markets' (Musset 2010, p. 3). Arguments such as this are well-known, positioning teachers and teacher education within a network of reform (Sahlberg 2011). Specific and dominant "positioning discourses" (Luttenberg, Imants and van Veen 2013) continually focus on the perceived inadequacies of teacher education (see Rowan, Mayer, Kline, Kostogriz and Walker-Gibbs 2015), with the field constantly balancing between PST desires for the concrete in what can be directly "used" in classrooms versus 'the larger academy who accuse teacher education of being bereft of theory or import' (Téllez 2007, pp. 544–545).

9.3 Disruptive innovation

Christensen (1997) has claimed that "disruptive innovation" in the form of 'changes in technology and market structure' (Christensen 1997, p. xiv) has always been responsible for company failure.

> In some cases the new technologies swept through quickly; in others, the transition took decades. In some, the new technologies were complex and expensive to develop. In others, the deadly technologies were simple extensions of what the leading companies already did better than anyone else.
>
> *(Christensen 1997, p. xiv)*

In teacher education, innovation is often closely linked to major policy-related change centred around entry and provision. There are now, for example, multiple pathways into teacher education and also a variety of providers, including de-regulated private providers such as in the U.S. and U.K. (see Ellis, Souto-Manning and Turvey 2019) which offer in most cases short-term or "narrow/instrumentalist" models of teacher education (see Zeichner 2016). This brand of teacher education often reflects traditional strands of teaching practice eschewing progressivist approaches. It pushes a "matter-of-fact" data-centric notion of teaching and learning exclusively focused on developing the affective interventionist strategies of classroom teachers to enhance student achievement, particularly for the socially and economically disadvantaged. An example is the New Teacher Project, modelled on Teach For America, the latter a program founded by Wendy Kopp[1], 'with the stated dual missions to fill teaching shortages in urban and rural districts and develop leaders for a movement to close the growing "achievement gap"' (Kretchmar, Sondel and Ferrare 2014, p. 742).

Innovation in teacher education is often connected to "problem setting" (Blackmore and Lauder 2004), meaning that a specific problem in or about teacher education is set, for which a specific solution is found. A recent Australian example involves the broad though vexed "problem" of quality schooling and by implication "quality teaching". "Students First" (SF) is the current Australian public school policy reform ensemble. It is comprised of four benchmark inputs: Teacher Quality, School Autonomy, Engaging Parents in Education and Strengthening the Curriculum. Each input contains particular points of reform or innovative programs, and the injection of more money into the school education system is not a primary focus. In other words, quality schooling is made possible through a focus on the four inputs listed earlier.

SF begins with the input of teacher quality. Teacher quality mirrors a standards-in-school-education agenda by casting doubt on the quality of initial teacher education (ITE) programs and so the preparation of future teachers. It represents an attempt at reinforcing "traditional" conceptions of teaching (direct instruction, for example) and focuses on curricular aspects considered of direct relevance to the Australian national economy. There are five points of reference listed under the input of teacher quality, each containing a series of innovative programs or reform efforts, these being Agriculture in Education, Flexible Literacy for Remote Primary Schools, Teach for Australia, the Teacher Education Ministerial Advisory Group and Literacy and Numeracy Test for Initial Teacher Education Students. A short description of each of these "innovation-based" programs and reform efforts follows.

> The Education in Agriculture Program is an Australian teaching program designed to professionally develop teachers' understanding and familiarity of agriculture and its importance to Australia. Resources for the program are made available through the Primary Industries Foundation of Australia and Agrifood Skills Australia. Both organisations promote the primary industries of mining and agriculture two industrial sectors of historical and current significance in the Australian economy. Mining and agriculture are traditional large-scale industries with historical roots in the early European settlement of the Australian nation.
>
> *(see Lowe 2016)*

The Flexible Literacy for Remote Primary Schools Program champions the merits of direct and explicit instruction techniques. The program is designed to support students in remote schools struggling to read. It quotes research findings based on an Australian Council of Educational Research (ACER) report, *Literacy and numeracy interventions in the early years of schooling: A literature review. Report to the Ministerial Advisory Group on Literacy and Numeracy* (2013). The report suggests that students struggling to read must master a variety of literacy-based skills, including the alphabetic code, via instruction in phonics, phonemic awareness, reading fluency, vocabulary and reading comprehension (see Department of Education and Training 2015).

One aspect of the SF policy that shifts the nature of the conversation about the teaching profession, by leveraging additional funding, is the Teach for Australia (TFA) Program, which rises out of discourse that 'claims that teacher education was broken but could be fixed by government intervention and national solutions' (Mayer et al. 2017, p. 3). The program, as it is realized in the Australian context, claims to recruit 'high calibre' (Windsor 2014, p. 98) university graduates seeking to enter the teaching profession who undertake a 'frantic six weeks of formal, intensive preparation over the summer break before disembarking into some of the most disadvantaged schools in Australia' (Evans 2016, p. 14). The bipartisan funding and support for the TFA program has steadily increased, with increases from 'A$22million to A$57 million' (Burns and McIntyre 2017, p. 29) and, more recently, a further '$20.5 million' (Department of Education and Training 2017). The Teach for Australia program valorizes teachers who are 'trained, accredited and managed to align their professional work with the language and practices of the private sector' (Knipe and Fitzgerald 2016, p. 366). Those who do so 'accept two-year employment contracts in disadvantaged secondary schools and teach with a reduced teaching load and a high level of support and training throughout a two-year placement period' (Department of Education and Training). Whilst the TFA program attempts "innovative disruption" and imagines an Australia 'where all children, regardless of background, attain an excellent education' (Teach for Australia 2017), it is perhaps better realized as 'merely a band-aide on neoliberalism's broken leg' (Windsor 2014, p. 154).

Also under the banner of teacher quality is the Teacher Education Ministerial Advisory Group (TEMAG), established in 2014 to report on the effectiveness of initial teacher education across Australia. The group, formed by the Australian government to advise the national Minister of Education on matters related to ITE, noted the 'concern regarding variability in the quality of teaching in Australian classrooms and the effectiveness of the preparation of new teachers for the profession' (TEMAG 2014, p. 1). It suggested reform of ITE in Australia through 'structural and cultural change' (TEMAG 2014, p. x) across courses and throughout the system and articulated a series of recommendations, key findings, key directions, key proposals and specific findings. The group also recommended a stronger emphasis on the process through which one becomes a teacher, emphasizing higher university admission standards, including greater levels of literacy and numeracy competence, verified now by the Literacy and Numeracy Test for all pre-service teachers prior to graduation. All initial teacher education students in Australia are now required to undertake the test in order to qualify for graduate teacher registration with their relevant state teaching authority. Australia has six states and two territories and they each maintain their own unique teacher registration mandates. The test represents a further point of reform (and innovative disruption) under the input of teacher quality.

Accountability is also inserted into the education/teacher education mix, prioritizing changes in pedagogy and curriculum. The motivating force at work is reduction scaling back education to a calculable score, ignoring the 'complexity of human consciousness' (De Lissovoy and McLaren 2003, p. 133) reifying pedagogy so that the primary benefits of learning purely serve instrumentalist ends. The exigence of most contemporary school education policy across the globe 'asserts the facticity of competition as the logos for the imperative to act' (Nicoll and Edwards 2004, p. 49), and it reifies teachers' work. To reify means 'to turn something abstract into a material thing' (Potter 1996, p. 107) and so 'naturalize or ontologically gerrymander it' (Nicoll and Edwards 2004, p. 48). This reification is about organizing and normalizing specific performance-oriented imperatives into the working lives of classroom teachers. It alters their professional interaction/s amongst themselves and their students, focusing quite pointedly on productivity. The relational in education is then viewed as a totality of observable and measurable outcomes 'lacking all psychic impulse or emotion' and signifying 'the opposite of engagement or recognition' (Honneth 2012, p. 58).

9.4 Continuous achievement

All of what has been outlined so far in this chapter is about highlighting a new performative habitus in teaching which centralizes teachers' work in enhancing levels of student achievement. The vast body of TER and global school education policy continue to maintain the argument that only highly committed, motivated and well-trained teachers matter the most in raising student learning outcomes. What perhaps might now be changing is the nature of the student-classroom teacher learning dynamic and how the latter is conceptualized and moreover what it signifies. In staying with an Australian school education example, *Through growth to achievement: Report of the Review to Achieve Educational Excellence in Australian Schools* (Department of Education 2018) – hereafter referred to as TGtA – a new direction in TE and TQ may potentially be emerging. TGtA is an Australian government-commissioned school education review. It presents perhaps a shift in emphasis around the conceptualization of learning and what it means and how classroom teachers should work with students to improve learning. The shift in emphasis incorporates a stronger and more stringent chronological element to learning where teachers are expected to focus specifically on 'attainment and acceleration' (Department of Education 2018, p. 56). A new model of education is proposed founded on 'the learning growth of every student every year' (Department of Education 2018, p. 56). This will entail development of a 'tailored teaching' (Department of Education 2018, p. 56) approach, meaning that each individual student has their learning growth mapped and documented against goals of achievement. The notion of "high-impact teaching" is introduced, connecting it with 'professional learning practices' (Department of Education 2018, p. 56) and aligning the two against specific actions designed for maximizing learning growth. TGtA lists three actions considered vital to support what it suggests is a growth focus:

- embedding professional collaboration as a necessity in everyday teaching practice
- developing a formative assessment tool that measures individual student growth and enables teachers to assess where individual students are on the various learning progressions, monitor student progress against expected outcomes and tailor teaching practices to maximise student learning growth
- providing a professional learning environment to enable, support and improve teaching practice that promotes individual student learning growth.

(Department of Education 2018, p. 57)

A growth focus which is specifically on a teacher's capability to tailor their teaching and so individualize student learning to enable maximum impact is given priority in the review. This is achieved through a teacher's capacity to:

- select, adapt and apply appropriate assessments to determine their students' current levels of attainment in particular learning areas;
- use assessment outcomes and data to diagnose and evaluate the diverse capabilities and learning needs of individual students in a classroom;
- analyse and use data and evidence about student learning to select appropriate resources and activities to tailor teaching to meet the personalised learning needs of students and;
- collaborate with, and support, colleagues to implement teaching methods that maximise individual student learning growth.

(Department of Education 2018, p. 67)

While TGtA acknowledges that suggested changes should be viewed in a context where schools, teachers and students are given space to "make mistakes", there is also the connection made to implementation of a broader educational reform agenda mimicking the accountability strategies of so-called high performing education systems such as Singapore and Shanghai (see Department of Education 2018).

This pressure to encapsulate teaching for continuous achievement is also about maintaining the "audit" squeeze on classroom teachers through continuous performance accountability. The structured career pathways of teachers are being re-defined to align with this aim so that an 'applied teacher expertise'

(Alterator, Deed and Prain 2018, p. 450) links more stringently to the allocation of responsibilities centred on individual student success.

> Teachers are expected to be both experts in enabling students to demonstrate acquisition of resolved knowledge for systemic testing, and also to enable students to participate as innovative, creative learners who use new methods to solve new problems.
>
> *(Alterator et al. 2018, p. 458)*

The digital revolution is now also an active element in how teachers' enactment of multiple roles and responsibilities hinges on demonstrating continuous quality and effectiveness. Alterator, Deed and Prain suggest that the

> digital revolution compels new teacher practices and new forms of teacher expertise. . . . Here teachers are expected to be experts at adapting these resources to motivate and customize learning for individuals and student groups. Learning is not simply offloaded to new technologies, but rather these technologies augment and complement teacher design, enactment, and review expertise.
>
> *(2018, p. 458)*

Teacher expertise in action is then about how well teachers work with competing demands where system recognition and reward hinge squarely on tangible and continuous student achievement outcomes (see Department of Education 2018).

9.5 Conclusion

A performative-habitus is now, we argue, a major component of contemporary education policy directing, in our view, not only how classroom teachers enact their practice but shapes the preparation of teachers as professionals. The performative-habitus is formed through an education policy differential where classroom teachers are afforded some professional agency as part of daily practice within the limits of specific priorities. Teacher practice is then modelled on an "autonomous", individualized platform where educational success is gained through constant attention to performance.

In this modern educational policy environment, the work of classroom teachers aligns closely with carefully crafted pedagogic designs of curriculum and assessment. Often highly centralized, the work of classroom teachers is limited to implementation and delivery. Responsibility for educational success is then shifted downwards to the classroom teacher. The taken-for-grantedness of their work is about teachers conforming without question to the shifting demands of a risk economy. The energy and direction of the individual classroom teacher then turns on a form of conduct focused perpetually on a type of homogeneity which is about classroom teachers taking responsibility for producing "results".

Note

1 Wendy Kopp is currently CEO and co-founder of Teach For All. Kopp initially founded Teach For America (TFA), the initiative taking root as part of her 1988 Princeton University thesis. TFA recruits and places high-performing college/university graduates in difficult-to-staff urban and rural schools, generally for a period of two years. Recruits undergo a summertime five-to-six-week "boot camp" of intensive pre-despatch training/preparation in readiness for their school placement.

References

Alterator, S., Deed, C. and Prain, V. 2018. Encapsulating teacher Expertise in action. *Teachers and Teaching*, 24(4), 450–460. https://doi.org/10.1080/13540602.2017.1399874

Australian Council for Educational Research. 2013. *Literacy and Numeracy Interventions in the Early Years of Schooling: A Literature Review Report to the Ministerial Advisory Group on Literacy and Numeracy*. NSW Department of Education and Communities.

Blackmore, J. and Lauder, H. 2004. Researching policy. In B. Somekh and C. Lewin (Eds.), *Research Methods in the Social Sciences* (pp. 97–104). London, UK: Sage.

Bourdieu, P. 1984. *Distinction: A Social Critique of the Judgement of Taste*. Cambridge, MA: Harvard University Press.

Bourdieu, P. 1990. *The Logic of Practice*. Cambridge, UK: Polity Press.

Bourdieu, P. 1998. *Practical Reason: On the Theory of Action*. Cambridge, UK: Polity Press.

Bourdieu, P. and Wacquant, L. 1992. *An Invitation to Reflexive Sociology*. Cambridge, UK: Polity Press.

Burns, D. and McIntyre, A. 2017. *Empowered Educators in Australia: How High-Performing Systems Shape Teaching Quality*. San Francisco, CA: Jossey-Bass.

Christensen, C. M. 1997. *The Innovator's Dilemma*. New York: Harper Business.

Churchward, P. and Willis, J. 2019 The pursuit of teacher quality: Identifying some of the multiple discourses of quality that impact the work of teacher educators. *Asia-Pacific Journal of Teacher Education*, 47(3), 251–264. https://doi.org/10.1080/1359866X.2018.1555792

Cochran-Smith, M. 2005. The new teacher education: For better or for worse? *Educational Researcher*, 34(3), 3–17.

De Lissovoy, N. and McLaren, P. 2003. Educational "accountability" and the violence of capital: A Marxian reading. *Journal of Education Policy*, 18(2), 131–143. https://doi.org/10.1080/0268093022000043092

Department of Education. 2018. *Through Growth to Achievement: The Report of The Review to Achieve Educational Excellence in Australian Schools*. Canberra, Australia: Commonwealth of Australia.

Department of Education and Training. 2015. *Students First Strategy: Teacher Quality*.

Department of Education and Training. 2017. *Teach for Australia*. Department of Education and Training. Retrieved from www.education.gov.au/teach-australia-0

Ellis, V. and McNicholl, J. 2015. *Transforming Teacher Education: Reconfiguring the Academic Work*. London, UK: Bloomsbury Academic.

Ellis, V., Souto-Manning, M. and Turvey, K. 2019. Innovation in teacher education: Towards a critical re-examination. *Journal of Education for Teaching*, 45(1), 2–14. https://doi.org/10.1080/02607476.2019.1550602

Evans, K. 2016. Melodie Potts Rosevear: Bringing passion for education to Teach for Australia. *The Age* (Melbourne), p. 14).

Honneth, A. (Ed.). 2012. *Reification: A New Look at an Old Idea*. Oxford: Oxford University Press.

Kanigel, R. 1997. *The One Best Way: Frederick Winslow Taylor and the Enigma of Efficiency.* New York: Penguin Books.

Knipe, S. and Fitzgerald, T. 2016. Policy reform: Testing times for teacher education in Australia. *Journal of Educational Administration and History*, 48(4), 358–369. https://doi.org/10.1080/00220620.2016.1210588

Kretchmar, K., Sondel, B. and Ferrare, J. J. 2014. Mapping the terrain: Teach For America, charter school reform, and corporate sponsorship. *Journal of Education Policy*, 29(6), 742–759. https://doi.org/10.1080/02680939.2014.880812

Lenglet, M. 2011. Conflicting codes and codings. How algorithmic trading is reshaping financial regulation. *Theory, Culture and Society*, 28(6), 44–66.

Lowe, I. 2016. *The Lucky Country? Reinventing Australia.* Brisbane, Australia: University of Queensland Press.

Luttenberg, J., Imants, J. and van Veen, K. 2013. Reform as ongoing positioning process: The positioning of a teacher in the context of reform. *Teachers and Teaching*, 19(3), 293–310. https://doi.org/10.1080/13540602.2012.754161

Maguire, M. 2014. Reforming teacher education in England: "An economy of discourses of truth". *Journal of Education Policy*, 29(6), 774–784, https://doi.org/10.1080/02680939.2014.887784

Mayer, D., Dixon, M., Kline, J., Kostogriz, A., Moss, J., Rowan, L., Walker Gibbs, B. and White, S. 2017. *Studying the Effectiveness of Teacher Education: Early Career Teachers in Diverse Settings.* Singapore: Springer.

Menter, I., Peters, Michael A., and Cowie, B. 2017. A companion to researh in teacher education. In Michael A. Peters, Bronwen Cowie and Iam Menter (Eds.), *A Companion to Research in Teacher Education* (pp. 1–15). Singapore: Springer.

Mills, C., Molla, T., Gale, T., Cross, R., Parker, S. and Smith, C. 2017. Metaphor as a methodological tool: Identifying teachers' social justice dispositions across diverse secondary school settings. *British Journal of Sociology of Education*, 38(6), 856–871. https://doi.org/10.1080/01425692.2016.1182009

Mockler, N. 2018. Early career teachers in Australia: A critical policy historiography. *Journal of Education Policy*, 33(2), 262–278. https://doi.org/10.1080/02680939.2017.1332785

Musset, P. 2010. *Initial Teacher Education and Continuing Training Policies in a Comparative Perspective: Current Practices in OECD Countries and a Literature Review on Potential Effects.* OECD Education Working Paper No. 48. Paris: OECD Publishing. Retrieved from http://dx.doi.org/10.1787/5kmbphh7s47h-en

Nicoll, K. and Edwards, R. 2004. Lifelong learning and the sultans of spin: Policy as persuasion? *Journal of Education Policy*, 19(1), 43–55. https://doi.org/10.1080/0268093042000182627

Osburn, J., Caruso, G. and Wolfensberger, W. 2011. The concept of "best practice": A brief overview of its meanings, scope, uses, and shortcomings. *International Journal of Disability, Development and Education*, 58(3), 213–222. https://doi.org/10.1080/1034912X.2011.598387

Potter, J. 1996. *Representing Reality: Discourse, Rhetoric and Social Construction.* London: Sage.

Rowan, L., Mayer, D., Kline, J., Kostogriz, A. and Walker-Gibbs, B. 2015. Investigating the effectiveness of teacher education for early career teachers in diverse settings: The longitudinal research we have to have. *Australian Educational Researcher*, 42, 273–298

Rowe, E. E. and Skourdoumbis, A. 2019. Calling for "urgent national action to improve the quality of initial teacher education": The reification of evidence and accountability in reform agendas. *Journal of Education Policy*, 34(1), 44–60, https://doi.org/10.1080/02680939.2017.1410577

Sahlberg, P. 2011. *Finnish Lessons: What Can the World Learn from Educational Change in Finland?* New York and London, UK: Teachers College Press.

Shacklock, G. 1998. Fast capitalist educational change: Personally resisting the images of school reform. *Discourse: Studies in the Cultural Politics of Education*, 19(1), 75–88. https://doi.org/10.1080/0159630980190105

Smyth, J. and Shacklock, G. 1998. *Re-making Teaching: Ideology, Policy and Practice*. London, UK: Routledge.

Stanfield, J. and Cremin, H. 2013. Importing control in initial teacher training: Theorizing the construction of specific habitus in recent proposals for induction into teaching. *Journal of Education Policy*, 28(1), 21–37. https://doi.org/10.1080/02680939.2012.682608

Swartz, D. 2002. *The Sociology of Habit: The Perspective of Pierre Bourdieu* (Vol. 22). Retrieved from www.bu.edu/av/core/swartz/sociology-of-habit.pdf

Teacher Education Ministerial Advisory Group. 2015. *Action Now: Classroom Ready Teachers*. Canberra: Department of Education. Retrieved from www.studentsfirst.gov.au/teacher-education-ministerial-advisory-group

Teach for Australia. 2017. Our vision and values. *Teach for Australia*. Retrieved from www.teachforaustralia.org/about-us/our-vision-values/

Téllez, K. 2007. Have conceptual reforms (and one anti-reform) in preservice teacher education improved the education of multicultural, multilingual children and youth? *Teachers and Teaching: Theory and Practice*, 13(6), 543–564. https://doi.org/10.1080/13540600701683457

TEMAG. 2014. *Action Now: Classroom Ready Teachers*. Canberra: Department of Education. Retrieved from http://www.studentsfirst.gov.au/teacher-education-ministerial-advisory-group.

Trippestad, T., Swennen, A. and Werler, T. (Eds.). 2017. *The Struggle for Teacher Education: International Perspectives on Governance and Reforms*. London, UK: Bloomsbury Academic.

Windsor, S. 2014. *Citizenship and Inequality: The Teach for Australia Program and the People Who Enter It*. PhD Thesis, University of Melbourne, Melbourne. Retrieved from http://hdl.handle.net/11343/52821(11343/52821)

Wiseman, A. R., Lingard, B. and Hardy, I. 2018. A critical examination of *Teach for Bangladesh's* Facebook page: "Social-mediatisation" of global education reforms in the "post-truth" era. *Journal of Education Policy*, 33(5), 632–661. https://doi.org/10.1080/02680939.2018.1445294

Zeichner, K. 2009. *Teacher Education and the Struggle for Social Justice*. London, UK: Routledge.

Zeichner, K. 2016. *Independent Teacher Education Programs: Apocryphal Claims, Illusory Evidence*. Boulder, CO: National Education Policy Center. Retrieved 20 September 2017 from http://nepc.color ado.edu/publication/teacher-education

10
CONCLUDING COMMENTS

Introduction

In this book we have sought to problematize the research constructs of teacher effectiveness (TE) and teacher quality (TQ) and argue that they are poor substitutes for measuring school productivity. In place of these metrics, this chapter proposes a focus on the transformative capacities of teachers as contributors to a larger and democratic social reality that links students' experiences to a broader social good beyond the needs of an economy. This discussion highlights how teachers can reposition their role as pedagogic experts so that the broad purposes of public education and its social contract can be acknowledged. The chapter will reinforce the dynamism of learning as a journey of becoming that is punctuated along the way by relational interactions.

10.1 Capacity

Teaching is hard work, but it is also work that, if encouraged, supports community. We take the view that teachers should reject simplistic notions of teaching practice which suggest a settled account of what makes for effective, quality and good teaching 'easily grasped . . . painlessly practiced, and quickly remediated by some supervising expert' (Ayers 1995, p. 220). Teaching we suggest is 'fundamentally ethical, political, and intellectual work' that at its core 'is characterized by uncertainty, mystery, obstacle, and struggle' (Ayers 1995, p. 220).

> Most teachers try to do their best in often difficult circumstances. Many of their circumstances are outside their direct control; they are often as much victims as their students. But while teachers can easily feel overwhelmed

by the enormity of the problems they face, they can still have a positive influence on the present and future lives of their students.

(Gale and Densmore 2003, p. 113)

To teach well means that teachers can make a difference to the lives and outcomes of their students and that they can contribute to transforming social inequities. Teachers, however, cannot correct all social ills nor should they be expected to.

The predicaments of classroom teaching are bound up in the uncertainties of practice and the unpredictability that accompanies working with young people. It is also connected to the practices, customs and structures evident in society at large. Teachers and teaching work are characterized by a professional and practitioner-led expertise that, if given room to grow and flourish, supports the productive engagement of students. This expertise we suggest is indicative of an enabling pedagogy that is cognizant of injustice, awake to social change and capable of critically reflecting on personal and system practice/s. The expertise required aligns with critical and socially just notions of pedagogy that support a framework for learning based on a series of conditions which:

- challenge students intellectually and foster their deep understanding
- encourage questioning about how knowledge is constructed
- allow opportunities for conversation and dialogue
- connect with students' lives and aspirations and the world beyond the classroom
- are supportive and inclusive, and encourage self-direction and autonomy
- recognise and value difference and diversity.

(Keddie and Churchill 2016, p. 607)

In other words, the championing and re-positioning of pedagogy away from 'so-called pure science, that is to say, a profoundly de-historicized and de-historicizing science' (Bourdieu 2004, p. 5) towards a broader vision of what is possible educationally. This broader vision, particularly of the role of classroom teachers, means a reclamation of professional space and the inclusion of 'more democratic ways of working' (Biesta 2017, p. 324). In saying this, we follow Gale and Densmore (2003), who state:

> teachers clearly have valuable skills and knowledge that schools and their communities need, but they do not have all that is needed. Working with and amongst communities, learning from them, teachers are better placed to make valuable contributions to the education of students and to a radical democratic agenda for western societies.
>
> *(p. 113)*

Encouraging a strong critical reflection, the socially just teacher thinks about themselves and their students in terms of what they have become, will become and why, particularly in an era of audit and surveillance accountability. The challenge for teachers, indeed for all educators enmeshed in a set-up of this kind, is to find ways around and out of the subjugating dictates of narrow audit measurements and the technical validation of 'what makes education *good*' (Biesta 2017, p. 316, emphasis in original).

A way out of "cause–effect" metrics connected to TE and TQ, we suggest, is for teachers to maintain a 'perpetual vigilance and skepticism' (Dean 1999, p. 4) about claims relating to their teaching practice/s. Problematizing wherever possible, criteria related to validation of their work by metrics of TE and TQ prioritizes the professional judgement of teachers, particularly about how their students engage and cope with the educational interactions that form schooling. Biesta asserts that for teaching 'to have any impact on students, it is because of the fact that students interpret and make sense of what they are being taught, not because the teaching would simply flow into their minds and bodies' (2012, p. 585). The learning that an education facilitates addresses the human being and the 'growth' (Dewey 1929) that stems from it. Growth in the sense used here refers to a Deweyan conception of human potential and the development of mind and action such that the orientation of human capacity makes full use of an intelligent reasoning. While the 'growth process' (Dewey 1929) is composed of phases, there is continuity from one phase to the next. A metricated characterization of student achievement at a specific point in time splits the growth process into parts, providing a false picture of change, if any, and characterizing educational development as independent of the conditions of the education system and of broader contextual influences.

10.2 Becoming

Teachers must be afforded the opportunity to move beyond the confining logic of contemporary accountability mechanisms. Their professional intellectual independence as teachers carries with it an ability to 'engage in an intelligent and informed way with the question of what is educationally desirable' (Biesta 2015, p. 676). An important consideration, then, is recognizing that learning and educational growth are unique to each individual. In imposing a seemingly infallible reliability on pedagogy via metrics such as TE and TQ to work against failure dispenses with the idea that students as human beings are 'subjects of action and responsibility' (Biesta 2015, p. 675). Questions of maturity and responsibility arise with these particular characteristics developing in students over time and dependent upon 'the challenges to which the individual is exposed' (Adorno and Becker 1999, p. 21).

The dilemma faced by educators at present is a seemingly intractable contradiction between, on the one hand, "commercial" education system pressures where learning outcomes of a training skill-based functionalist kind are promoted over 'the notion of education as democratic practice' (Stengel 2016, p. 245). The latter configuration of education allows for the creation of 'situations for educative teacher-learner interaction in practice' (English 2013, p. 148) denoting meaningful and flexible school and classroom environments rich in learning potential. This for teachers means a focus on the present and what is currently absent or under-developed in their students but with an eye to the future and what might become. The payoff is a return to reflective experience where the student begins with experiences of doubt perhaps or perplexity. The "doing", as such, with the emphasis on end-point results, is not what matters most. Underlying any "doing" in schooling is the connection to learning via cultivation of an internalized dialogue between student and the subject matter at hand. In other words, a concern with subject matter per se is superfluous if the former is not 'a related factor in a total and growing experience. Thus to see it is to psychologize it' (Dewey in Hickman and Alexander 1998, p. 243).

Inquiry will have a role here. When John Dewey spoke of inquiry, he stressed dealing in the immediate. An important aspect of inquiry is how it helps in guiding and determining reflective action. While the 'aim of education, Dewey argued, was to enable people to *continue* their education' (Garrison 1998, p. 64, emphasis in original), the role and work of educators is to help students make sense of the world around them. Ends in themselves if alleging penultimate fixed truths 'detached from all specific content . . . disconnected from the means' (Dewey 1998, p. 255) should be abandoned in favour of inquiry as effective action for the 'development of a creative imagination capable of envisioning future possibilities' (Garrison 1998, p. 75). This represents an important foundation upon which a re-examination of 'quantitative reductionism' (Gutierrez and Lipman 2016) provides an opportunity for advancing critique, particularly of conduct and conditions that undermine social progress and democracy. While we don't doubt a link between effective and quality classroom teachers and educational productivity, too strong an attachment to the dictates of mathematical constructions for the evaluation of educational performance destroys our sense of contextual perspective. In other words, holding fast to a statistical methodological puritanism 'which holds that there is an external reality, a methodology of observational representation which holds that external reality can be observed, and that it is best represented with languages like mathematics that clearly distinguish facts from value statements, and a correspondence theory of causality' (Wyly 2009, p. 314) hollows out the lived experience of classroom teachers and students.

So, to finish, what we have tried to do in this book is to grapple with the complexities connected to the research constructs of TE and TQ and to highlight some of the underlying and broader issues involved in their figuration. In talking of the need for a 'strategic positivism' (2009), Elvin Wyly means that researchers interested in advancing a critical progressivist educational agenda engage with statistics critically. There is an urgent need, we would argue, for a fresh look at how all of us interested in notions of educational performance and teacher practice should engage with the calculable and to perhaps draw upon a stronger sense of what we term a "critical statistical reflexivity" when dealing with notions of teacher effectiveness and teacher quality in education.

References

Adorno, T. W. and Becker, H. 1999. *Education for Maturity and Responsibility* (Translated by R. French, J. Thomas and D. Weymann). London, UK: Sage Publications.

Ayers, W. 1995. Ten alternative classrooms. In W. Ayers (Ed.), *To Become a Teacher: Making a Difference in Children's Lives* (pp. 215–221). New York: Teachers College Press.

Biesta, G. 2012. Philosophy of education for the public good: Five challenges and an agenda. *Educational Philosophy and Theory*, 44(6), 581–593. https://doi.org/10.1111/j.1469-5812.2011.00783.x

Biesta, G. 2015. Teaching, teacher education, and the humanities: reconsidering education as a *geisteswissenschaft*. *Educational Theory*, 65(6), 665–679.

Biesta, G. 2017. Education, measurement and the professions: Reclaiming a space for democratic professionality in education. *Educational Philosophy and Theory*, 49(4), 315–330. https://doi.org/10.1080/00131857.2015.1048665

Bourdieu, P. 2004. *Science of Science and Reflexivity*. Cambridge: Polity Press.

Dean, M. 1999. *Critical Effective Histories: Foucault's Methods and Historical Sociology*. London, UK and New York: Routledge.

Dewey, J. 1929. *Experience and Nature*. New York: W.W. Norton and Co.

Dewey, J. 1998. Aims in education. In L. A. Hickman and T. M. Alexander (Eds.), *The Essential Dewey: Volume 1 Pragmatism, Education, Democracy* (pp. 250–256). Bloomington and Indianapolis, IN: Indiana University Press.

English, A. R. 2013. *Discontinuity in Learning: Dewey, Herbart and Education as Transformation*. Cambridge and New York: Cambridge University Press.

Gale, T. and Densmore, K. 2003. *Engaging Teachers: Towards a Radical Democratic Agenda For Schooling*. Maidenhead, UK: Open University Press.

Garrison, J. W. 1998. John Dewey's philosophy as education. In L. A. Hickman (Ed.), *Reading Dewey: Interpretations for a Postmodern Generation* (pp. 63–82). Bloomington and Indianapolis, IN: Indiana University Press.

Gutierrez, R. R. and Lipman, P. 2016. Toward social movement activist research. *International Journal of Qualitative Studies in Education*, 29(10), 1241–1254. https://doi.org/10.1080/09518398.2016.1192696

Keddie, A. and Churchill, R. 2016. The future of teaching: schooling, equity and social change. In R. Churchill et al. (Eds.), *Teaching Making a Difference* (3rd ed., pp. 592–621). Queensland, Australia: John Wiley & Sons Australia Ltd.

Stengel, B. S. 2016. Educating *Homo Oeconomicus*? "The disadvantages of a commercial spirit" for the realization of *democracy and education*. *Educational Theory*, 66(1–2), 245–261.

Wyly, E. 2009. Strategic positivism. *The Professional Geographer*, 61(3), 310–322. https://doi.org/10.1080/00330120902931952

INDEX

Note: Entries denoted with an n are attributed to a note at the end of the chapter. Entries in **bold** indicate a table. NCLB is an acronym for No Child Left Behind and RTTT is an acronym for Race to the Top.

accountability: defined 38; high-stakes 38; linked politically and economically 33, 83; student performance data 17–18, 29; teacher education, pedagogy/curriculum 138; TE/TQ 2, 33; via standardized testing 77
adaptive teaching: to contextual needs of students 121–122; England's Teaching Standard 5 122
"adding value": to knowledge 48; teacher focus 17
algorithm limitations 64–65
analysis of master narratives 81–84, **85–86**
Angus, Laurie 7
Arrighi, Barbara 124
assessment: beyond standardized minimums 10; at expense of individual child 73; favored term of the 1990s 101; fortify social divisions 126; impeded teacher judgement 112; intensification 74; international regime of performance verification 102; large scale, comparative measure of choice for governments 50; NCLB 91; new techniques of 39; normalizing processes evident 53; overuse of student 71, 72; performance monitoring and 39; policy implementation in schools 121; RTTT new standards and **86**, 91; served a selection function for military/college admissions 101; student development, formal 65; teachers' beliefs about 122; technologies of intervention 103; tool to measure student growth 139
Australian Council of Trade Unions (ACTU) 24
Australian Institute for Teaching and School Leadership (AITSL) 74
Australia Reconstructed (ACTU) 24

Ball, Stephen 38, 40, 58, 123
Barker, B. 112
Barrow, R. 15
Bauman, Z. 48
behavioural modification 78
behavioural psychology, Edward Thorndike 104–105
Berliner, D. 6
"best practice": benchmark against 70; "conditioning" the right kind of teacher 10; education policy encapsulating 131; global idea in teaching 134–135; identification and implementation 75; pedagogies at odds with 111; policy production which leads to 88; in teacher education 134; teacher's need to gain understanding 90–91

Biddle, B. 6
"big data" 35–36
Blomqvist, P. 56
Bosworth, B. 21
Bourdieu, Pierre: accountability metrics 3; conceptions of power 4–6; inequality gaps, hierarchy of "gifts" 125, 126; "logic(s) of practice"/"doxa" 4, 71; objectivism limitations 28–29; teacher effectiveness research 63
Bush, George W. 83

caring: emotional/empathetic qualities 127; teacher for students 126–127
"cause-effect" metrics 146
charter schools: advocated by teachers/union leaders 92; corporate interests 40; focus on outcomes of schooling 39; NCLB converting public schools 92; RTTT increasing/removing cap on number 94, 95
choice/competition 39–40; approach to social services 38; economically driven reforms 23; family rights 36; judicious consumers exercising 6; market mechanisms/school markets 25; NCLB, enhanced parental choice 93; parental responsibilities 57; public school dissolution 39; resulting in tensions 112; tutoring, remediation, enrichment activities 92; undermining drive for equal opportunities 112
Clarke, C. 101
classroom: affective interventionist strategies 136; environments 147; pedagogic adaptability context 117; practices of teachers in 7–10; predicaments of teaching 145; variability in quality of teaching in Australia 137
Clinton, J. M. 13
Cobb-Douglas production function 41
Cochran-Smith, M. 133
Coleman Report 18–19, 42, 102
"commensuration" 17
communication 107
comparability 50
competencies 107
competitiveness: economic and political 82, 96; and educationalization 51–52; education as a global "race" for economic 50; international economic 24, 47, 48, 59; manufactured uncertainty 49; perceived national success and 102; skills/competencies 107

compliance: with competencies 101; principal immersed in 39; purpose of education 102; regime, teacher 111
Connell, Raewyn 75
continuous achievement 138–139
corporatism 39
creativity 107
Cremin, H. 132, 133
'crises in state education': economic in origin, Australia 24; perceived failure and under-performance 6, 22, 23; in student performance 81–82; teachers and teaching 25, 40
'crises of legitimation' 4
critical thinking 10, 107, 122
Cronin, C. 4
curriculum: design, approaches to 29, 90; fostering generalized competence 107; Pearson, reductive effects on 109; relevant to Australian national economy 136; response to knowledge-based economy 48; source of the "sacred" 107; standardized testing 102; theorizing 103–104; values-based 36; what should be taught 106

data: distorting effects 18; "scientific" evidence-base 16; utilization, comparison/evaluation 17
"datafication" 71, 101
Day, C. 119
de-centering responsibility 50–51
decentralization 112
De Lissovoy, N. 50–51
Densmore, K 124, 145
Deweyan: conception of human potential 146; progressivist approach 105, 109
Dewey, John: inquiry, dealing in the immediate 147; teachers engaged in formation of proper social life 120; "theory of experience" 118
digital revolution 140
discursive 82
disruptive innovation 135
doxa: questionable beliefs of teaching 63; self-evident order 70–71
Duffy, G. 120

economic: crises 33–34; functions 5; inequities 8; transformation 33
education: defined as an industry 24; as democratic practice 146; research, Coleman Report 42, 102; social/economic problems 51; training, job-ready skills 24

educational approaches: instrumentalist/behaviourist 105; in U.S., Deweyan progressivist 105, 109
education policy: discursive rhetoric 88; incorporation of context 123; large-scale intergovernmental organizations 88
education policy reforms: decentralization/marketization 112; economically driven 23, 38; Education Reform Act of 1988 23; focus on type of teacher needed 133–134; National Defense Education Act (NDEA) 23; new public management (NPM) 38; parent choice, consumers 57; RTTT teacher policy 94; social disadvantages 112; testing at centre 100
education production function: input-to-output, labour and capital 41, 42; methodological problems 43; pre-eminent measurement technique 43
Education Reform Act of 1988, United Kingdom 23
Efficacy Framework 108
Egeberg, H. 58
Elementary and Secondary Education Act (ESEA) 91
endogenous privatization 40
"enterprising self" 39
Equality of Educational Opportunity (Coleman) 42
evaluation: Coleman Report 42; NCLB requirements of teacher/school system 92, 93; of pedagogy 33; production function analyses 42; school productivity 1, 4, 8, 12–13, 19–21; systems and people 27–29; teacher effectiveness 14, 28; teacher performance 4, 14, 63, 71; teacher productivity 10, 13, 19–21; teacher to student test scores 94; teaching practice 76, 78
evidence-based innovation 133
exogenous privatization 40

fast policy 84
Flexible Literacy for Remote Primary Schools Program 136–137
Foucault, Michel: accountability metrics 3; conceptions of power 4–6; governmentality 28, 103; "normalization" 108; teacher effectiveness research 63; "technologies of power" 18, 78
Foulcauldian "technologies of power" 18, 78

Gale, Trevor 25, 68, 71, 110, 124, 145
Gates Foundation 58
Gibboney, R. 105
Gleeson, D. 53
global education industry (GEI) 101
Global Financial Crisis (GFC) 35
globalization: of economy and education 24; formation of world system and interconnections 34; 'practices of governing' 35; shaping education 37; technology usage needed 48
Goals 2000: Educate America Act 102
Gofen, A. 56
Goodson, I. 37
government: minimalist ideology of 40; neoliberal, "audit society" 76
governmentality: heightened performance measures 43; manage behaviour of human beings 103; skills development 51
governmentalization: defined 28; reconstruction of self, "self-care" 51
Griffith, Morwenna 72, 119
Gu, Q. 119
Gunter, H. 53

Hannus, S. 5, 6
Hargreaves, A. 37
"high-impact teaching" 139
Hoffman, J. 120
Hogan, A. 108, 109, 110
Holloway, J. 71
How the world's best-performing school systems come out on top (Moursed and Barber) 9, 81, 83, **85**, 88–89
Hoxby, C. 40
human capital: concept of education 101; global companies driven by 36; KBE importance of investment in 48, 49; preparation, professional learning of teachers 83; specify skills and competencies 50; two sides to 51
human development 110

improving teacher quality/effectiveness 89
inclusion 112, 145
Index of Community and Socio-Economic Advantage (ICSEA) 43–44n1
initial teacher education (ITE) 136
inputs: in education and productivity 20, 21; measures 3, 29; productivity, growth 19
instruction: defined 9; versus pedagogy 100, 103–104; polarization between pedagogy 104

instrumentalist/behaviourist approach 105
intangible capital 35–36
International Large-Scale Assessments (ILSAs), government comparative measures used 50
intervention: artificial, manipulation of data 64; control over teaching practice 78; to increase effectiveness of teachers 7; intrusive, high-stakes testing 37; NCLB, professional development **85**; policy 2; policy as 'textual interventions into practice' 84; reformist, current political/economic 33; research geared towards specific knowledge outcomes and 71; teaching practices 76

Keynesian: political framework and education reform 37; post-war capitalism 33
knowledge: and assessment 10; content 14; "know-how" of the future, STEM 48; needed for successful transition into adulthood 36; versus skills 104; teacher 17; what is most important 102
'knowledge-based capital' 36
knowledge-based economy (KBE): driving education reform 9, 47; education now a directly economic factor 48; national and personal prosperity depend upon 49; teachers responsible for 47
Kopp, Wendy 136, 141n1

Lagemann, E. 106
Larsen, M. 25
leadership: school, importance of 91; through head teachers/principals 52–53
learner centred education 107
Lewis, S. 71
lifelong education KBE requires 48, 49
Lingard, B. 108
literacy and numeracy 19, 36, 48, 111, 137
Literacy and numeracy interventions in the early years of schooling: A literature review (ACER) 137
Literacy and Numeracy Test 137
Lubienski, C. 101
Luttrell, W. 127

Maguire, M. 101
Malthus, Thomas Robert 41
managerialism: business, symbolic policy 95; connected to market models 38–39; one of the pillars of reform 58

market economy 17
'market forces' 6
marketization: reform in education 37, 112; stratified, unequal schools 40
master narrative: analyses of four documents 82–83; increased school autonomy, heightened accountability 83; policy symbolism, teacher performance 96; there is no alternative (TINA) 81–82
McConney, A. 58
McKinsey Report 83, 88
measurement: and comparison of skills within nations 50; of outputs 39; pre-eminent, production function 43; of student achievement 78; surveillance used in TER 9, 63; of teaching practice 5; value-added 95
mechanistic view of learning 105
metrics TE/TQ 10
Mills, C. 124
Ministerial Council on Education, Employment, Training and Youth Affairs (MCEETYA) 73
Mitra, Dana 57
Mockler, N. 119
models: contextual value-added (CVA) 67; process-product 65–66; quantitative growth designs 67
Molla, T. 110
Morley, L. 39
MySchool, new public management (NPM) 38

National College in School Leadership (U.K.) 91
National Defense Education Act (NDEA) 23
Nation at Risk, A (U.S. Dept. of Education) 102
neoliberal economics 125
neoliberal ideas of education 54, 58
neoliberalism: education bound to free market 35; political settlement, defined 34; 'practices of governing' 35; TFA program 137
new managerialism 38–39
new public management (NPM) 38
New Teacher Project 136
"No Child Left Behind" (NCLB) (2002) 9, 81, 83, **85**
normalization: employable, competent learner worker 108; processes, education systems 53
Nussbaum, Martha 110

Oakeshott, Michael 109
Obama, Barack 83
objectivism: methodological, artificial adjustment of data 68; reduces complexity and specificity 28
O'Connor, K. E. 127
Organization for Economic Co-Operation and Development (OECD): influencing education 33, 50; promoting large-scale testing 82
orthodoxy 59, 71
outputs: of education 15; in education and productivity 20, 21; productivity, growth 19–20; set of techniques 7; student achievement 17

Page, D. 55, 58
parental empowerment 56–57
parents: as consumers, "parental voice" 56; increased educational involvement 56; and teacher interaction, social class 55
Pearson: edu-business 108; Efficacy Framework 108–109
pedagogic adaptability: "in the moment" teacher's responses 120–121; relational narrative 117, 118
pedagogical relation: four domains 109–110; between teachers, students, subject matter 119
pedagogy: favored by Thorndike 106; narrowing 7, 59; streamlined process 59; via metrics 146
'perceived failings' 110
performance: continuous, accountability 139; culture 27, 74; linked to student learning outcomes 54; measures, 'intensifications of governmentality' 43; monitoring 39; regimes, education systems 53; reviews 2; teacher, "productive autonomy" 54
performative habitus in teaching: Bourdieuian notion defined 131; educational policy directing teacher priorities 140
performativity: defined 37–38; panoptic 54; reform pillar 58
Phillips, D. 15
policy assumptions 17
policy case studies 86–95
policy documents: *How the world's best-performing school systems come out on top.* 9, 81, 83, **85**, 88–91; "No Child Left Behind" 9, 81, 83, **85**, 91–93; "Race to the Top" 9, 81, 83, **86**, 93–95; *Teachers*

matter: Attracting, developing and retaining effective teachers. 9, 81, 83, **85**, 86–88
policy shortcuts 84
political mobilization 4
"positivist" research 100
power: Bourdieu's analyses 5; contingencies, socio-economic 124–125; disciplinary 103; institutional supervision 54–55
presuppositions 71, 91, 133
pre-testing 68
Principles of Teaching (Thorndike) 106
privatization: endogenous/exogenous 40; link education to modern economy 41; in public education 40
productivity: celebrated, quality ignored 112; education focused on 138; how to define 20; school 4, 8, 10, 12, 13, 19–21, 144
'professional compliance' 59
professional learning 91
professional metrics 2
public education: crises in state education 6; crisis, failure, under-performance 6, 22–23; crisis in student performance 81–82; crisis of teachers and teaching 25, 40

quality teaching: changes focused on 12; defined 2; research construct 15

"Race to the Top" (RTTT) (2009) 9, 81, 83, **86**; value-added models (VAMs) 84, 93
randomized control trial studies (RCT) 68, 71
Ranson, Stewart 78
Rassool, N. 39
Rawolle, S. 34
Reay, Diane 55–56, 124
reform: based on economics/demographics 37; pillars of 58; three periods defined 37
relational narrative 117–119
reports: *Australia Reconstructed* (1987) 24; *Teachers matter: Attracting, developing and retaining effective teachers* 9, 81, 83, **85**
research: ignores 'storied phenomenon' 118; policy seeking evidence or authentic research 26; "positivist" 100
responsibilization 50–51
Ricardo, David 41
Rizvi, F. 40
Rowe, Emma 35
Rowlands, J. 34

Saltmarsh, Sue 56
school: autonomy 19; continual 'contextual change' 123–124; effectiveness/improvement 6–7; four key elements of 36; funding linked to enrolment 23
school choice: admission 40; family rights 36; NCLB, enhanced 93; parental responsibilities 57; public school dissolution 39; resulted in tensions 112
school effectiveness/school improvement (SESI): defined 3; focus on measurable factors 118; measures to address failure 7; quality teaching 14–15
school markets 25
schools, successful systems 88–89
science, technology, engineering, mathematics (STEM) 48
scoring teacher's work 1
Seddon, Terri 25, 123
Sellar, S. 108
Sen, Amartya 110
Simola, H. 5, 6
"singularity" 17
skills and competencies 106–109
Slee, R. 6
Smyth, J. 6
social class 19, 125
"social fields" 3
social justice: agenda influencing teacher education reforms 134; enhancing, politically driven 107; goals, measures misapplied 4
socio-economic: disparity 107, 125; inputs, no effect 91; status and class, power contingencies 124–125
standardization of education 37
standardized testing: NCLB required 92; power through data 54–55; RTTT punitive measure tied to 93
Stanfield, J. 132, 133
"statistically controllable" 16
Steiner-Khamsi, G. 101
Stillwaggon, J. 112
Streeck, W. 33
student: develop capabilities more than competencies 109; learning growth mapped/documented 139; self-management 108
student achievement: audits, culture of performance 27; Coleman Report 18–19, 42, 102; function of school autonomy 19, 83; learning and 2; marginal gains 121; responsibility and blame attributed to teachers/schools 7; school context impacts 124; school/teacher productivity 19–20; social class determines 19; standardized tests 19; teacher affects 19; teacher contributes more versus student 65; teacher responsible for 47
"Students First" (SF) 136
student voice 57–58
surveillance: accountability, teacher reflection 145–146; neoliberal ideas 54–55; normalization, instrument of power 18; qualify, classify, punish 103; teachers' work 38, 57
Swartz, David 133
symbolic policy forms: connected to "master narratives" 95–96; symbolic logic education policy 95

teacher: affects student achievement 19; autonomy 53–54; comparison to peers 59; disposition 132, 133; education, linked to policy changes 135; education/preparation 84, 133–134, 135, 137–138, 140; enabler of performance management objectives 113; identity, professional 72, 119, 122; impacted by digital revolution 140; learning facilitator/collaborator 9–10, 100; led instruction/process-product oriented 70; narrowed role in productivity calculations 8; new teacher education, "best practice/s" 133–135; as pedagogic experts 144; performance evaluations 4, 14, 54, 94; power 5; preparation, Literacy and Numeracy Test 137; recruitment 84, 85, 91, 93; reform pillars governing teacher subject 58; responsible for student achievement 47; role 111; self-concept 72; standards 14, 74–75
"teacher blame" 25
Teacher Education Ministerial Advisory Group (TEMAG) 137
teacher effectiveness (TE): adaptive teaching 122; defined 1–2, 12; measures, distorting 4, 5; measuring student progress 74; metrics devoid of emotional or personal dimension 127; pedagogic adaptability 117–118; rhetorical device 3
Teacher Effectiveness and Teacher Education (Gage) 65
teacher effectiveness research (TER): adheres to positivist methodology 78; caring variable not figured into metrics

127; daily administrative accountability 77; determined by effective teacher guidance 63; doxic logic 71; evidence-based interventionist approach 76; focus on student achievement 16; framed by quantification 15; measurement/surveillance used 9, 63; one size fits all 75; research eliminates sociological effects 124; value-added/contextual/value-added research 67; "what works" policy advice 16–17
teacher quality (TQ): affects performance 89; defined 1–2, 12; measures, distorting 4, 5; measuring student progress 74; pedagogic adaptability 117–118; rhetorical device 3
Teachers matter: Attracting, developing and retaining effective teachers (Organization for Economic Co-Operation and Development) 9, 81, 83, **85**
teacher work: effective/highly effective, ineffective 28, 94, 95; sacking ineffective 86
Teach for America 136
Teach for Australia (TFA) Program 137
testing: accountability via standardized 77; centre of education reforms 100; data proliferation 17; distorts perceptions of teacher effectiveness 72; effect on curricula 102; evaluative judgement 101; example of governmentalization 28; globalization 37; governing what knowledge is most valued 103; NCLB standardized testing 91–92; OECD promoting large-scale 82; power through surveillance 54–55; selection function for military/college admission 101; spread in U.S. post Sputnik 101; standardized 19; standardized relationship to instruction 100; term versus assessment 101
there is no alternative (TINA) 81–82

Thorndike, Edward: instrumentalist/behaviourist approach 104–106; *The Principles of Teaching* 106
Through growth to achievement: Report of the Review to Achieve Educational Excellence in Australian Schools (Department of Education) 138
Tripplett, J. 21
two-factor input/output 41

unintended consequences 121
U.S. educational thinking: Deweyan progressivist approach 105, 109; instrumentalist/behaviourist approach 105
U.S. federal government funding 94–95

value-added measures (VAMs): education policy, school productivity gains 95; RTTT teacher evaluation system 93
values: fixed calculable entity 59; used in decision making 5
Verger, C. 101
verification 102
vocational training 54

Wacquant, Löic 4
Weiner, G. 6
"what works": comparison/evaluation 17, 93; data/evidence-base prescribed policy 16; governmentalization 28; idea of singular process 91; instrumentalist approaches to teacher embedded in 120; NCLB, accountability **85**; NCLB policy 93, 94; policy shortcuts, readymade examples of 84; political mobilization to 4; set of procedures that prioritizes 7; teacher interviews/notions of 63
working-class parents 55

Yates, Lyn 36, 104
Youdell, D. 40
Young, Michael 107